# Measuring the Psychological and Electrophysiological Attributes of Human Personality:

## Emerging Research and Opportunities

Sanja Tatalović Vorkapić
*University of Rijeka, Croatia*

A volume in the Advances in Psychology, Mental Health, and Behavioral Studies (APMHBS) Book Series

IGI GLOBAL
DISSEMINATOR OF KNOWLEDGE

www.igi-global.com

Published in the United States of America by
IGI Global
Information Science Reference (an imprint of IGI Global)
701 E. Chocolate Avenue
Hershey PA 17033
Tel: 717-533-8845
Fax: 717-533-8661
E-mail: cust@igi-global.com
Web site: http://www.igi-global.com



Library of Congress Cataloging-in-Publication Data

Names: Vorkapic, Sanja Tatalovic, 1972- author.
Title: Measuring the psychological and electrophysiological attributes of human personality : emerging research and opportunities / by Sanja Tatalovic Vorkapic.
Description: Hershey PA : Information Science Reference, [2017] | Includes bibliographical references.
Identifiers: LCCN 2016057757| ISBN 9781522522836 (h/cr) | ISBN 9781522522843 (eISBN)
Subjects: LCSH: Neuropsychology. | Personality.
Classification: LCC QP360 .V67 2017 | DDC 612.8/2--dc23 LC record available at https://lccn.loc.gov/2016057757

This book is published in the IGI Global book series Advances in Psychology, Mental Health, and Behavioral Studies (APMHBS) (ISSN: 2475-6660; eISSN: 2475-6679)

British Cataloguing in Publication Data
A Cataloguing in Publication record for this book is available from the British Library.

# Advances in Psychology, Mental Health, and Behavioral Studies (APMHBS) Book Series

ISSN:2475-6660
EISSN:2475-6679

Editor-in-Chief: Bryan Christiansen, PryMarke, LLC, USA

Mission

The complexity of the human mind has puzzled researchers and physicians for centuries. While widely studied, the brain still remains largely misunderstood.

The **Advances in Psychology, Mental Health, and Behavioral Studies (APMHBS)** book series presents comprehensive research publications focusing on topics relating to the human psyche, cognition, psychiatric care, mental and developmental disorders, as well as human behavior and interaction. Featuring diverse and innovative research, publications within APMHBS are ideally designed for use by mental health professionals, academicians, researchers, and upper-level students..

Coverage

- Neurological Disorders
- Anxiety
- Counseling & Therapy
- Trauma & Stress
- Mental Health & Disorders
- Socialization
- Cognition
- Human Interaction
- Addiction
- Psychiatry

IGI Global is currently accepting manuscripts for publication within this series. To submit a proposal for a volume in this series, please contact our Acquisition Editors at Acquisitions@igi-global.com or visit: http://www.igi-global.com/publish/.

The Advances in Psychology, Mental Health, and Behavioral Studies (APMHBS) Book Series (ISSN 2475-6660) is published by IGI Global, 701 E. Chocolate Avenue, Hershey, PA 17033-1240, USA, www.igi-global.com. This series is composed of titles available for purchase individually; each title is edited to be contextually exclusive from any other title within the series. For pricing and ordering information please visit http://www.igi-global.com/book-series/advances-psychology-mental-health-behavioral/110200. Postmaster: Send all address changes to above address. 

## Titles in this Series

*For a list of additional titles in this series, please visit:*
*http://www.igi-global.com/book-series/advances-psychology-mental-health-behavioral/110200*

***Emerging Research in Play Therapy, Child Counseling, and Consultation***
Rheta LeAnne Steen (Loyola University New Orleans, USA)
Information Science Reference • ©2017 • 436pp • H/C (ISBN: 9781522522249) • US $205.00

***Workforce Development Theory and Practice in the Mental Health Sector***
Mark Smith (Te Pou o te Whakaaro Nui: National Workforce Center for Adult Mental Health, Addiction and Disability, New Zealand) and Angela F. Jury (Te Pou o te Whakaaro Nui: National Workforce Center for Adult Mental Health, Addiction and Disability, New Zealand)
Information Science Reference • ©2017 • 378pp • H/C (ISBN: 9781522518747) • US $190.00

***Improving the Quality of Life for Dementia Patients through Progressive Detection...***
Jinglong Wu (Okayama University, Japan)
Medical Info. Science Reference • ©2017 • 353pp • H/C (ISBN: 9781522509257) • US $205.00

***Police Psychology and Its Growing Impact on Modern Law Enforcement***
Cary L. Mitchell (Pepperdine University, USA) and Edrick H. Dorian (Los Angeles Police Department, USA)
Information Science Reference • ©2017 • 345pp • H/C (ISBN: 9781522508137) • US $190.00

***Seduction in Popular Culture, Psychology, and Philosophy***
Constantino Martins (Nova University of Lisbon, Portugal) and Manuel Damásio (Lusófona University, Portugal)
Information Science Reference • ©2017 • 332pp • H/C (ISBN: 9781522505259) • US $175.00

***Chronic Mental Illness and the Changing Scope of Intervention Strategies...***
Barre Vijaya Prasad (Dharwad Institute of Mental Health and Neurosciences, India)
Medical Info. Science Reference • ©2017 • 404pp • H/C (ISBN: 9781522505198) • US $220.00

*For an enitre list of titles in this series, please visit:*
*http://www.igi-global.com/book-series/advances-psychology-mental-health-behavioral/110200*

IGI GLOBAL
DISSEMINATOR OF KNOWLEDGE

www.igi-global.com

701 East Chocolate Avenue, Hershey, PA 17033, USA
Tel: 717-533-8845 x100 • Fax: 717-533-8661
E-Mail: cust@igi-global.com • www.igi-global.com

# Table of Contents

# Foreword

Personality as a topic of psychological study is a variegated field. A daunting number of theoretical perspectives have emerged since Sigmund Freud articulated a three-dimensional view of the human psyche. His fundamental ideas spurred the scientific analysis of personality factors that was derived primarily from questionnaire inventories completed by normal individuals—often undergraduates at major universities. Using sophisticated statistical methodology, personality researchers were able to categorize groups of related behaviors, beliefs, and fundamental attributes of individual differences. Such findings are the theoretical basis about the organization of personality traits.

Several of the major perspectives are highlighted in this book and provide the background for a review of neuroelectric assessment findings for personality structure. The application of electroencephalogram (EEG) and event-related potential (ERP) measures to characterize personality constructs in normal populations was a major breakthrough for the topic area. For the first time, personality researchers could study the biological underpinnings of affective and cognitive differences governing personality traits. Indeed, the application of these methods produced a much needed connection to the ultimate source of personality differences—human brain function.

The text provides a good overview of how EEG measures can reflect these differences. The major findings are reviewed with sufficient detail to give the reader a solid sense of dynamic personality research by assessing the underlying neural events associated with theoretical assumptions. However, the explication of biological findings from personality EEG patterns was much more complicated and convoluted than behavioral implications suggested. The background neural brain activity was too ambiguous for precise assessment of hypothesized constructs. This difficulty occurred primarily because EEG sources and intra-brain communications were are nebulous to ascertain. Mapping putative neuroelectric sources to behavioral personality findings required a more pellucid technique than basic brainwave patterns could provide.

Following the development of information processing theory and computing advances, personality researchers adopted the emerging cognitive neuroscience field. This paradigm shift induced a scientific evolution of personality research with the adoption of ERP methods. Application of these techniques to characterize personality was powerful as the specificity of ERP component amplitude and latency reflected the affective/cognitive events related to individual differences. The text comprehensively reviews the relevant methods and clearly highlights major findings to provide a much needed portrait of contemporary personality research. This challenging task has been addressed in an assessable scholarly fashion. The overarching theoretical perspective and detailed contents will become a must read for future scientists using neuroelectric assays of personality's origins.

*John Polich*
*The Scripps Research Institute, USA*

# Preface

Modern psychology and understanding of individual differences have made extraordinary progress in the last 60 years. A large number of theoretical models of personality has been largely empirically validated, and some of them have even experienced certain modifications due to scientific testing. So, even though they have been generally accepted and widely applied, theories of personality traits have in recent times been unduly dominant (McAdams & Pals, 2006; Tatalović Vorkapić, 2014), which means that identity models could give a more complete understanding of the human personality and pave the way to create an integrative science of personality. This is also corroborated by the attempts to create a single-factor model of personality (Musek, 2007). On the other hand, significant progress has been made in the creation of research designs and methodologies applied in current personality research (Robins, Fraley & Krueger, 2007). While there is no standard research on personality, the existing research methods and statistical procedures allow better insight into the understanding of the human personality today. Canli (2006) thereby emphasized the importance of neurogenic personality base and emotions without using a combination of cognitive-behavioral paradigms, and non-invasive techniques of imaging the brain, such as the functional magnetic resonance imaging. On the other hand, Stelmack (2004) explained the comprehensive nature of human personality by using a review of various psychophysiological methods, which resulted in a thorough presentation of electrophysiological studies of extraversion and neuroticism.

But what is evident as a deficiency in the existing world and Croatian literature in the field of personality psychology is a complete manuscript that describes the possibilities for studying human personality by means of different psychophysiological indicators, among which the method of evoked brain potentials is particularly prominent. And here lies the main contribution of this book that aims to show the positive and negative aspects of the application of the method of evoked potentials in research in relation to different theoretical frameworks of research of the human personality. Hugdahl (1995) and Robins, Fraley and Krueger (2007) showed in great detail and explained the advantages and disadvantages of the evoked brain potentials method in relation to the possibility of understanding human personality by summarizing the results of the existing dominant psychophysiological research.

The novelty of this manuscript is precisely the analysis of human personality from the perspective of two dominant biological theory of personality, Eysenck's (1967) and Strelau's (1983), and exogenous and endogenous components of evoked brain potentials that have been tested with the implementation of the visual oddball paradigm. Furthermore, this book represents a significant step forward in Croatia for the reason that after the book by the late Professor Anthony Fulgosi, "Biological basis of personality traits" (1994) there have been no similar books. Also, although it contains a large number of previous studies presented in the field of electrophysiology personality, it is essentially a scientific research book and is strongly empirically oriented, thus providing an insight into the theoretical background of the biological basis of personality and methods of evoked potentials, and the results of conducted research, which partially responded to research questions and partly to the many open questions for future research and advances in this area.

## ORGANIZATION OF THE BOOK

The book is organized into five chapters, which are concerned with the following:

Chapter 1 presents an introduction to the book and empirical research that has been run. It provides an analysis of historical dana in the field of personality psychology. Therefore, various personality theories and measurement methods have been presented in detail as the theoretical and methodological frame in understanding human personality. Besides that, the examples of applied different psychophysiological methods were described with the aim of explaining human personality. The emphasis of this chapter is on a detailed overview on psychophysiology of human personality along with the most intriguing research questions.

Chapter 2 described the theoretical background of applied personality theories in presented empirical research. Therefore, the well-known Eysenck's dimensional personality theory (1967) is introduced since biological basis of personality is thoroughly explored within this theory. The main postulations of this theory were presented with a special accent on the biological bases of personality, i.e. extraversion and neuroticism. Besides that, Strelau's temperament theory (1983) is presented as well, regarding its theoretical postulations, main temperament dimensions, and its explanation within the frame of understanding the functioning of the Central Nervous System.

Chapter 3 provides a brief overview of evoked brain potentials, as well as the bases of electrophysiology of the brain. The main research findings on evoked potentials and other psychological variables such as cognition, emotion, motivation, and personality are also presented. Emphasis is given to the relationship between evoked brain potentials and personality, operationalized by previously presented two personality theories: Eysenck's and Strelau's. Therefore, all complexity about the relationship between evoked brain potentials and human personality and relevant research methodology is discussed in this chapter.

Chapter 4 deals with a clearly presented research aim, problems, and hypothesis with the methods and determined research results. The correlational design research that was run on a sample of N=54 students in Croatia is described. The main findings regarding the relationship between personality traits of extraversion and evoked brain potentials are presented. The relationship between personality traits (extraversion, neuroticism, psychoticism, social desirability, addiction, criminality, empathy, impulsivity, adventurousness, strength of excitation, strength of inhibition, mobility, and depression) and latencies and amplitudes in two trials for these evoked brain potentials: N1, P2, N2, P3, and Slow wave activity is described within the determined research results. Also, the visual oddball paradigm that was applied for evoking brain activity measured on two occipital and two parietal electrodes is presented as well. Results on behavioral variables, such as age, sight characteristics, coffee drinking, smoking, taking medications, alcohol and drugs consumptions, and body exercises are also introduced. Basically, due to a too simple and monotonous visual task that was used, correlation analyses revealed a significant relationship between personality traits and evoked brain potentials, especially in the trait adventurousness and social desirability. Determined findings from the PCA factor analysis with the Varimax rotation and fifteen individual Hierarchical regression analyses are presented.

Chapter 5 is written with the aim of concluding the main research findings and it presents the main questions for future research. Therefore, certain psychological and electrophysiological attributes of human personality and their relationship are presented. The contribution of this research and the whole book is described here. Also, focus is given to the novelty of research findings. In addition, like many other studies, this study has provided some answers, but at the same time it has revealed many more questions. Therefore, various guidelines for future research and some innovative measurement and/or methodology proposals are presented in this last section.

*Sanja Tatalović Vorkapić*
*University of Rijeka, Croatia*

## REFERENCES

Canli, T. (2006). *Biology of Personality and Individual Differences*. London: The Guilford Press.

Eysenck, H. J. (1967). *Biological basis of personality*. Springfield, IL: Charles C Thomas Publisher.

Fulgosi, A. (1994). *Biološke osnove ličnosti [Biological bases of personality]*. Jastrebarsko, Croatia: Naklada Slap. In Croatian

Hugdahl, K. (1995). *Psychophysiology: The Mind-Body Perspective*. Harvard University Press.

McAdams, D. P., & Pals, J. L. (2006). A New Big Five: Fundamental Principles for an Integrative Science of Personality. *The American Psychologist, 61*(3), 204–217. doi:10.1037/0003-066X.61.3.204 PMID:16594837

Musek, J. (2007). A general factor of personality: Evidence for the Big One in the five-factor model. *Journal of Research in Personality, 41*(6), 1213–1233. doi:10.1016/j.jrp.2007.02.003

Robins, R. W., Fraley, R. C., & Krueger, R. F. (2007). *Handbook of Research Methods in Personality Psychology*. London: The Guilford Press.

Stelmack, R. M. (2004). On Personality and Arousal: A Historical Perspective on Eysenck and Zuckerman. In *On the Psychobiology of Personality: Essays in Honor of Marvin Zuckerman* (pp. 17–28). Elsevier Ltd. doi:10.1016/B978-008044209-9/50003-8

Strelau, J. (1983). *Temperament, Personality, Activity*. London: Academic Press.

Tatalović Vorkapić, S. (2014b). Je li privilegirani status modela osobina ličnosti u psihologiji ličnosti opravdan? – Prikaz modela identiteta [Is privileged status of personality traits' models in personality psychology justified? – Description of identity models]. *Suvremena Psihologija, 17*(2), 181–198.

# Acknowledgment

The author of the book would like to acknowledge the help of all the people involved in this research. First, many thanks to prof. Ksenija Willheim, M.D. Ph.D. and prof. Ante Jurjević, M.D. Ph.D. for enabling the electrophysiological measurement at the Department of Neurology at Clinical Hospital Center Rijeka. Special thanks to the assist. prof. Josip Rudež, M.D. Ph.D. and the medical nurse Snežana Kovačić who have provided technical and expert support in ERP-measurement.

Furthermore, the author of the book wish to acknowledge the valuable contributions of prof. Mladenka Tkalčić, Ph.D. for research organization and coordination at the Department for Psychology at Faculty for Humanities and Social Sciences in Rijeka. Manny thanks to all professors who helped her, with this study and all psychology students who have participated in the research. Special thanks to prof. Igor Kardum, Ph.D. and prof. Jasna Hudek-Knežević, Ph.D. for their great support. Also, she wishes to acknowledge the special support of the Academician Daniel Rukavina, M.D., Ph.D., prof. emeritus, who knows how to recognize the real scientist.

The author of the book greatly appreciate all the support accepted from her mentor at Scientific Master degree program in Psychology and Scientific Doctoral degree program in Psychology, prof. Meri Tadinac, Ph.D. She has embraced author's research idea and helped her to realize it. Thank you Meri! Also, many thanks to other professors from the Department of Psychology at Faculty for Humanities and Social Sciences in Zagreb: prof. Vesna Buško, Ph.D., prof. Zvonimir Knezović, Ph.D. and prof. Denis Bratko, Ph.D. Her special thanks are given to prof. Ante Fulgosi, who strongly influenced on her scientific focus.

In addition, the author of the book wish to acknowledge the valuable contributions of two eminent scientists whose advices helped her a great deal in this research and shaping this book: prof. John Polich, Ph.D. and prof. Ksenija

Marinković, Ph.D. Many thanks for valuable contributions of the reviewers regarding the improvement of quality, coherence, and content presentation of chapters. Special thanks to MA Matea Butković for her great support in translation and proofreading of the whole book.

Finally, the author is more than thankful to her husband Stjepan and her two children Enea and Erik for never ending inspiration and love, and her loving parents and sister Maja for unconditioned support.

Without the support of all these great people, this book would not have become a reality.

*Sanja Tatalović Vorkapić*
*University of Rijeka, Croatia*

# Chapter 1
# Introduction to Psychophysiology of Human Personality


## ABSTRACT

*The analysis of historical data has shown that there have been numerous attempts in exploring and understanding individual differences in human personality. Many of them have been using the arousal construct seemed as the most dominant one. Since then, personality psychology has revealed many personality theories and measurement methods as a theoretical and methodological frame in understanding human personality. Besides that, the same researchers and many others have tried to explain human personality and its various psychological concepts using different psychophysiological methods. Therefore, contemporary psychophysiology of personality includes all research on the biological basis of personality underlying trait-like differences in psychological functioning. This section will provide a detailed overview of the psychophysiology of human personality along with the most intriguing research questions.*


DOI: 10.4018/978-1-5225-2283-6.ch001

## INTRODUCTION TO BIOLOGY OF HUMAN PERSONALITY AND INDIVIDUAL DIFFERENCES

*A systematic study of the physiological basis of individual psychological differences is not only desirable, it is absolutely essential for true scientific understanding of human psychological differences. (Teplov, 1961, according to Fulgosi, 1997, p. 414)*

Since there is generally a certain amount of disagreement about how to define psychology as a science (Nyborg, 1997), it is not uncommon that a similar situation is also present within the inner fields of psychology of personality. Some authors define psychology as a social science, others as a biological science. Some universities place it as a field of humanities, others as a medical, social or political science, while some understand it as a part of information technology, sociology, anthropology, philosophy, and computer science. Opinions also differ about what the real subject of study in psychology is, which directly reflects the type of selected methodology applied in the efforts to find answers to research questions. The aforementioned has its logical roots in the very beginning of the formulation of psychology as a science. Plato, Aristotle, and Democritus thereby played key roles, whereas Democritus's materialistic-atomistic approach to man stood opposite Plato's and Aristotle's visions of man who was explained based on his own shadow, not on his own characteristics. Also, the latter represents the foundation of today's philosophical and psychological-humanistic worldview, where abstraction becomes an essential element in explaining man, but also poses a methodological obstacle.

Pursuant to the aforementioned, in the opinion of many psychologists (Nyborg, 1997), the field of personality represents a central place in modern psychology because, unlike others, it requires a systematic scientific study and complete coverage of man, with all his characteristics. It is clear that the aforementioned implies a high complexity. It is important to note that these characteristics interact with each other, and as such should be studied, however, not in isolation. It is, this synthetic approach to the study of human personality that allows a higher level of understanding of human nature and human behavior (Fulgosi, 1997). The English word personality has its roots in the Latin word *persona* which can be translated as mask, and it indicates all the external characteristics of a person, or the Latin word *per se una*, meaning to contain yourself (Eysenck, 1967). Consequently, when applying the top down analysis, it is necessary to start from a general definition of personality as: "... a set of consistent, distinctive thoughts, emotions, and behaviors that characterize the way in which individuals adapt to the world around them" (Santrock, 1997, p. 402), and have a different interaction with their physical and social environment (Atkinson et al., 1996).

A number of theoretical frameworks, which todays' field of personality is full of, more or less indicate an agreement in relation to this definition of personality. However, although one of the established general definitions of personality is the behavioral stability of people in different situations (Feldman, 1997, p. 373), the question is how it is possible that some individuals show different characteristics and behaviors in the same situations, which has been the targeted topic of discussion from the very beginning of the development of this area. The answer to this question can be found in a wide range of theories - from the fact that biological and genetic factors are responsible for these inter-individual variations, to the fact that the responsibility for them can be fully attributed to different life experiences. It is important to emphasize the scientific discourse on the development of human personality and the vague definition of the difference between temperament and personality, or more precisely, the confusing number of aspects in which these two important terms in psychology are overlapping (Shiner et al., 2012). Therefore, the current development of personality psychology is marked by numerous controversies, whether in terms of theory or research methodology. The main problems in the context of personality psychology relate to several factors. First, they relate to the existence of an extremely large number of theories or attempts of postulating theories. Second, they relate to the significant differences between these theories and to the way in which they arise (e.g. statistical versus clinical approach). Third, they relate to the unclear relations between those theories, and the lack of a generally accepted model of personality (Mlačić & Knezović, 1997), as well as the general lack of agreed research methods, standards of proof and rejection of evidence, and methods of experimental research - or the lack of a paradigm (Eysenck, 1997).

In addition, Canli (2006) points out that, although there is a significant progress in the methodology and results of the research of personality and individual differences regarding the fields of genetics and neuroscience, a lack of communication between researchers who are divided into various scientific fields prevents quality improvement in understanding of the human personality. In fact, geneticists, neuroscientists, and psychologists rarely come to the same conferences and congresses, which makes it impossible to adequately approach scientific research on individual differences in personality. But for that very reason, a conference titled *"Biological basis of personality and individual differences"* was organized, which presented the research on mapping the personality in biology, the biology of personality traits, the genetic markers of individual differences and the vulnerability towards psychopathology, the functional magnetic resonance approach, and the connection between human and animals' personalities. Consequently, Canli (2006) wrote a book, which, by starting from a holistic approach to understanding the human personality, manages to link certain areas of contemporary research on the biology of personality and individual differences by using various neuroimaging techniques. As will be described in this book, Canli pointed out that the research of Gray (1970, 1991) and Zuckerman (2006) gave a more than significant contribution to understanding the biology of the human personality, especially in the development of theoretical models. However, unlike this book, Canli (2006) provided a significant contribution in the display of the genetic research of personality, and those, which apply to exploring the functional MRI. Given the fact that the methodological direction of this book does not include the application of evoked brain potentials in studies of personality, research will seek to contribute to the understanding of human personality, i.e. its biology by using methods of evoked brain potentials.

Specifically, regarding different approaches to the study of human abilities and personalities, H. Nyborg (1995 to 1997) highlighted their importance for the understanding of human nature. The examples of *All surface analysis approach*, which has a descriptive nature and uses correlation analysis, refers to behaviorism, information theory, the theory of social learning, phenomenology, cultural anthropology and cultural relativism, descriptive, lexical and psychology factor personality traits, and classical psychometrics. *The top-down analysis approach* includes analyses that range from the study of phenotypic surface to the identification of their biological foundations, which is also the main type of analysis used in this study. In contrast, *the bottom-up analysis approach* includes analyzes that range from certain experimental manipulations of some biological parameters to the use phenotypic behavior as dependent measures. *The Gene-environment analysis approach* represents a more precise tool than the abovementioned one, but also falls within the scope of another dualistic rhetoric (it typically uses Fisher's analysis of variance and assumes independent proportions of genetic and environmental variance to explain 100 percent of phenotypic variance) - the most popular type of this analysis is behavioral genetics. The last three central analyses require a hierarchical solution. Finally, the All bottom analysis approach, which allows causal analysis, represents the future in psychological research, and according to Nyborg's thinking (1997), it will be fully occupied with studies of biological parameters of human nature, which he called molecular research in psychology, as pointed out also in Canli's book (2006).

*Science is limiting itself and creating progress by attacking only those problems that it can attack, considering the knowledge and methods at its disposal. Psychology has made significant progress in this century, and that progress is accelerating. However, psychology is limited, and it should be if it wants to continue with its progress - limited to asking questions, but certain of its results (Hebb, 1974; p.74).*

## INDIVIDUAL DIFFERENCES IN PERSONALITY

The beginnings of research on individual personality differences were focused on the development of a questionnaire for (self)assessment of personality (Eysenck, 1990). These only available assets were used for the description and prediction of behavior. Models of personality traits, which tried to move away from the level of personality to higher levels that represent a causal explanation form, were developed somewhat later. As Gale and Eysenck (1992) pointed out, psychometric methods achieved an average level of predictive validity for psychological and social importance of human behavior. This sort of success in describing personality supported the attempts to identify biological substrate obtained from psychometric measures of individual variations that followed (De Pascalis, 2004). However, despite this, self-assessment measures were the first applications and are commonly used in personality research (Robins, Fraley & Sherman, 2007).

Results obtained using psychometric instruments were analyzed using a variety of methods to record bioelectrical signals. These include procedures for monitoring the activities of the autonomic nervous system, such as electro dermal and cardiovascular recording, and the recording of the central nervous system, such as EEG recording and recording of evoked brain potentials (Diamond & Otter-Henderson, 2007). Therefore, nowadays it is possible to investigate various physiological processes in different cognitive processes, emotional states, and social interactions. A series of neurophysiological studies, which have so far formed the basis of psychophysiology of personality, has provided a very large amount of data about the fact that neurophysiological or neuro biochemical events or changes lay in the base of every mental state or process (Hugdahl, 1995a). These techniques enable an (un)limited insight into physiological processes and neurological generators of bioelectrical activity (Cacioppo, Tassinary & Bernstone, 2000). A significant number of different psychophysiological responses and methods were used to test hypotheses and to explain the biological basis of temperament and basic personality traits, especially extraversion, neuroticism, and sensation seeking (Stelmack &

Geen, 1992). Studies of biological and psychophysiological determinants of temperament and personality stemmed from specific hypotheses proposed by Pavlov and Eysenck in their classic experimental studies of personality (Eysenck, 1963, 1967; Nebylitsyn and Gray, 1972; Strelau, 1983a). In a way, these authors laid the foundations of psychophysiology of personality, although the concept of excitation, which found its special place in each of their personality theories, was explored in other areas of psychology, such as emotion and motivation (Duffy, 1962). For an obvious reason, these personality theories will represent the conceptual framework of this book, but prior to their description, it is necessary to provide a more detailed overview of the concept of arousal.

## AROUSAL AND PERSONALITY

Elizabeth Duffy (1904-1970) made a significant contribution to the field of emotion and motivation in her 40 years of research activity (Stelmack, 2004). Her work on physiological arousal and behavior in children has found continuity in mobilizing energy with emotional and motivated behavior. In addition, she was a pioneer in the application of psychophysiological methods in the research on the level of physiological arousal of different people in different situations. Based on her research, she concluded that the description of behavior at a given moment requires two aspects: a) direction – an approach or retreat to people, things, ideas, or any element of the environment; and b) activation, arousal or intensity (Duffy, 1972). In connection with this, activation or arousal may be general or specific, in which changes are continuously occurring in the physiological functioning of the body of an individual who is trying as efficiently as possible to meet the demands of his environment. Based on this consideration, Duffy (1972) proposed a continuum of psychological conditions that can be understood in terms of their correspondence with the mobilization of energy continuum, with which her colleagues Lindsley (1951) and Malmo (1959) quite agreed. The activation or arousal dimension represented a dimension as described in that continuum of neurophysiological conditions, which were ranked from deep sleep to strongly excited states. So, arousal is presenting a continuous state of an individual, while excitation presents a temporarily state that is closely related with a certain stimulus. At that time, research reticular formation was marked as a significant progress in neurophysiology excitation. It was found that low amplitude and high frequency electroencephalographic (EEG) activity are associated with wakefulness and attention, and a high amplitude and low frequency EEG are associated with the activity of sleep and sleepiness (Jasper, 1949). Moruzzi and Magoun (1949) showed that these measures of arousal are moderated by the activity of the ascending reticular activation system (ARAS-a). In the study of functional importance of ARAS, it was suggested that the relationship between the state of excitation in this continuum and performance could be described using the inverted U-curve (Hebb, 1949).

Arousal is a very specific concept because it is ubiquitous. In other words, almost every physiological response can be considered as an indicator of the degree of activation (Duffy, 1972). Therefore, it is recommended to apply multiple psychophysiological recording methods to identify systems and patterns of responses that correspond to specific phenomena in the continuum excitation, as well to interact with environmental conditions and individual differences in behavior. Therefore, it is quite clear that arousal system is being viewed as a system that is not homogeneous, but is composed of a large number of subsystems with different functions (Hebb, 1949). Malmo (1959) also pointed to the shaky foundation of defense of those viewpoints that claimed that ARAS is a unique intensity moderated mechanism. He claimed that ARAS is actually not a homogeneous anatomical system, but unfortunately, he never managed to empirically verify his hypothesis. Later studies that resulted in a low inter-correlation between psychophysiological indicators of arousal, for example, the conductivity of the skin of the thumb, heart rate, muscle potentials and EEG desynchronization that are observed under certain conditions, greatly served as significant evidence against the one-dimensionality of the construct of arousal (Elliott, 1964; Lacey, 1967; Kaplan, 1964).

As for the areas of personality psychology, Duffy (1966) pointed out that the degree of activation affects the sensory sensitivity and motor response, and that it is involved in all the consistencies of behavior, which are called personality traits. The greatest interest was on the application of psychophysiological recording techniques for the study of anxiety - individual differences in this personality trait, which is assumed to be characterized by patterns of high activation (Duffy, 1972). However, the dominating conclusion of a large number of extensive review papers on the results of these studies was ambiguous. Duffy (1962) concluded that a fairly small number of studies have found a significant correlation between physiological and behavioral measures in the normal population. In addition, since there is almost no significant positive relationship between behavioral changes and those that occur in the activation response, researchers were directed to seek explanations of those significant negative correlations that were mainly found in the same research. However, the crucial fact is, according to Duffy (1962), that researchers in the field of psychology of personality are constantly making the same mistakes - constantly examining the direct relationship between physiological activation measures and measures guiding aspects of behavior, such as for example, attitudes, values, aggression, and shyness. Nevertheless, with the approach they ignore the fact that behavior steering and the intensity or mobilization of energy that occur with certain conducts are relatively independent aspects of human responses. In addition, the already existing confusion becomes even greater with the inadequate implementation of physiological and psychometric measures in the research literature (Fulgosi, 1994, 1997).

Today's two very influential personality theories, Gray's Reinforcement sensitivity theory (1982, 1987, 1991) and Zuckerman's Sensation Seeking Theory (1969, 1979), demonstrate just how significant this construct is. Although both theoretical frameworks don't represent the focus of this research, they have played a very important role throughout the history of the development of personality psychology, as well as in contemporary discourses about the biology of personality. Gray's model of personality (1970, 1972, 1982) resulted from the efforts to find a compromise between Pavlov's and Eysenck's theory of personality, and it was obtained based on the rotation of Eysenck's personality factors of neuroticism and extraversion in 45°. The obtained factors of anxiety (neuroticism introverts: N + E) and impulsivity (extravert neuroticism: N + E +), which he connected with the process of punishment and rewards, were two basic dimensions of personality. In connection with this, an increased level of anxiety reflects the high degree of sensitivity to signals of punishment, non-rewarding and novelties, and a high degree of impulsivity reflects a high degree of sensitivity to signals of reward and impunity. Gray believed that both dimensions are associated with the level of extraversion in a way in which extraverts are more reactive to award signals, and introverts to signals of punishment (1983). In other words, the difference between introverts and extraverts is caused by the functioning of the nervous system, or by its attitude accessibility, which is higher in introverts (Tadinac, Vukosav & Bunjevac, 1984). He tried to explain their relationship on the basis of the physiological system, the so-called "behavioral inhibition system" (BIS), which controls the level of anxiety and consists of a set of interactive structures "septum-hippocampal system," its monoamine afferent pathways from the brain stem and neocortical projection in the frontal lobe (Gray, 1983). By adding it to the existing "behavioral inhibition system" (BIS), the construct "behavioral activation system" (BAS), Gray (1991) set a theory of personality called Reinforcement Sensitivity Theory. However, although the contribution of Gray's model was significant in the physiological sense, and there is a number of researches that verified the set theory of personality

(Matthews & Gilliland, 2001), the idea of the rotating Eysenck's personality dimensions in meaningful constructs did not maintain for a long time.

Besides that, psychophysiological researches are trying to determine the physiological processes that are correlated with certain personality factors, which the Cattell factor-analytic model has a lot of, e.i. sixteen. This process is called Physiological (biochemical) indexation of certain personality traits (Cattell, 1973, according to Fulgosi, 1994), and some of such organic correlates are the events of arousal, practical indicators and others. Catell developed two concepts somatic activation, based on his own and other research: autonomously - endocrine (functioning ANS) and cortical (Fulgosi, 1994), whose measures were included in the above process. The physiological indexation factor of personality is still far from its finality, but the inclusion of a growing number of physiologic variables can certainly contribute to a better discrimination of personality factors based on physiological functioning. As mentioned before, this theoretical model of personality describes the use of two main axes of human behavior: the Behavioral Inhibition System - BIS, and the Behavioral Activation System - BAS. Persons whose behavior prevails within the BIS usually show behavioral avoidance and withdrawal, and a high sensitivity to punishment. In contrast, individuals with a dominant BAS often exhibit behaviors of interest and accession, and a high sensitivity to reward. When compared to the orthogonal display of Eysenck's extraversion and emotional stability, both the BIS and the BAS pass diagonally. Thus, the BIS diagonal, which passes between the high levels of extraversion and emotional stability, indicates low anxiety, and when passing between high neuroticism and high introversion, it shows a very high level of anxiety. In contrast, if an individual with his personality traits is located between high extraversion and high neurotic, he or she exhibits high impulsiveness, and if the traits are located between high introversion and high emotional stability, this indicates a low level of impulsiveness. The Revised reinforcement sensitivity theory (Gray & McNaughton, 2000) empirical research has shown that people with dominant BAS behaviors are sensitive to the conditioned and unconditioned stimuli of rewards; they tie their emotions and anticipation of pleasure, and exhibit impulsive optimism. In contrast, people with dominant BIS behaviors often associate emotions with concern; they tend to be anxious, try to solve all internal conflicts and put themselves in a non-confrontational situation, and quickly recognize the situation of vulnerability for themselves.

On the other hand, arousal presented the main theoretical concept in Eysenck's (1967) theory of extraversion and Zuckerman's theory of sensation seeking (1969). The main difference between their understandings of arousal as a psychological construct was also the fact that Eysenck incorporated it within his conditioning theory and Zuckerman within the effects of sensory deprivation on both the physiological and psychological processes. In other words, Eysenck (1967) was focused on stimulus intensity as the significant mediator and arousal, based on which the physiological foundation of differences between introverts and extraverts and learning could be determined. The difference, as Zuckerman stated, lies in the fact that the main predictor of arousal is the need or hunger for a stimulus. This need has been established in laboratory experiments, where after increased isolation (or sensory deprivation) the increased reactions to receiving more stimuli that are different have been determined (Zuckerman & Haber, 1965). Therefore, he created the Sensation Seeking Scale with the aim of defining "an operational measure of the optimum level of stimulation and the optimum level of arousal" (Zuckerman, 1979, p.91).

The main postulation within his theory is that individual differences are determined with specific levels of stimulation and arousal. Therefore, high-sensation seeking individuals are those who have the optimal functioning when they are on the high tonic level of arousal, as they constantly seek for more stimulation. With this in line, low-sensation seekers are individuals who are the happiest when they achieve the low tonic level of arousal, as they avoid high stimulation. First definition of sensation seeking stimuli included three properties that were favored by high sensation seekers: complexity, novelty, and variety. Later on, he added the intensity of stimuli. A variety of studies has demonstrated the differences between low and high sensation seekers regarding early-evoked brain potentials. Zuckerman, Murtaugh, and Siegel (1974) determined that high disinhibits showed higher amplitudes of the early-evoked potentials, and Buchsbaum (1971) determined that low sensation seekers showed decrease in that same amplitude. Thus, the aforementioned optimum level of stimulation in psychological research was operationalized as a trait of sensation seeking for which various physiological, organic, and biochemical correlates have been defined. Individuals who are hungry for excitement have a greater need and are more inclined to experiencing various high-exciting situations, experiences, and sexual excitements. They have a bigger total amount of sex hormones (they inhibit the production of monoamine oxidase), and a lower level of MAO enzyme in the brain. Monoamine oxidase - affects the breakdown of monoamines, which have an important role in emotions and affecting the general level of activation in the body, and is inversely related to norepinephrine and dopamine, which are excreted during positive affective brain experiences in the brain center for positive stimulation. Correlation analyses have shown the most significant positive correlation between sensation seeking traits and psychoticism (Zuckerman, 1991). Based on the aforementioned, Zuckerman set up a biochemical model of personality that included: sex hormones, brain norepinephrine and dopamine, as well as peripheral and cerebral MAO with their genetic base, the limbic system of rewards, ARAS, cortex, physiological parameters: the amplitude of the orientation reflex (OR), electro dermal response and heart rate, an increase of mean values of evoked brain potentials and ultimately manifested the trait of sensation-seeking behavior in individuals (1979 to 1983).

## PSYCHOPHYSIOLOGY OF PERSONALITY

Psychophysiology of personality is related to research on the biological basis of personality, which primarily uses psychophysiological techniques of various durations and extents of the provided information. It is based on a series of neurophysiological studies of human behavior and functioning, which deal with the study of connections and dependencies between mental and physical, which so far have provided an extremely large amount of data that claims that neurophysiological or neuro biochemical event or change are behind virtually every mental state or process. Other things were investigated and established, such as the differential forms and morpho-physiological substrates and numerous command centers in the brain that determine the ways of learned/innate behaviors and responses, experiences and personality traits, both at the level of the cerebral cortex, as well as the subcortical levels - up to the brainstem. In addition to the mentioned determining of the typical neurophysiological patterns associated with a particular type of behavior, the main goal of this study is to determinc the actual mechanisms of neural functioning that are in the background of this same behavior and individual differences (Fulgosi, 1994). They are possible due to a variety of techniques of registering every activity of the autonomic nervous system - ANS-a (electro dermal, temperature, cardiovascular and gastrointestinal measures) and the central nervous system - CNS (electro cortical and magneto cortical measures and measures of cerebral blood flow and metabolism). With a detailed study of the field of psychophysiology of individual differences in humans and the biological basis of personality, or more specifically, electroencephalographic correlates of different personality traits, it is possible to spot two dominant aspects, depending on the initial theoretical framework. On the one hand, there is one which is characterized by persistent quite clear and understandable theoretically substantiated efforts in carrying out neurophysiological researches within psychology, which today represents one of the most developed and most dynamic areas of research (Hugdahl, 1995a) of connections and dependencies between the mental and the physical (Fulgosi, 1994). On the other hand, the same research has resulted not only in rich knowledge in the context of the confirmation of the hypotheses or outside the framework, but it has also produce a large amount of unenviable questions directed to (un)solved methodological problems. In the attempts to find a way out of these methodological mazes, previous studies of psychophysiology of human behavior, showed in the scientific research literature in both psychology, but also other related disciplines, were trying to satisfactorily answer most of these questions, in the most reliable way of applying the combination of the shown psychophysiological methods.

By studying the literature in the field of personality psychology, to this day the most common and most detailed researched are the psychophysiology Eysencks extraversion (E) and neuroticism (N), and Zuckermans personality dimensions – sensation seeking (SS) (Stelmack & Geen, 1992). In the last three decades, most of the literature has been increasingly focused on extraversion. There is strong evidence that extraversion is genetically determined (Zuckerman, 1995). In addition, most of the factor-analytic theories of personality agree that extraversion has a definite place among the fundamental dimensions of personality, although there are still disagreements about the number and nature of other characteristics from which it varies (Costa & McCrae, 1985; Zuckerman, 1995). Finally, extraversion is associated with biological concepts, which is discussed in detail in the context of Eysenck's well-known theory of personality (1967).

The psychophysiological measures are: electro dermal activity, cardiovascular activity, body temperature, pupillometry, electroencephalography, and evoked brain potentials. The following findings were obtained by indexing the concept of arousal with the aforementioned psychophysiological measures and by applying them in the study of extraversion:

1. **Extraversion and Electro Dermal Activity:** The whole electro dermal activity was recorded as a change in the electrical resistance of the skin (Hugdahl, 1995b). In relation to these variables, there is an equal number of different findings. The conditions of the experiment included: just noticeably stimulation, low intensity stimuli, less arousing conditions, and simple task requirements or placebo conditions (Fowles, Nagel & Roberts, 1977; Smith, Jones & Wilson, 1983; all according to Zuckerman, 1991), the individual differences in activity between electro dermal activity between introverts and extraverts occurred rarely (Coles, Gale & Kline, 1971; Nielsen & Petersen, 1976; Davis & Cowles, 1988; all according to Stelmack & Geen, 1992). On the other hand, while high

demanding and challenging tasks were set during the experiment, such as assignments with arithmetic problems or tasks that require long-term retention of attention (Fowles, Roberts & Nagel, 1977; Smith, Rockwell-Tischer & Davidson, 1986; all according to Stelmack & Geen, 1992), as well as those with high tones and large doses of caffeine (Fowles, Roberts & Nagel, 1977; Smith, Wilson & Jones, 1983; all according to Zuckerman, 1991), significantly higher levels of skin conductance were measured in introverts than extraverts. Regarding the relation of extraversion and sensitivity to stimulation (auditory, visual, etc.), in experiments where some activities were performed, introverts preferred quieter, less excitable environment with fewer opportunities for socializing than extraverts, so they choose to study in the library with lower levels of visual and auditory stimulation; introverts are also more sensitive and have a lower tolerance to stimulation than extraverts; extraverts set the sound intensity to 20dB higher than introverts when they were offered a choice in that sense (Campbell & Hawley, 1982; Campbell, 1983, 1992; Dornic & Ehehammar, 1990; Green, 1984; all according to Stelmack, 1997).

2. **Extraversion and Cardiovascular Activity:** A number of studies have examined the study of differences between introverts and extraverts in their cardiovascular activity measured by electrocardiogram (ECG), which resulted in a series of inconsistent results, mainly due to different types and intensity of the applied stimulus (Zuckerman, 1991). Specifically, Stelmack and associates (1979; according Stelmack & Geen, 1992) did not find comparable differences in the heart rhythm of extraverts and introverts. On the other side, authors Gange, Geen, and Harkins (1979, according to Stelmack & Geen, 1992) found higher heart rates in introverts than extraverts in all experimental conditions including the tasks of attention and control tasks, which did not have any set tasks. However, since they did not detect differences in the heart rate between the two groups of participants when their basic rhythm was studied, it was concluded that the obtained results indicate differences in the heart rate to a certain extent and reflect the reactions of participants to a certain form of applied experimental procedure.
3. **Extraversion and Body Temperature:** The measured body temperature during the duration of 24 hours (from 4.00 P.M. to 4.00 A.M.) in two groups of participants showed the following. Blake's research (1967, according to Stelmack, 1981) showed that body temperature in the morning was higher in introverts than in extraverts, but this changed in the evenings when it was determined that the body temperature is higher in

extraverts than in introverts. This finding is also confirmed by another research from Folkard (1975, according to Stelmack, 1981), who applied the measure of subjective evaluation levels of alertness during the day both in introverts and extraverts. A group of introverts was estimated to be more awake in the morning hours, and a group of extraverts in the afternoon and evening.

4. **Extraversion and Pupillary Reaction:** The so-called pupillometry is a relatively new developed psychophysiological measure (Stelmack, 1981). The iris muscle that surrounds the pupil of the eye is reciprocally innervated by the ANS, and the effect of that system is especially dominant in the pupil reflex to light (pupillary reflex). In the case of pupil reflex to light, by recording pupils at various time intervals after giving them a light stimulus, differences between extraverts and introverts were observed. Most studies demonstrated, that participants who showed a wider and faster constriction of the pupils in different experimental conditions, also had a low score on a scale of extraversion (Eysenck & Eysenck, 1985). This suggested that they were more excited and reactive, and had greater amounts of acetylcholine in the cholinergic synapses, which is associated with a higher reactivity to the environment and faster conditioning (Holmes, 1967; Frith, 1977; all according to Stelmack, 1981).
5. **Extraversion and Electroencephalography:** Development and application of EEG represents a significant technological advantage, that has allowed researchers from different disciplines an objective method of recording bioelectrical brain signals to electrodes on the surface of the head (Faber, 1980; Gale & Edwards, 1983a,b, 1986; Gale, 1986, 1987; Eysenck, 1990; Stelmack & Geen, 1992; Dabić-Jeftić & Mikula, 1994a; Hugdahl, 1995c; Wilson, 1995; Šantić, 1995; Judaš & Kostović, 1997; Pinel, 1997a). In the psychophysiological studies of personality traits, more specifically of extraversion, the basic hypothesis was that higher levels of cortical arousal are inherent to introverts as opposed to extraverts. The higher cortical arousal in EEG studies is operationalized and described as a brain activity of low amplitude and high frequency in the alpha brain rhythm: 8 -13 Hz (Stelmack, 1981; Eysenck & Eysenck, 1985). Starting from this hypothesis, A. Gale (1980, 1983) and colleagues (1969) showed thirty-three studies containing a total of thirty-eight experimental comparisons: in twenty-two of them extraverts were less induced than introverts, i.e. they had $\alpha$-rhythm of lower frequencies; in five of them introverts were less excited than extraverts; and in eight of them, there was no significant difference between introverts and extraverts.

For an explanation of inconsistent findings obtained, Gale (1981, 1983) listed three methodological reasons: a) the use of techniques that rely on manually scoring (unreliable and subject to systematic errors); b) high variability of research in relation to the used technical support (electrodes, defining α-activity); c) and a significant variation in the complexity of tasks that they have had to perform in these studies. Therefore, he suggested that the effects of extraversion on EEG are influenced by a level of excitation, that is induced by experimental conditions. Therefore, he believed that introverts would probably be more excited than extraverts in medium-arousing experimental conditions, so experimental situations with extremely low and high levels of arousal should be avoided when testing the hypotheses. In addition, Venturini, de Pascalis, Imperiali and Martini (1981; according to Eysenck, 1990) did not find any significant differences in the basic α-rhythms of extraverts and introverts, but they did find them in the declining of the α-rhythm. Extraverts adapted to the auditory stimulants, while introverts did not, which implies that introverts are generally more sensitive to stimulation. Although this is a range of inconsistent findings, there is a majority of those who are in favor of Eysenckov's premise that extraverts will have an α-rhythm of high amplitude and low frequency introverts an α-rhythm of low amplitude and high frequency, and neurotics slow y- and fast β - brain waves (Eysenck, 1967).

Some studies (Sternberg, 1992, 1994) showed that a personality trait of a lower order - impulsivity, which forms most of the dimensions of extraversion, shows a stronger association with low excitation than extraversion. However, in addition to those already disclosed, Gale and Edwards (1983a) cited other reasons which lay under the inconsistent psychophysiological findings related to personality, collectively called "the seven deadly sins in the psychophysiology of individual differences". They are: theoretical over-simplicity; obsession with the correlation rather than with the process; poor psychometrics; poor physiology; trivial experimentation; procedural insensitivity; low level of knowledge in the processing and interpretation of results; and highlighted the advantages of using the paradigm in psychophysiological research personality traits. Although Stelmack (1997) pointed out the comforting fact of proven heritability of extraversion, which he stated was a good enough reason to believe in the fact that the biological basis of extraversion will finally be fully determined and clearly defined, to the stated he also added the following (1981): limitations of data obtained through self-assessment questionnaires as EPQ, the division of participants into groups of extraverts and introverts, and ignoring sexual differences, which is further discussed in the discussion paper.

6. **Extraversion and Brain Evoked Potentials:** This is a measure of electro cortical activity. It is recorded in relation to a specific and controlled stimulation from the environment, while the kind and intensity of the applied stimuli are significant (Cobb & Morocutti 1966; Bergamini, Bergamasco, Gastaut & Sprague, 1967; Donchin & Lindsley, 1968; Begleiter, 1979; Faber, 1980, Picton, 1980; Stelmack, 1981; Loveless, 1983; Eysenck, 1990; Kenemans, 1990; Stelmack & Geen, 1992; Dabić-Jeftić & Mikula, 1994a; Hugdahl, 1995d; Šantić, 1995; Judaš & Kostović, 1997; Pinel, 1997a; Stelmack, 1997). Its advantage is that it provides an insight into the changes in the amplitude and latency of brain waves specific timely related to set stimulus. In general, it was found that by increasing the intensity of the given stimuli of any modality from the environment, the amplitude of evoked brain potentials increases (Regan, 1972; according to Stelmack, 1981), which also reflects, according to Näätänen (1975) and Teder (1994), an elevated level of included attention. Since it has been proved that evoked brain potentials serve as reliable indicators of changes in sensitivity to stimuli and attention, they represent a suitable technique to study the difference between psychophysiological differences between extraverts and introverts. Overall, Stelmack (1997) reported about a series of studies published during 1960 and 1970 in which he examined the sensitivity to stimuli in introverts and extraverts, where it resulted in higher sensitivity in the case of introverts according to extraverts to low intensity stimulation in the auditory (Stelmack & Campbell, 1974) and visual modalities (Siddle, Morris, Manganese & White, 1969). Furthermore, in the application of evoked brain potentials, and in experiments with moderate sensory stimulation, greater amplitudes of brain waves were mostly recorded in introverts than in extraverts (Stelmack, 1981), but such differences did not exist in experimental situations with high intensity stimuli regardless of the type of modalities (visual, auditory, somatosensory). However, given the particular specificity and peculiarities of each wave within a group called evoked brain potentials, it is not reliable to show generalized and general results in the study of the differences between introverts and extraverts. Therefore, the results of individual differences between the two groups of participants in previous researches will be more clearly presented in the later division of exogenous and endogenous evoked brain potentials.

Finally, several authors emphasized the need for a holistic approach in the study of human personality, which is nowadays attempted to be operationalized and measured under the identity theory (Tatalović Vorkapić, 2014b). Although the basis of his theory is psychobiological, Zuckerman pointed out the existence of two pathways and individual differences in human personality: the biological and social one (Zuckerman, 2003). Within that, Zuckerman (1992) emphasized that psychobiology of personality consists of complex, hierarchical relations between several elements: personality traits, social behavior, learning (conditioning and modeling), physiology, biochemistry, neurology and genetics, which were presented as seven turtles. Starting from the common ground of evolution, the social pathway consists of culture, society, neighborhood, family, and observational learning and social reinforcement. Regarding the biological pathway, it consists of genetics, neurology, biochemistry, physiology, and conditioning. These two pathways lead to behavioral traits that consequently lead to personality traits. Similarly, in some aspects, Eysenck (1997) pointed out that the only truly comprehensive and meaningful psychological research framework in the study of human behavior and functioning consists of three basic disciplines: correlation, experimental and psychophysiological, all with the aim of uniting the science of psychology, and the possibility of creating a paradigm within the same. He established the existence of five basic components (Eysenck, 1981b; to 1997). With the goal of explaining the human person in an integral way, each of the models of personality structure should have these components listed, which he tried to elaborate in detail within his Dimensional typology of personality and its main dimensions (extraversion, neuroticism, and psychoticism), which also represent the initial theoretical framework in this research. By displaying this biological model of personality, whose fundamental characteristic is the integrity of the study of human behavior and functioning, it was attempted to argue the validity of explanations and analyzing the relationship between endogenous ERP components P300, the recorded latencies and amplitudes, and its personality traits of extraversion/introversion.

With regards to this model, the entire personality consists of the following components: the so-called distal (distant) causative factors that precede or are the genetic basis of a certain behavior and relate to the genetically determined personality factors (DNA); proximal (near) causing factors related to biological intermediates as the arousal of the limbic system, and this order of personality mediators would also include the P300 component (and other evoked brain potentials), which is interesting for this study, as a delayed wave long provoked by an external stimuli, which is a part of the endogenous brain potentials; known psychometric constellation of personality traits: extraversion (E), neuroticism (N) and psychoticism (P); proximal (closer) factors consequences that are experimentally studied in the context of the process of conditioning, sensitivity, attention, perception, memory and recall; and distal (distant) factors of consequences which are manifested and studied in the form of social behavior: sociability, crime, creativity, psychopathology and sexual behavior (Eysenck, 1997). If we now pay attention to the study of the relationship between evoked brain potentials and the E-I dimension of personality, i.e. the possible differences between extraverts and introverts in the amount of the P300-amplitude (cognitive EP-component), as well as the initial restriction on the result explanations obtained in research, it is important to point out which segment of personality is being discussed and how big it is, The ideal would be the creation of such a research draft that would cover behavioral genetic studies of personality, studies of biological mediators, experimental studies, and the studies of social behavior. Also, one of the most important problems in this area of research are the vagueness and arbitrariness in determining the neural mechanisms and anatomic-physiologic structures, which in many cases have a descriptive, not an explanatory meaning, and they often have a hypothetical character (Fulgosi, 1994). Regardless of these difficulties, the general strategy of research is extremely important in this field for associating such neural mechanisms with individual differences in behavior, i.e. with personality traits that have been identified in an independent way - by applying psychological tests.

## REFERENCES


Atkinson, R. L., Atkinson, R. C., Smith, E. E., Bem, D. J., & Nolen-Hoeksema, S. (1996). Individual Differences. In *Hilgard's introduction to psychology* (12th ed.; pp. 408–445). Harcourt Brace & Company.

Begleiter, H. (1979). Evoked brain potentials and behavior.*Proceedings of a Conference on Evoked brain potentials and behavior held at the Downstate Medical Center, State University ofNew York*. Plenum Press. doi:10.1007/978-1-4684-3462-0

Bergamini, L., Bergamasco, B., Gastaut, H., & Sprague, J. M. (1967). *Cortical evoked potentials in man*. Charles C. Thomas Publisher.

Buchsbaum, M. S., & Stevens, S. S. (1971). Neural events and the psychophysical law. *Science*, *172*(3982), 502. doi:10.1126/science.172.3982.502 PMID:5550509

Cacioppo, J. T., Tassinary, L. G., & Bernston, G. G. (2000). Psychophysiological science. In *Handbook of Psychophysiology* (2nd ed.; pp. 3–23). Cambridge, UK: Cambridge University Press.

Canli, T. (2006). *Biology of Personality and Individual Differences*. London: The Guilford Press.

Cobb, W., & Morocutti, C. (1966). The evoked potentials: Proceedings of an International Meeting held in Siena (Italy). *Electroencephalography and Clinical Neurophysiology, 26.*

Costa, P. T., & McRea, R. R. (1985). *The NEO-Personality Inventory: Manual Form S and Form R.* Psychological Assessment Resources, Inc.

Dabić-Jeftić, M., & Mikula, I. (1994a). Evocirani potencijali kore mozga – Osnovne postavke i klinička primjena [Evoked brain potentials – Fundamental postulates and clinical application]. Školska knjiga.

De Pascalis, V. (2004). On the Psychophysiology of Extraversion. In R. M. Stelmack (Ed.), *On the Psychobiology of Personality: Essays in Honor of Marvin Zuckerman* (pp. 295–327). Elsevier Ltd. doi:10.1016/B978-008044209-9/50017-8

Diamond, L. M., & Otter-Henderson, K. D. (2007). Physiological Measures. In R. W. Robins, R. C. Fraley, & R. F. Krueger (Eds.), *Handbook of Research Methods in Personality Psychology* (pp. 370–388). London: Guilford Press.

Donchin, E., & Lindsley, D. B. (1968). Average evoked potentials: Methods, results and evaluations. National aeronautics and space administration.

Duffy, E. (1962). *Activation and Behavior*. New York: Wiley.

Duffy, E. (1966). The nature and development of the concept of activation. In R. N. Haber (Ed.), *Current research in motivation* (pp. 278–281). New York: Holt, Rinehart and Winston.

Duffy, E. (1972). Activation. In N. S. Greenfield & R. A. Sternbach (Eds.), *Handbook of psychophysiology* (pp. 577–622). New York: Holt, Rinehart and Winston.

Elliot, R. (1964). Physiological activity and performance: A comparison of kindergarten children with young adults. *Psychological Monographs, 78*(10).

Eysenck, H. J. (1963). *Experiments with Drugs*. Oxford, UK: Pergamon Press.

Eysenck, H. J. (1967). *Biological basis of personality*. Springfield, IL: Charles C Thomas Publisher.

Eysenck, H. J. (1990). Biological Dimensions of Personality. In L. E. Pervin (Ed.), *Handbook of Personality* (pp. 244–276). John Wiley & Sons, Inc.

Eysenck, H. J. (1997). Personality and Experimental Psychology: The Unification of Psychology and the Possibility of a Paradigm. *Journal of Personality and Social Psychology*, *73*(6), 1224–1237. doi:10.1037/0022-3514.73.6.1224

Eysenck, H. J., & Eysenck, M. W. (1985). Chapter eight: The psychophysiology of personality. In *Personality and individual differences: A natural science approach* (pp. 217–236). New York: Plenum Press. doi:10.1007/978-1-4613-2413-3_8

Faber, B. (1980). Artefakti u elektroencefalografiji [Artifacts in Electroencephalography]. Psychiatric Hospital Jankomir.

Feldman, R. S. (1997). Personality. In *Essentials of understanding psychology* (3rd ed.; pp. 371–400). The McGraw-Hill Companies, Inc.

Fulgosi, A. (1994). *Biološke osnove ličnosti [Biological bases of personality]*. Jastrebarsko, Croatia: Naklada Slap.

Fulgosi, A. (1997). Psihologija ličnosti: teorije i istraživanja [Personality Psychology: Theory and research]. Školska knjiga.

Gale, A. (1980). Electroencephalographic Correlates of Extraversion-Introversion. In R. Sinz & M. R. Rosenzweig (Eds.), *Psychophysiology* (pp. 237–256). Berlin: Springer-Verlag.

Gale, A. (1981). EEG studies of extraversion-introversion: what's the next step? In R. Lynn (Ed.), *Dimensions of personality: Papers in honour of H. J. Eysenck* (pp. 181–207). Oxford, UK: Pergamon.

Gale, A. (1983). Electroencephalographic Studies of Extraversion-Introversion: A Case Study in the Psychophysiology of Individual Differences. *Personality and Individual Differences*, *4*(4), 371–380. doi:10.1016/0191-8869(83)90002-8

Gale, A. (1986). Extraversion-introversion and spontaneous rhythms of the brain: Retrospect and prospect. In J. Strelau, F. K. Farley, & A. Gale (Eds.), *The biological bases of personality and behavior: Psychophysiology, performance, and application* (Vol. 2, pp. 25–57). Hemisphere Publishing Corporation.

Gale, A. (1987). The Electroencephalogram. In A. Gale & B. Christie (Eds.), *Psychophysiology and the Electronic Workplace* (pp. 223–237). John Wiley & Sons, Ltd.

Gale, A., Coles, M., & Blaydon, J. (1969). Extraversion-introversion and the EEG. *British Journal of Psychology*, *60*(2), 209–223. doi:10.1111/j.2044-8295.1969.tb01194.x PMID:5787680

Gale, A., & Edwards, J. A. (1983a). Psychophysiology and Individual Differences: Theory, Research, Procedures and the Interpretation of Data. *Australian Journal of Psychology*, *35*(3), 361–379. doi:10.1080/00049538308258749

Gale, A., & Edwards, J. A. (1983b). The EEG and Human Behaviour. In Physiological Correlates of Human Behaviour: Vol II: Attention and Performance (pp. 99-127). Academic Press Inc.

Gale, A., & Edwards, J. A. (1986). Individual differences. In M. G. H. Coles, E. Donchin, & S. W. Porges (Eds.), *Psychophysiology: Systems, Processes and Applications* (pp. 431–507). New York: The Gulford Press.

Gale, A., & Eysenck, M. W. (1992). *Handbook of Individual Differences: Biological Perspectives*. New York: Wiley.

Gray, J. A. (1970). The psychophysiological basis of introversion–extraversion. *Behaviour Research and Therapy*, *8*(3), 249–266. doi:10.1016/0005-7967(70)90069-0 PMID:5470377

Gray, J. A. (1972). The psychophysiological nature of introversion-extraversion: a modification of Eysenck's theory. In V. D. Nebylitsyn & J. A. Gray (Eds.), *Biological bases of individual behavior* (pp. 182–205). London: Academic Press. doi:10.1016/B978-0-12-515350-8.50017-X

Gray, J. A. (1982). *The neuropsychology of anxiety: An enquiry into the functions of the septo-hippocampal system*. Oxford, UK: Oxford University Press.

Gray, J. A. (1983). Anxiety, Personality and the Brain. In A. Gale & J. A. Edwards (Eds.), Physiological Correlates of Human Behaviour: Vol III. Individual Differences and Psychopathology (pp. 31-43). Academic Press Inc.

Gray, J. A. (1987). *The psychology of fear and stress* (2nd ed.). Cambridge, UK: Cambridge University Press.

Gray, J. A. (1991). Neural systems, emotion and personality. In J. Madden IV, (Ed.), *Neurobiology of learning, emotion and affect* (pp. 273–306). New York: Raven Press.

Gray, J. A., & McNaughton, N. (2000). *The neuropsychology of anxiety: An enquiry into the functions of the septo-hippocampal system* (2nd ed.). Oxford, UK: Oxford University Press.

Hebb, D. O. (1949). *Organization of behavior*. New York: Wiley.

Hugdahl, K. (1995a). An overview of psychophysiology: Introduction. In *Psychophysiology: The Mind-Body Perspective* (pp. 3–31). Harvard University Press.

Hugdahl, K. (1995b). Collecting and analyzing data: Electrodermal activity. In *Psychophysiology: The Mind-Body Perspective* (pp. 101–130). Harvard University Press.

Hugdahl, K. (1995c). Collecting and analyzing data: The Electroencephalogram. In *Psychophysiology: The Mind-Body Perspective* (pp. 234–265). Harvard University Press.

Hugdahl, K. (1995d). Event-related potentials. In *Psychophysiology: The Mind-Body Perspective* (pp. 266–308). Harvard University Press.

Jasper, H. H. (1949). Diffuse projection system: The integrative action of the thalamic reticular system. *Electroencephalography and Clinical Neurophysiology, 1*(1-4), 405–419. doi:10.1016/0013-4694(49)90213-8 PMID:18421831

Judaš, M., & Kostović, I. (1997). Opće moždane funkcije: uzlazni aktivacijski sustavi, EEG, stupnjevi budnosti i stanja svijesti [General brain functions: ascending activation systems, EEG, degree of alertness and states of consciences]. In The basics of neuroscience (pp. 295-319). MD.

Kaplan, A. (1964). The conduct of inquiry: Methodology for behavioural science. Scranton, PA: Chandler.

Kenemans, J. L. (1990). *Event-related brain potential manifestations of orienting* (Doctoral Dissertation). Rijksuniversiteit, Den Hag, Netherlands.

Lacey, J. I. (1967). Somatic response patterning and stress: some revisions of activation theory. In M. H. Appley & R. Trumbull (Eds.), *Psychological stress: Issues and research*. New York: Appleton-Century-Crofts.

Lindsley, D. B. (1951). Emotion. In S. S. Stevens (Ed.), *Handbook of experimental psychology*. New York: Wiley.

Loveless, N. E. (1983). Event-related brain potentials and human performance. In: A. Gale & J. A. Edwards (Eds.), Physiological Correlates of Human Behaviour: Vol II. Attention and Performance (pp. 79-97). Academic Press Inc.

Malmo, R. B. (1959). Activation: A neurophysiological dimension. *Psychological Review, 66*(6), 367–386. doi:10.1037/h0047858 PMID:14420402

Matthews, G., & Gilliland, K. (2001). Personality, biology and cognitive science: A reply to Corr (2001). *Personality and Individual Differences, 30*(2), 353–362. doi:10.1016/S0191-8869(00)00029-5

Mlačić, B., & Knezović, Z. (1997). Struktura i relacije Big-Five markera i Eysenckova upitnika ličnosti: Empirijska usporedba dvaju strukturalnih modela ličnosti [The structure and relations of the BigFive markers and Eysenck's personality questionnaire: Empirical comparison of two structural personality models]. Društvena istraživanja, 1(27), 1-21.

Moruzzi, G., & Magoun, H. W. (1949). Brainstem reticular formation and activation of the EEG. *Electroencephalography and Clinical Neurophysiology, 1*(1-4), 455–473. doi:10.1016/0013-4694(49)90219-9 PMID:18421835

Näätänen, R. (1975). Selective attention and evoked potentials in humans: A critical review. *Biological Psychology, 2*(4), 237–307. doi:10.1016/0301-0511(75)90038-1 PMID:1156626

Nebylitsyn, V. D., & Gray, J. A. (1972). *Biological Bases of Individual Behavior*. New York: Academic Press.

Nyborg, H. (1997). *The scientific study of human nature: Tribute to Hans J. Eysenck at eighty*. Pergamon, Elsevier Science Ltd.

Picton, T. W. (1980). The use of human event-related potentials in psychology. In I. Martin & P. H. Venables (Eds.), *Techniques in psychophysiology* (pp. 357–395). John Wiley & Sons, Ltd.

Pinel, P. J. J. (1997a). What Biopsychologists do: The Research Methods of Biopsychology. In Biopsychology (pp. 105-129). University of British Columbia, Allyn & Bacon.

Robins, R. W., Fraley, R. C., & Krueger, R. F. (2007). *Handbook of Research Methods in Personality Psychology*. London: The Guilford Press.

Šantić, A. (1995). Biomedicinska elektronika [Biomedical electronics]. Školska knjiga.

Santrock, J. W. (1997). Personality. In *Psychology* (5th ed.; pp. 399–439). Dallas, TX: Brown and Benchmark Publishers, University of Texas.

Shiner, R. L., Buss, K. A., McClowry, S. G., Putnam, S. P., Saudino, K. J., & Zentner, M. (2012). What Is Temperament Now? Assessing Progress in Temperament Research on the Twenty-Fifth Anniversary of Goldsmith et al. (1987). *Child Development Perspectives*, *0*(0), 1–9. doi:10.1111/j.1750-8606.2012.00254.x

Siddle, D. A., Morris, R. B., White, K. D., & Mangan, G. L. (1969). Relation of visual sensitivity to extraversion. *Journal of Experimental Research of Personality*, *3*, 264–267.

Stelmack, R. M. (1981). The psychophysiology of extraversion and neuroticism. In H. J. Eysenck (Ed.), *A model for personality* (pp. 38–63). Springer-Verlag Berlin Heidelberg. doi:10.1007/978-3-642-67783-0_2

Stelmack, R. M. (1997). The Psychophysics and Psychophysiology of Extraversion and Arousal. In H. Nyborg (Ed.), *The Scientific Study of Human Nature: Tribute to Hans J. Eysenck at Eighty* (pp. 388–403). Oxford, UK: Pergamon Press.

Stelmack, R. M. (2004). On Personality and Arousal: A Historical Perspective on Eysenck and Zuckerman. In *On the Psychobiology of Personality: Essays in Honor of Marvin Zuckerman* (pp. 17–28). Elsevier Ltd. doi:10.1016/B978-008044209-9/50003-8

Stelmack, R. M., & Campbell, K. B. (1974). Extraversion and auditory sensitivity to high and low frequency. *Perceptual and Motor Skills*, *38*(3), 875–879. doi:10.2466/pms.1974.38.3.875 PMID:4842444

Stelmack, R. M., & Geen, R. G. (1992). The Psychophysiology of Extraversion. In A. Gale & M. W. Eysenck (Eds.), *Handbook of Individual Differences: Biological Perspectives* (pp. 227–254). New York: John Wiley & Sons, Ltd.

Stenberg, G. (1992). Personality and the EEG: Arousal and emotional arousability. *Personality and Individual Differences*, *13*(10), 1097–1113. doi:10.1016/0191-8869(92)90025-K

Stenberg, G. (1994). Extraversion and the P300 in a Visual Classification Task. *Personality and Individual Differences*, *16*(4), 543–560. doi:10.1016/0191-8869(94)90182-1

Strelau, J. (1983a). *Temperament, Personality, Activity*. London: Academic Press.

Tadinac, M., Vukosav, Ž., & Bunjevac, T. (1984). Snaga živčanog sustava i Eysenckova dimenzija ekstraverzije – introverzije [The strength of nervous system and Eysenck's dimensions of extraversion-introversion]. Revija za psihologiju, 14(1-2), 21-26.

Tatalović Vorkapić, S. (2014b). Je li privilegirani status modela osobina ličnosti u psihologiji ličnosti opravdan? – Prikaz modela identiteta [Is privileged status of personality traits' models in personality psychology justified? – Description of identity models]. *Suvremena Psihologija*, *17*(2), 181–198.

Teder, W. (1994). *Selective attention and auditory event-related potentials* (Doctoral Dissertation). University of Helsinki, Helsinki, Finland.

Wilson, G. F. (1995). Preface: EEG in basic and applied settings. *Biological Psychology*, *40*(1-2), vii–viii. doi:10.1016/0301-0511(95)90013-6 PMID:7647171

Zuckerman, M. (1969). Theoretical formulations. In J. P. Zubek (Ed.), *Sensory deprivation: Fifteen years of research* (pp. 407–432). New York: Appleton-Century-Crofts.

Zuckerman, M. (1979). *Sensation seeking: Beyond the optimal level of arousal*. Hillsdale, NJ: Erlbaum.

Zuckerman, M. (1983). *Biological basis of sensation-seeking, impulsivity and anxiety*. Hillsdale, NJ: Erlbaum.

Zuckerman, M. (1991). Psychobiology of personality. Cambridge University Press.

Zuckerman, M. (1992). What is a basic factor and whch factors are basic? Turtles all the way down. *Personality and Individual Differences*, *13*(6), 675–682. doi:10.1016/0191-8869(92)90238-K

Zuckerman, M. (1995). Good and Bad Humors: Biochemical Bases of Personality and its Disorders. *Psychological Science*, *6*(6), 325–332. doi:10.1111/j.1467-9280.1995.tb00521.x

Zuckerman, M. (2003). Biological bases of personality. In Handbook of psychology: Vol. 5. Personality and social psychology (pp. 85–116). New York: Wiley. doi:10.1002/0471264385.wei0504

Zuckerman, M. (2006). Sensation seeking in entertainment. In J. Bryant & P. Vorderer (Eds.), *Psychology of entertainment* (pp. 367–387). Mahwah, NJ: Lawrence-Erlbaum.

Zuckerman, M., & Haber, M. M. (1965). Need for stimulation as a source of stress response to perceptual isolation. *Journal of Abnormal Psychology*, *70*(5), 371–377. doi:10.1037/h0022462 PMID:5832760

Zuckerman, M., Murtaugh, T. M., & Siegel, J. (1974). Sensation seeking and cortical augmenting-reducing. *Psychophysiology*, *11*(5), 535–542. doi:10.1111/j.1469-8986.1974.tb01109.x PMID:4415722

# Chapter 2
# Biologically Based Personality Theories

## ABSTRACT

*In this section, the theoretical background of applied personality theory in presented empirical research will be introduced. Biological bases of personality are thoroughly explored within well-known Eysenck's dimensional personality theory (1967). The main postulations of this theory will be presented with the special accent on biological bases of personality, i.e. extraversion and neuroticism. This will bring light on understanding the arousal theory and Brebner-Cooper's model of extraversion. In addition, Strelau's temperament theory (1983) will be presented, regarding its theoretical postulations, main temperament dimensions and its explanation within the frame of understanding the Central Nervous System functioning.*

## INTRODUCTION TO EYSENCK'S DIMENSIONAL PERSONALITY THEORY

McAdams and Palls (2006, p. 3) said that: "Theory is at the heart of science." Although throughout the history of the development of personality psychology it is evident that there is a large number of personality theories, they all have three common elements: emphasis on individual personality characteristics, motivation, and the holistic approach to the study of human personality.

DOI: 10.4018/978-1-5225-2283-6.ch002

The first component seeks to answer the question what and how do people differ from each other, and what is the structure of their personality. It is attempted to provide answers to these questions through correlation-research drafts and the traditional concepts in the context of theories are personality traits, temperament, and personality types. Within the framework of the second elements, it is attempted to answer the questions about why people do what they do, what they want, what directs their behavior, and what are the dynamics of their actions. Traditional concepts within these questions are values, needs, goals, instincts, conflicts, defenses, etc., and laboratory experiments are used in the attempt to test them. The third element is focused on the understanding of the entire person, the meaning of a person's life, and what integrates it. Traditional concepts are the concept of ego, self-esteem, lifestyle, identity, and structure of life, which are tested by using case studies. One of the most important constructs that has experienced the longest and strongest empirical validation and whose creation is the central function of personality theories refers to extraversion. This construct is also one of those that mostly relate to biological determinants of human functioning, which is evident in biological theories that follow.

The roots of biological personality theories are associated with the first data on the theories of temperament and personality, which sought to establish basic types of personality or temperament, i.e. a limited number of typical patterns by which it would be possible to describe any person, and to find the causes of individual differences (according Tadinac, 1986). Thus, the Greek physician Hippocrates (5/4. C. BC. AD) and the Roman physician Galen (2$^{nd}$ century, AD) considered that the personality characteristics of the individual are the result of the functioning of his body, and the differences between personality characteristics of individual people are the result of differences in the functioning of their organisms. This statement formed the foundation for the understanding of the four temperament types that are associated with the four main types of body fluids (blood, slime, yellow bile, and black bile): sanguine (bright and lively), phlegmatic (hardly exciting and indifferent), choleric (easy exciting, sudden and abrupt), and melancholic (pessimistic and depressed). They are described in Table 1, in which the relation between Hippocratic-Galen's temperaments and Pavlov's basic types of nervous system (NS) is also observable. Hippocrates-Galen's temperament typology was not only interesting to Pavlov, but also to Kant (1912), who provided a detailed description of the four temperaments in terms of behavior and divided them into temperament emotions: melancholic and sanguine, and temperament activities: phlegmatic and choleric.

*Table 1. Relation of Hippocrates-Galen's temperament typology, Pavlov's nervous system typology, and Eysenck's fundamental personality dimensions E and N*

| Hippocrates-Galen's Typology | Pavlov's Nervous System Typology | Eysenck's Fundamental Personality Dimensions E and N |
|---|---|---|
| Melancholic | Weak | Unbalanced, introvert |
| Choleric | Strong, unbalanced | Unbalanced, extravert |
| Phlegmatic | Strong, balanced, slow | Stabile, introvert |
| Sanguine | Strong, balanced, mobile | Stabile, extravert |

Source (Ruch, 1992)

Unlike him, Wundt's (1903) interest in this temperament typology resulted in the creation of dimensional systems with orthogonal dimensions: "strength of emotion" and "rate of emotion change." Their combination forms four types of temperament, which have the following features: melancholic have intense emotions and their slow changes; choleric have also intense emotions but their changes are rapid; phlegmatic have weaker emotions and their changes are slow; and sanguine also have weaker emotions but their changes are quick. In addition, Theophrastus described different characteristics in terms of lines, emphasizing the role of the environment in their formation. N. Wundt also believed that there are four types of temperament, while Shelldon's, Kretschmer's and Conrad's constitutional psychology brought personality traits into connection with the physical characteristics of the individual.

Furthermore, due to a later discussion of the research results, it is significant to mention again Gray's personality research and his reinterpretation of the strength concept of NS in the context of the arousal theory. A weak NS can be more easily and more intensely aroused, so the personality dimension known as the NS strength can be described as a dimension of arousal level or accessibility attitude (1972). Gray equalized the concept of arousal with the strength of excitation. However, if the stimulus intensity and the environmental effects (e.g. fatigue, hunger, etc.) maintain constant, greater excitation would determine higher levels of arousal of the cortex as would the strength of excitation (SE), which in Eysenck, who understood it as a state, would determine higher levels of excitation of the nerve processes. The level of this arousal is associated with strength and number of nonspecific nerve impulses coming into the cortex from ARAS, which represents the physiological substrate of extraversion. This hypothesis has served him, as well as Eysenck (Eysenck & Eysenck, 1985), to explain the relation between the strength of excitation and extraversion, and not only that relation but also the relation between the two-dimensional system of extraversion and neuroticism with four types of temperament. Eysenck assumed that introverts and people with a weak NS generally have higher arousal levels and strong excitatory potential, and extraverts a strong NS and a weak excitatory potential. This would mean that extraverts, because they are less excited to certain stimuli, could tolerate the growth of the stimulus intensity longer without falling into a state of trans-marginal inhibition.

As for introverts, they would reach the border point sooner after which the intensity of the response drops, due to a higher cortical excitation of certain stimuli. This was confirmed in a series of studies that established a significant positive correlation between SE and extraversion (Strelau, 1996, 1997; Strelau & Zawadzki, 1997). In addition, research of the relation between Pavlov's CNS properties and Eysenck's personality dimensions resulted with the following median correlation coefficients: between SE and extraversion $r$ =.40, between SE and neuroticism $r$ = -. 46, (which again confirms Eysenck's and Gray's assumptions), between the strength of inhibition (SI) and neuroticism $r$ = -. 38, between the SI and psychoticism $r$ = -. 27, between mobility (MO) and extraversion $r$ =.54, and between mobility and neuroticism $r$ = -. 22 (Strelau, Angleitner & Ruch, 1989; Ruch, Angleitner & Strelau, 1991; Corulla, 1989; San Martini & Mazzoti, 1990), which was also confirmed in the Croatian research sample (Čekolj, 2007).

With the aim of studying the relationship between Eysenck's basic personality dimensions and temperament dimensions, the same analysis will be carried out in this study. Besides previously described relationships, Table 1 shows the assumed, but also empirically confirmed relation between Hippocrates-Galen's personality typology, Eysenck's basic personality dimensions, and Pavlov's temperament typology. A melancholic is characterized by glumness, anxiety, rigidity, sobriety, pessimism, restraint, and antisocial behavior; a choleric is characterized by restlessness, sensitivity, aggressiveness, irritability, impermanence, impulsivity, optimism, and activities; a phlegmatic is characterized by passivity, carefulness, thoughtfulness, peacefulness, restrain, reliability, and gentleness; a sanguine is characterized by sociability, accessibility, talkativeness, receptivity, frivolity, liveliness, peace of mind, and leadership (Čekolj, 2007). Mood researches in such classifications of personality types (Howarth, 1988; Howarth & Zumbo, 1989) and the factor analysis of personality traits (Eysenck & Eysenck, 1985) have provided a confirmation of the assumed relationship.

## Theoretical Framework of Eysenck's Dimensional Personality Theory

Due to its empirical confirmation, wide application and so far most clearly elaborated and clarified biological background, Eysenck's theory of personality (1967) is one of the initial theoretical basis figures in this work. It is based on the results of the factor analysis and correlation among a number of indicators and measurement instruments of behavior and personality traits. Considering that it is based on the results of objective tests, it is empirical in its character and based on three sets of data: a) results of the factor analysis; b) data obtained through experimental research; and c) Pavlov's theory of classical conditioning and its physiological and neurological explanations and interpretations of individual differences in individual's personality. As a real incidence can be reduced to elements, behavior can also be reduced to such factors as determinants.

Thus, Eysenck (1965, p. 2) defined personality as:

*... A more or less stable and permanent organization of the individual's character (connotative attributes), temperament (emotions), intellect (cognitive behavior), and physical characteristics (physical configuration), which determines its original way to adapt to the environment.*

Every science requires some form of classification of the fundamental phenomenon it studies. Therefore, personality traits are in the very framework of personality psychology set as its basic unit, from which Eysenck started in his research structures (1943 to 1967). Soon he noticed that lines are not independent and do not represent personality dimensions. Based on a later conducted factor analysis of data, he determined the existence of two fundamental personality dimensions, which take the form of a continuum and bipolarity, and are mutually orthogonal or independent: extraversion and introversion dimensions (E-I), and neuroticism dimensions, i.e. emotional stability (N-ES). Based on the obtained factors, Eysenck compiled the list of attributes that characterize individual types on the level of characteristics. These personality traits are determined by correlations of two or more related habits, i.e. habitual or customary responses, behaviors, or actions that consistently appear in the repertoire of the individual's behavior in the same or similar situations.

Finally, the level of habit is determined by the lowest levels of an individuals' specific procedures or reactions (relation between individuals' stimuli (Stimulus) and individuals' reactions (Reaction): S-R relation). Eysenck has therefore, shown that there are four levels in the personality structure that are hierarchically organized. As mentioned above, the extraversion factor correlates with the strengths of excitation and inhibition of the central nervous system (CNS). In Eysenck's personality model, higher levels of extraversion are interpreted as an indicator of cortical inhibition, sociability, impulsiveness, risk-taking, and optimism. On the other hand, low levels of extraversion reflect cortical excitation, introspection, reserve, seriousness, and pessimism. In addition to the primary description of the two poles of extraversion factors, Eysenck (1967) gave a description of the neuroticism factors, which indicates the level of emotions, and emotional stability that is related to the lability of the autonomic nervous system (ANS).

Elevated levels of neuroticism reflect characteristics such as moodiness, anxiety and concern, while reduced levels reflect a predisposition to calmness, emotional control, and adjustment (according to Taub, 1998). The next factor analysis of results collected on the sample of psychiatric patients (with diagnoses of schizophrenia and bipolar disorder) in the research from 1952, Eysenck (1967) established the existence of another personality dimension: the psychoticism factor (P), which was independent of previous two factors. The main indicators of this factor are: stubbornness, social withdrawal or isolation, delusions of guilt, and unworthiness, impulsivity or aggression, self-centeredness, lack of insight, mood disturbances, suspiciousness, damage thinking and memory, motor disorders, mental retardation, hallucinations, delusions, and disordered ideas about a relationship, size or significance, depression, suicidality, manic behaviour, and the existence of a family history of psychosis.

Markedly higher levels of psychoticism reflect a predisposition to schizophrenia or mood disorder, a moderately higher level of antisocial personality disorder (psychopathy), which are found in prisoners, schizophrenics, alcoholics, and opiate addicts (Eysenck, 1997). Thus, the psychoticism dimension differs normal people from mentally ill, and extends from psychoticism to normality. On the basis of such records, Eysenck (1976, according to Fulgosi, 1997, p. 394) concluded that psychotic disorders differ from neurotic ones:

*Neurotic disorders are an expression of excessive anxiety, distress, agitation, concerns, and emotional reactivity, while a psychotic person is "crazy" in the sense that his cognitive processes are disturbed to a greater or lesser degree, while a neurotic person completely disposes of his mental capabilities, but cannot control his/her emotions.*

In conclusion, Eysenck's personality model assumes the existence of three described factors of personality (P, E, N), with occasional interpretation of the L-scale (Lie-scale or Social desirability scale) as factor of social conformity. Seeking to provide physiological and neurological explanations, Eysenck was initially related the established and proven three dimensions of personality with the old Hippocratic classification of personality types and found that there is great similarity between them, so that modern mathematical methods of the factor analysis confirm this division and descriptions (Eysenck & Eysenck, 1969, according to Fulgosi, 1997).

## Physiological Basis of the E-I Dimension

Viennese doctor O. Gross tried to determine the physiological basis for the dimensions of extraversion/introversion, conceiving emotional processes and states as primary and secondary functions. The primary function is in the basis of sensation and perception, and the secondary reflects the perseverance of primary functions. Due to this, people differ in the length of secondary process, but among introverts, the duration is longer than among extraverts. Although it is speculative, Eysenck believed this typology to be the forerunner of modern physiological mechanism of extraversion/introversion: ARAS, the Ascending Reticular Activation System. In addition of Gross's contributions, Eysenck believed that Jung was significant, because he related extraversion with a group of neurotic disorders, and introversion with psychostenic or dysthymic disorders (anxiety, anguish, agitation, reactive depression, phobias, etc.).

In addition to empirical studies and the factor analysis, Eysenck's theory is based on Hull's neo-behavioral learning theory and Pavlov's reflexology, i.e. the contemporary Soviet psycho-neurology, and on modern neurological concepts on the functioning of the nervous system, i.e. the brain (according to Fulgosi, 1997). The basic concept that connects Hull's and Pavlov's theory is the neurophysiological process of inhibition, i.e. basic physiological dimensions of the individual's nervous system (NS) as mentioned before, and it refers to the strength of the NS, where it differentiates between a strong or stable and weak or unstable NS. Pavlov's concept of NS strength is the first physiological support to the E-I dimension. In addition to this concept, furthermore, "arousability," a term from Western psychology, is important for Eysenck's theory, which is described in the first part of the book. The term "arousal" or activation refers to intensity variations of behavior, including the level of vigilance and alertness, the measure of readiness of the organism to respond (Gray, 1983). Gray believed that this term could be equated with

Pavlov's term of nervous system strength, where the weak NS is more excited by a certain intensity stimulus than a strong NS. After that, first Gray, and then Eysenck himself, related "arousal" to the dimensions of extraversion/introversion. By explaining that a strong and weak NS are mutually different in the degrees of arousal and ease of arousal, Gray, followed by Eysenck (1967), considered that individual differences in E-I are caused by the functioning of the NS, i.e. NS arousal - which is higher among introverts compared to extraverts. This would mean that E-I and the intensity of the NS are the same thing, and that introverts have a weak and extraverts a strong NS.

Strelau (1983a,b) also gave an overview of eight studies on the relationship of NS-strength measured with the construct of strength of excitation (SE) from its own STI (Strelau Temperament Inventory) and dimensions of E-I, where significant positive correlations were produced in all eight. In addition, the concept of equilibrium in dynamism, Eysenck (1957; according Fulgosi, 1997) is related to the concept of excitatory-inhibitory balance underlying the E-I dimensions. Excitation dominance would correspond to introversion and extraversion, and dominance of inhibition to extraversion. In his experimental research, it was found that introverts condition easier and form positive reflexes easier than extraverts do. Thus, introverts would be those individuals who generate excitatory potential more easily than extraverts generate, and generate inhibitory potential with more difficulty (Eysenck, 1957 according to Fulgosi, 1997). These differences in the possibility of conditioning extraverts and introverts, Gray (1983) explained through differences in sensitivity to punishment and frustration caused by restraint in rewarding, which is higher among introverts than extraverts are.

Other physiological support to the E-I dimension is located in Hull's theory of reactive inhibition. Reactive inhibition is present in each repetition of an action. According to Eysenck's theory, extravert's reactive inhibition develops rapidly, it is strong and difficult to lose, i.e. disappear. He characterized introverts with the opposite, and pointed out that for precisely this reason, extraverts cannot hold a constant in a particular activity; they are prone to change, impermanent; they are constantly looking for new content and are difficult to condition. The model ARAS (Ascending reticular activating system) was set by Moruzzi and Magoun (1949), and was also mentioned by Gray. By observing their psychophysiological studies of EEG synchronization, they noticed from the instructions to the participants that from a peaceful and relaxing situation they focus attention on the stimulus or a new change of stimuli in the environment that the sample of their EEG activity changes from a slow synchronized into a fast and non-synchronized. This change in EEG activity was found in those electrodes that recorded cortical excitation caused by activity in ARAS, and was transferred through contralaterals. They concluded that the reticular formation plays an important role in the initiation and maintenance of motivation, emotions and conditioning, maintenance of vigilance and attention, and regulation in receiving sensory information. ARAS is localized in the reticular formation of the brain stem and the central gray bark brain stem, and has a grid shape, which is made up of folds of nerve cells, which are interspersed with normal sensory cortical pathways of a specific thalamic system.

Determination of extraversion and neuroticism, as the main psychometric factors, represented a significant improvement in the typology of personalities whose author was H. Eysenck (1959). However, this typology carried an important restriction, which Duffy discussed. Precisely because both extraversion and neuroticism significantly correlate with anxiety, which has been defined with most anxiety questionnaires, which were applied in early studies of personality and activation, it was impossible to clearly interpret the findings. In the scheme Eysenck (1967) proposed, intensity that modulates the excitation construct, as Duffy set it, stretched along the continuum of introversion – extraversion. Specifically, behavioral differences related to extraversion are identified with "differential sensitivity thresholds in different parts of ARAS." In his book, *The biological bases of personality* (1967), Eysenck explained in detail the individual differences in extraversion and neuroticism, as well as the neurophysiological basis of the original theory behind excitation-inhibition, and then then arousal theory of extraversion or cortical-reticular arousal, and excitation theory of neuroticism or limbic arousal. Although it was started from a rather vague assumption that introverts characteristically have a high activity level or a lower level of excitation and the cortical-reticular system, this theoretical context was sufficiently seductive and has inspired thousands of experiments until today, as can be seen here. The interest in the theory of extraversion arousal has survived despite significant modifications created by Gray (1972) and Brebner and Cooper (1974), and a very large number of research has resulted in findings that can be classified into three major categories of findings.

First, psychophysiological literature has found that introverts and extraverts do not differ in tonic or basic levels of physiological activity. This conclusion stems from the absence of differences in the measurement of skin conductance in situations before stimulation and later in situations that have a low potential for attitude accessibility. In addition, differences in EEG measurements during low excitation or during sleep are rare. Therefore, Eysenck's hypothesis about the differences in the basic level of arousal between introverts and extraverts has no support in studies using psychophysiological methods of measurement (Matthews & Gilliland, 1999; Stelmack, 1990). Secondly, an extremely large number of findings demonstrated a significantly higher sensitivity or reactivity among introverts to a specific physical stimulation than among extraverts (Stelmack, 1981; Stelmack & Geen, 1992; Stelmack & Houlihan, 1995). These effects are found in some social situations in which introverts prefer a quieter environment and solitude, and during learning, they avoid noisy and intense stimulation (Campbell & Hawley, 1982; Grenn, 1984).

Increased reactivity among introverts due to physical stimulation is determined in different experimental paradigms with the use of different methods, and it was concluded that introverts characteristically have:

1. A lower absolute sensory sensitivity (Stelmack & Campbell, 1974);
2. Lower pain thresholds (Barnes, 1975; Schalling, 1971);
3. Lower noise thresholds (Dornic & Ekehammar, 1990);
4. A higher skin conductance response to short and moderately strong tones (Smith, 1983; Stelmack, 1979);
5. Higher EP auditory amplitudes on simple physical stimuli (Stelmack, Achorn & Michaud, 1977; Stelmack & Michaud- Achorn, 1985; Stenberg, Rosen & Risberg, 1990);
6. A faster latency fear reflex in moderate noisy bangs (Britt & Blumenthal, 1992); and
7. Faster auditory evoked potentials (Bullock & Gilliland, 1993; Stelmack & Wilson, 1982; Swickert & Gilliland, 1998).

Thirdly, introverts and extraverts differ in their study of motor behavior. Sources of these differences, in Stelmack's opinion (2004), are attributed to a faster movement initiative among extraverts than introverts. The effects of these differences are reflected in spontaneity, physical and social, which is quite distinctive from extraverts to introverts (Barrat & Patton, 1983). Extraverts are much more talkative and more likely to initiate conversations during an interview than introverts (Campbell & Rushton, 1978), and they are restless in limited environments (Gale, 1969). Extraverts are more focused on physical activity and sports than introverts (Eysenck, Nias & Cox, 1982; Kirkcaldy, 1982).

These findings imply basic differences between extraverts and introverts in the performed motor tasks:

1. Faster reaction time among extraverts (Barrat, 1959; Robinson & Zahn, 1988);
2. Better recollection effects among extraverts (Eysenck & Frith, 1977);

3. More false positive errors among extraverts with the time reactions tasks (Brebner & Flavell, 1978);
4. Faster movement in extraverts in reaction time tasks (Doucet and Stelmack, 1997, 2000; Stelmack, Houlihan, McGarry-Roberts, 1993);
5. An increased CNV amplitude (EP-measure of preparation for response) among extraverts (O'Connor, 1982);
6. A slower recovery of the motor reflex among extraverts (Pivik, Stelmack & Bylsma, 1988; Stelmack & Pivik, 1996).

Any theory of extraversion simply must adapt to the sensory and motor effects that are consistently demonstrated in researches. Given this information, the task of identifying the neural circuits and neurochemical characteristics remains in the foundation of these effects and functions that differ introverts from extraverts. In addition, some psychophysiological research has truly provided an answer to the demands of the task. Moreover, there have been several experiments, which indicate that dopamine - a neurotransmitter that is believed to modulate the probability and effect of behavioral responses to sensory input (Le Moal & Simon, 1991), affects variations in extraversion (Rammsayer, Netter & Vogel, 1993). In addition, it is important to mention that psychophysiological methods are rather unsuccessful in distinguishing between individuals on the dimension of neuroticism, at least in the paradigms that use physical stimulation, such as in extraversion studies (Fahrenberg, 1987; Matthews & Gilliland, 1999). Evoked brain potentials, conductivity of the skin, and changes in heart rhythm are measures, which are quite sensitive to changes in physical stimulation. Application of these techniques recorded under physical stimulation conditions, such as e.g. short sounds or flashes of light, reveals that the introverts' sensory systems are more reactive and sensitive than those among extraverts'. Identical procedures, however, do not differentiate individuals in the neurotic dimension, indicating that sensor sensitivity is not a factor that underlies this construct. Failure to reach a consistent difference in sensory sensitivity for individuals who differ in the neuroticism dimension by using psychophysiological methods, such as e.g. sensory thresholds and pain thresholds or psychological statements, also corroborate the previous point of view.

## PAVLOV'S THEORY OF CENTRAL NERVOUS SYSTEM PROPERTIES AS THE BASICS OF STRELAU'S TEMPERAMENT THEORY

The basic postulate of Pavlov's theory of the Central nervous system types is that a highly organized nervous system has a number of dimensions that are responsible for the dynamic functioning of excitation and inhibition processes. The author believed that there are three such dimensions, which in various combinations with each other form such a neurophysiological basis on which individual' nervous systems may vary, which is then reflected in their behavior, i.e. personalities. These are dimensions, which are partly inherited and partly formed during the embryonic development and the postpartum early pre-school period, considering the continuation of intensive development of the brain (Tadinac, 1986). The first dimension is the strength of the nervous system (strength of excitatory and inhibitory processes), the second is the balance of these processes, and the third is their mobility (Strelau, 1983a,b; Strelau, Farley & Gale, 1985).

Pavlov (1955) defined the strength of excitation (SE) as "the working capacity of brain cells", because he observed that the intensity of the response increases with stimulus intensity to a certain limit beyond which it starts to decrease. This decrease is explained by a process called trans-marginal or protective inhibition, which is considered to be inherited. In contrast, the strength of inhibition (SI), that relates to to the cell ability to reach and maintain the conditioned state of inhibition, is not inherent but rather conditioned. Given that Pavlov gave less importance to this kind of strength in his research, his followers somewhat neglected it and studied it only so that they could assess the dimensions of equilibrium (balance). Pavlov defined this dimension as the ability to comply with the requirements of the environment to inhibit certain responses to the initiatives of other reactions, which are indirectly measured by strength of excitation and inhibition ratio (Strelau, 1987). For example, people who have a too low equilibrium have high excitation concerning inhibition. Finally, Pavlov defined mobility as the ability of NS to respond adequately and in a timely manner to the constant changes in the environment. In other words, it represents the possibility of favoring inhibition or excitation in the given situation, and thus the temporal aspect of the NS functioning, and includes all forms of measurable speed.

Since Pavlov defined NS dimensions and defined them in relation to the individual's adaptation ability to his environment, Pavlov's theory is of behavioral nature because it does not relate the processes of excitation and inhibition to the biological structures in the brain. In addition, it should be noted that Pavlov considered these dimensions as lines, not as states. Therefore, if the intensity of stimulation and level of arousal of the cortex are kept constant, people who have a high excitation conceived as a line will be resistant to intense or prolonged stimulation, but excitation understood as a condition for the same person will be low. This should be taken into consideration while interpreting the results, which include testing Pavlov's CNS properties.

As shown in Table 1, there is a weak internal inhibition, low extinction, and habituation in an individual whose excitatory processes in the brain are dominating the equilibrium; this process is reversed in individuals with a dominant inhibitory. Pavlov distinguished four basic types of people under the influence of Greek philosophers: a) weak type, b) strong and unbalanced type, c) strong, balanced and slow type, and d) a strong, balanced and mobile type of people who correspond to the classic types of temperament, which were suggested by Hippocrates and Galen: a) melancholic, b) choleric, c) phlegmatic, and d) sanguine. Dimensions of NS are within Pavlov's theory understood as its inherent features, which in combination with environmental factors develop a distinctive pattern of behavior - visible in a particular type of NS (Strelau, 1997). Melancholic are characterized by weak processes, excitation and inhibition, i.e. a weak NS with a limited range of action. Pavlov considered them as a type in which NS does not work properly, so he considered them less adaptive. Choleric are characterized by strong excitation and inhibition processes, in which the excitation is predominant, i.e. strong and NS is unbalanced. Pavlov thought of phlegmatic (strong, balanced or inert NS) and sanguine (strong, balanced and mobile NS) are being most adaptive.

## Modifications of Pavlov's Theory

Pavlov's CNS typology had a considerable heuristic value and over time prompted a series of studies that were mostly led by three research groups: the Leningrad group, the Moscow Group (Teplov and Nebylitsyn), and the Ural Group (Merlin). Specific studies of the Moscow group have led to the contemporary concept that is called the neo-Pavlovian school. Their value was that they modified Pavlov's constructs in four basic dimensions of CNS: strength, mobility, instability, and dynamism (Nebylitsyn, 1972), and operationalized them better, which has eliminated the difficulties which Pavlov encountered himself. His basic method for testing CS functioning was experimenting and applying psychophysiological methods, but experimental methods can only partially but not globally determine the properties of NS. However, in the experiments, those stimuli were applied that affect the postcentral part of the brain, which forms the basis of neurophysiological and sensory perception (e.g. measurement of caffeine amounts that are necessary to cause trans-marginal inhibition), which does not affect the anterior-central part of the brain that is responsible for the organization of active and goal-oriented behavior. That is why there is a different definition of NS dimensions: NS strength is manifested in the resistance to strong stimuli and high sensitivity thresholds, and the low reactivity to events; NS mobility is reflected in rapid/slow alternation or excitation transformation into inhibition and vice versa; NS lability represents a high speed/slowness of excitation, transfer arousal, concentration, and duration of these processes; dynamism of NS is a fast/slow development of conditioned responses, which can be positive or negative (dynamism of the excitatory process would identify the ability to form positive conditioned reflexes, dynamism of the inhibitory process identifies forming negative conditioned reflexes, the so-called equilibrium in dynamism represents the superiority of either excitatory or inhibitory processes in dynamism).

Since according to Nebylitsyn (1972) each of these dimensions is measured with three indexes (relative to excitation, inhibition, and balance between the two processes), a wholesome profile of NS dimensions in individuals consists of twelve measurements. In the early 1970s, the Warsaw group carried out a modification of the neo-Pavlovian typology, led by Jan Strelau. Jan Strelau implies with term "temperament" relatively stable characteristics of the organism, primarily biologically determined, that are shown in the formal aspects of the response and determine the behavior characteristics with regard to the energy level and time (1983a). Considering the energy level, Strelau differentiates two basic dimensions of temperament: reactivity, which is regulated with a mechanism that transforms the intensity of the stimulus into central arousal, and activity, which is regulated by the acquired behavioral mechanism located in the cortical and subcortical structures, and it consists of learned strategies for amplifying or damping stimulation. In other words, temperament plays a significant role in regulating the relation between the individual and his environment, which in 1993 was described in detail in *The Regulation Theory of Temperament* (RTT, Strelau, 1993, 1996).

Considering the time features, Strelau mentioned dimensions arising from neo-Pavlovian dimensions of NS mobility and instability. The first dimension of temperament, strength of excitation (SE), refers to the functional capacity of nerve cells and is reflected as the ability to withstand very intense and very long-lasting stimulations without having a trans-marginal or protective inhibition, which protects against cell damage/exhaustion. With an increase in stimulus intensity, the response magnitude increases to a certain limit (the so-called tin trans-marginal inhibition) after which the reaction size decreases with additional increase in stimulus intensity. In other words, protective inhibition is reflected in the reduction of the response amplitude or even termination of the reaction, and in behavioral disorders, it is of a mostly emotional nature.

The strength of inhibition (SI) is manifested as the ability to interrupt or postpone certain behavior if it is needed, and to refrain from any behavior and reaction when the situation requires it. In real life, people with a low strength of inhibition will not be able to successfully inhibit/delay the reaction in accordance with the requirements of the situation, thus their adaptation to environmental conditions will be worse than among people with a high strength of inhibition.

Mobility (MO) of the nerve processes is evident in their fast and adequate response to environmental change, which, in accordance with the requirements of the environment, gives advantage to impulse A before B, which then leads an individual to more appropriate adjustments (Strelau, Angleitner & Ruch, 1990; Ruch, Angleitner & Strelau, 1991).

The final result of Strelau's work has led to the development of Strelau's temperament inventory (STI). However, the main objection to this Russian school is that it is extremely difficult to achieve replicability of their findings (Eysenck, 1990). Strelau, Angleitner, and Ruch (1990) established poor psychometric characteristics based on the meta-analysis of data obtained by STI, and also that the content of the particles docs not constitute a representative form of human behavior because it is too limited to situations and behaviors in the workplace. As a result, a new survey called The Pavlovian Temperament Survey (PTS) was constructed with the aim of testing the basic temperament characteristics and their cross-cultural comparisons (Strelau, Angleitner & Newberry, 1999). What today could be considered as the biggest objection to this theory is the fact that it is fully characterized as a biological personality theory, but with a very low empirical validity, and a very small number of researches examining its environmental and constructive validity, or the place it in relation with various psychophysiological measures. Therefore, in addition to Eysenck's theory, it was logical to examine the relation between the theoretical model and the evoked brain potentials in this work.

Finally, regarding the biological personality theories, it is important to mention Cloninger's model (1986), which initially developed three hereditary and mutually independent personality dimensions, each associated with a specific central neurotransmitter (dopaminergic activity with activation, serotonergic with inhibition, and noradrenergic with maintaining behavior). However, many authors believe that it is highly unlikely that personality can be simplified and reduced to interactive work of three types of neurotransmitters (Eysenck, 1990). He later developed and expanded his model with four personality dimensions that are evaluated by using a Temperament and Character Inventory (TCI) (Cloninger, Svrakic & Przybeck, 1991, 1993). In addition, R. Plomin (1990), in the context of the so-called behavioral genetics, pointed out the importance of hereditary factors in certain personality traits in humans, identifying specific genes for specific traits by conducting a correlation analysis of DNA samples and measured personality traits, and tried to determine in detail the complex interaction of environmental and hereditary factors on individual personality.

## REFERENCES

Barnes, G. (1975). Extraversion and pain. *The British Journal of Social and Clinical Psychology*, *14*(3), 303–308. doi:10.1111/j.2044-8260.1975.tb00182.x PMID:1182410

Barrat, E. (1959). Anxiety and impulsiveness related to psychomotor efficiency. *Perceptual and Motor Skills*, *9*(3), 191–198. doi:10.2466/pms.1959.9.3.191

Barrat, E. S., & Patton, J. (1983). Impulsivity: Cognitive, behavioral, and psychophysiological correlates. In M. Zuckerman (Ed.), *Biological bases of sensation seeking, impulsivity, and anxiety* (pp. 77–116). Hillsdale, NJ: Erlbaum.

Brebner, J., & Cooper, C. (1974). The effect of a low rate of regular signals upon the reaction times of introverts and extraverts. *Journal of Research in Personality*, *8*(3), 263–276. doi:10.1016/0092-6566(74)90037-3

Brebner, J., & Flavel, R. (1978). The effect of catch-trials on speed and accuracy among introverts and extraverts in a simple RT task. *British Journal of Psychology*, *69*(1), 9–15. doi:10.1111/j.2044-8295.1978.tb01627.x PMID:626808

Britt, T. W., & Blumenthal, T. D. (1992). The effects of anxiety on motoric expression of the startle response. *Personality and Individual Differences*, *13*(1), 91–97. doi:10.1016/0191-8869(92)90224-D

Bullock, W. A., & Gilliland, K. (1993). Eysencks arousal theory of introversion/ekstraversion: A converging measures investigation. *Journal of Personality and Social Psychology*, *64*(1), 113–123. doi:10.1037/0022-3514.64.1.113 PMID:8421248

Campbell, A., & Rushton, J. P. (1978). Bodily communication and personality. *The British Journal of Social and Clinical Psychology*, *17*(1), 31–36. doi:10.1111/j.2044-8260.1978.tb00893.x PMID:620103

Campbell, J. B., & Hawley, C. W. (1982). Study habits and Eysencks theory of extraversion-introversion. *Journal of Research in Personality*, *16*(2), 139–146. doi:10.1016/0092-6566(82)90070-8

Čekolj, T. (2007). *Usporedba Eysenckove i Pavlovljeve tipologije temperamenta* [The comparison between Eysenck's and Pavlov's temperament typology] (Thesis). Department of Psychology, Faculty of Humanities and Social Sciences, University of Zagreb, Zagreb, Croatia.

Cloninger, C. R. (1986). A unified biosocial theory of personality and its role in the development of anxiety states. *Psychiatric Developments*, *3*, 167–226. PMID:3809156

Cloninger, C. R., Przybeck, T. R., & Svrakic, D. M. (1991). The Tridimensional Personality Questionnaire: U.S. normative data. *Psychological Reports*, *69*(3), 1047–1057. doi:10.2466/pr0.1991.69.3.1047 PMID:1784653

Cloninger, C. R., Svrakic, D. M., & Przybeck, T. R. (1993). A psychobiological model of temperament and character. *Archives of General Psychiatry*, *50*(12), 975–990. doi:10.1001/archpsyc.1993.01820240059008 PMID:8250684

Corulla, W. J. (1989). The relationship between the Strelau Temperament Inventory, sensation seeking and Eysencks dimensional system of personality. *Personality and Individual Differences*, *10*(2), 161–173. doi:10.1016/0191-8869(89)90200-6

Dornic, S., & Ehehammar, B. (1990). Extraversion, neuroticism, and noise sensitivity. *Personality and Individual Differences*, *11*(9), 989–992. doi:10.1016/0191-8869(90)90283-W

Doucet, C., & Stelmack, R. M. (1997). Movement time differentiates extraverts from introverts. *Personality and Individual Differences*, *23*(5), 775–786. doi:10.1016/S0191-8869(97)00104-9

Doucet, C., & Stelmack, R. M. (2000). An event-related potential analysis of extraversion and individual differences in cognitive processing speed and response execution. *Journal of Personality and Social Psychology, 78*(5), 956–964. doi:10.1037/0022-3514.78.5.956 PMID:10821201

Eysenck, H. J. (1959). *Manual of the Maudsley Personality Inventory*. London: University of London Press.

Eysenck, H. J. (1965). *The Structure of Human Personality*. London: Methuen & Co. Ltd.

Eysenck, H. J. (1967). *Biological basis of personality*. Springfield, IL: Charles C Thomas Publisher.

Eysenck, H. J. (1990). Biological Dimensions of Personality. In L. E. Pervin (Ed.), *Handbook of Personality* (pp. 244–276). John Wiley & Sons, Inc.

Eysenck, H. J. (1997). Personality and Experimental Psychology: The Unification of Psychology and the Possibility of a Paradigm. *Journal of Personality and Social Psychology, 73*(6), 1224–1237. doi:10.1037/0022-3514.73.6.1224

Eysenck, H. J., & Eysenck, M. W. (1985). Chapter eight: The psychophysiology of personality. In *Personality and individual differences: A natural science approach* (pp. 217–236). New York, London: Plenum Press. doi:10.1007/978-1-4613-2413-3_8

Eysenck, H. J., & Frith, C. D. (1977). *Reminiscence, motivation and personality*. New York: Plenum Press. doi:10.1007/978-1-4684-2244-3

Eysenck, H. J., Nias, D. K., & Cox, D. N. (1982). Sport and personality. *Advances in Behaviour Research and Therapy, 4*(1), 1–56. doi:10.1016/0146-6402(82)90004-2

Fahrenberg, J. (1987). Concepts of activation and arousal in theory of emotionality (neuroticism). In J. Strelau & H. J. Eysenck (Eds.), *Personality dimensions and arousal* (pp. 99–120). New York: Plenum Press. doi:10.1007/978-1-4899-2043-0_6

Fulgosi, A. (1997). Psihologija ličnosti: teorije i istraživanja [Personality Psychology: Theory and research]. Školska knjiga.

Gale, A. (1969). "Stimulus hunger": Individual differences in operant strategy in a button-pressing task. *Behaviour Research and Therapy, 7*(3), 263–274. doi:10.1016/0005-7967(69)90006-0

Gray, J. A. (1972). The psychophysiological nature of introversion-extraversion: a modification of Eysenck's theory. In V. D. Nebylitsyn & J. A. Gray (Eds.), *Biological bases of individual behavior* (pp. 182–205). London: Academic Press. doi:10.1016/B978-0-12-515350-8.50017-X

Gray, J. A. (1983). Anxiety, Personality and the Brain. In A. Gale & J. A. Edwards (Eds.), Physiological Correlates of Human Behaviour: Vol III. Individual Differences and Psychopathology (pp. 31-43). Academic Press Inc.

Green, R. G. (1984). Preferred stimulation levels in introverts and extroverts: Effects on arousal and performancedoi. *Journal of Personality and Social Psychology*, *46*(6), 1303–1312. doi:10.1037/0022-3514.46.6.1303

Howarth, E. (1988). Mood differences between the four Galen personality types. *Personality and Individual Differences*, *9*(1), 173–176. doi:10.1016/0191-8869(88)90044-X

Howarth, E., & Zumbo, B. D. (1989). An empirical investigation of Eysencks typology. *Journal of Research in Personality*, *23*(3), 343–353. doi:10.1016/0092-6566(89)90006-8

Kant, I. (1912). *Anthropologie in Pragmatischer Hinsicht*. Leipzig: Meiner. (Original work published 1798)

Kirkcaldy, B. D. (1982). Personality profiles at various levels of athletic participation. *Personality and Individual Differences*, *3*(3), 321–326. doi:10.1016/0191-8869(82)90052-6

Le Moal, M., & Simon, H. (1991). Mesocorticolimbic dopaminergic network: Functional and regulatory roles. *Psychological Review*, *71*, 155–234. PMID:1986388

Matthews, G., & Gilliland, K. (1999). The personality theories of H. J. Eysenck and J. A. Gray: A comparative review. *Personality and Individual Differences*, *26*(4), 583–626. doi:10.1016/S0191-8869(98)00158-5

McAdams, D. P., & Pals, J. L. (2006). A New Big Five: Fundamental Principles for an Integrative Science of Personality. *The American Psychologist*, *61*(3), 204–217. doi:10.1037/0003-066X.61.3.204 PMID:16594837

Moruzzi, G., & Magoun, H. W. (1949). Brainstem reticular formation and activation of the EEG. *Electroencephalography and Clinical Neurophysiology*, *1*(1-4), 455–473. doi:10.1016/0013-4694(49)90219-9 PMID:18421835

Nebylitsyn, V. D. (1972). *Fundamental properties of human nervous system*. New York: Plenum Press. doi:10.1007/978-1-4684-1881-1

OConnor, K. (1982). Individual differences in the effect of smoking on frontal-central distribution of the CNV: Some observations on smokers control of attentional behaviour. *Personality and Individual Differences*, *3*(3), 271–286. doi:10.1016/0191-8869(82)90048-4

Pivik, R. T., Stelmack, R. M., & Bylsma, F. W. (1988). Personality and individual differences in reaction times between introverts and extraverts. *Personality and Individual Differences*, *14*, 701–712.

Plomin, R. (1990). *Nature and nurture: An introduction to human behavioral genetics*. Belmont, CA: Thomson Brooks/Cole Publishing Co.

Rammsayer, T., Netter, P., & Vogel, W. H. (1993). A neurochemical model underlying differences in reaction times between introverts and extraverts. *Personality and Individual Differences*, *14*(5), 701–712. doi:10.1016/0191-8869(93)90118-M

Robinson, T. N. Jr, & Zahn, T. P. (1988). Preparatory interval effects on the reaction time performance of introverts and extraverts. *Personality and Individual Differences*, *9*(4), 749–761. doi:10.1016/0191-8869(88)90064-5

Ruch, W. (1992). Pavlovs types of nervous system, Eysencks typology and the Hippocrates-Galen temepraments: An empirical examination of the asserted correspondence of three temperament typologies. *Personality and Individual Differences*, *13*(12), 1259–1271. doi:10.1016/0191-8869(92)90168-O

Ruch, W., Angleitner, A., & Strelau, J. (1991). The Strelau Temperament Inventory – Revised (STI-R): Validity studies. *Europe's Journal of Psychology*, *5*, 287–308.

San Martini, P., & Mazzoti, E. (1990). The relationship between the factorial dimensions of the Strelau Temperament Inventory and the EPQ-R. *Personality and Individual Differences*, *11*(9), 909–914. doi:10.1016/0191-8869(90)90271-R

Schalling, D. (1971). Tolerance for experimentally induced ain as related to personality. *Scandinavian Journal of Psychology*, *12*(1), 271–281. doi:10.1111/j.1467-9450.1971.tb00630.x PMID:5150861

Smith, B. D. (1983). Extraversion and electrodermal activity: Arousability and the Inverted-U. *Personality and Individual Differences*, *4*(4), 41–419. doi:10.1016/0191-8869(83)90007-7

Stelmack, R. M. (1979). Extraversion orienting reaction habituation rate and sensitivity to stimulation. In H. D. Kimmel, E. H. Van Olst, & J. R. Orlebeke (Eds.), *The orienting reflex in humans* (pp. 647–656). New York: Erlbaum.

Stelmack, R. M. (1981). The psychophysiology of extraversion and neuroticism. In H. J. Eysenck (Ed.), *A model for personality* (pp. 38–63). Springer-Verlag Berlin Heidelberg. doi:10.1007/978-3-642-67783-0_2

Stelmack, R. M. (1990). Biological basis of extraversion: Psychophysiological evidence. *Journal of Personality*, *58*(1), 293–311. doi:10.1111/j.1467-6494.1990.tb00917.x PMID:2198340

Stelmack, R. M. (2004). On Personality and Arousal: A Historical Perspective on Eysenck and Zuckerman. In *On the Psychobiology of Personality: Essays in Honor of Marvin Zuckerman* (pp. 17–28). Elsevier Ltd. doi:10.1016/B978-008044209-9/50003-8

Stelmack, R. M., Achorn, E., & Michaud, A. (1977). Extraversion and individual differences in auditory evoked response. *Psychophysiology*, *14*(4), 368–374. doi:10.1111/j.1469-8986.1977.tb02966.x PMID:882616

Stelmack, R. M., & Campbell, K. B. (1974). Extraversion and auditory sensitivity to high and low frequency. *Perceptual and Motor Skills*, *38*(3), 875–879. doi:10.2466/pms.1974.38.3.875 PMID:4842444

Stelmack, R. M., & Geen, R. G. (1992). The Psychophysiology of Extraversion. In A. Gale & M. W. Eysenck (Eds.), *Handbook of Individual Differences: Biological Perspectives* (pp. 227–254). New York: John Wiley & Sons, Ltd.

Stelmack, R. M., & Houlihan, M. (1995). Event-Related Potentials, Personality, and Intelligence: Concepts, Issues, and Evidence. In D. H. Saklofske & M. Zeidner (Eds.), *International Handbook of Personality and Intelligence* (pp. 349–365). New York: Plenum Press. doi:10.1007/978-1-4757-5571-8_17

Stelmack, R. M., Houlihan, M., & McGarry-Roberts, P. A. (1993). Personality, reaction time, and event-related potentials. *Journal of Personality and Social Psychology*, *65*(2), 399–409. doi:10.1037/0022-3514.65.2.399

Stelmack, R. M., & Michaud-Achorn, A. (1985). Extraversion, attention, and habituation of the auditory evoked response. *Journal of Research in Personality, 19*(4), 416–428. doi:10.1016/0092-6566(85)90009-1

Stelmack, R. M., & Pivik, R. T. (1996). Extraversion and the effect of exercise on spinal motoneuronal excitability. *Personality and Individual Differences, 21*(1), 69–76. doi:10.1016/0191-8869(96)00034-7

Stelmack, R. M., & Wilson, K. G. (1982). Extraversion and the effects of frequency and intensity on the auditory brainstem evoked response. *Personality and Individual Differences, 3*(4), 373–380. doi:10.1016/0191-8869(82)90003-4

Stenberg, G., Rosen, I., & Risberg, J. (1990). Attention, and Personality in Augmenting/Reducing of Visual Evoked Potentials. *Personality and Individual Differences, 11*(12), 1243–1254. doi:10.1016/0191-8869(90)90151-G

Strelau, J. (1983a). *Temperament, Personality, Activity*. London: Academic Press.

Strelau, J. (1983b). Pavlov's Nervous System Typology and Beyond. In A. Gale & J. A. Edwards (Eds.), Physiological Correlates of Human Behaviour: Vol III. Individual Differences and Psychopathology (pp. 139-154). Academic Press Inc. doi:10.1016/B978-0-12-273903-3.50014-6

Strelau, J. (1987). Personality Dimensions Based on Arousal Theories. In J. Strelau & H. J. Eysenck (Eds.), Personality Dimensions and Arousal (pp. 269-286). New York: Plenum Press. doi:10.1007/978-1-4899-2043-0_16

Strelau, J. (1993). The location of the regulative theory of temperament (RTT) among other temperament theories. In J. Hettema & I. J. Deary (Eds.), *Foundations of personality* (pp. 113–132). Dordrecht: Kluwer. doi:10.1007/978-94-011-1660-2_9

Strelau, J. (1996). The Regulative theory of temperament: Current status. *Personality and Individual Differences, 20*(2), 131–142. doi:10.1016/0191-8869(95)00159-X

Strelau, J. (1997). The contribution of Pavlovs typology of CNS properties to personality research. *European Psychologist, 2*(2), 125–138. doi:10.1027/1016-9040.2.2.125

Strelau, J., Angleitner, A., & Newberry, B. H. (1999). Pavlovian Temperament Survey (PTS): An international handbook. Göttingen: Hogrefe & Huber Publishers.

Strelau, J., Angleitner, A., & Ruch, W. (1989). Strelau Temperament Inventory (STI): General review and studies based on German samples. In C. D. Spielberger & J. N. Butcher (Eds.), *Advances in Personality Assessment* (Vol. 8, pp. 141–187). New York: Erlbaum, Hillsdale.

Strelau, J., Angleitner, A., & Ruch, W. (1990). Strelau Temperament Inventory (STI): General Review and studies based on German samples. In J. N. Butcher & C. D. Spielberger (Eds.), *Advances in personality assessment* (pp. 187–241). Hillsdale, NJ: Lawrence Erlbaum Associates Publishers.

Strelau, J., Farley, F. H., & Gale, A. (1985). The Biological Bases of Personality and Behavior: Vol I. Theories, Measurement, Tehniques, and Development. Hemisphere Publishing Corporation.

Strelau, J., & Zawadzki, B. (1997). Temperament and personality: Eysenck's three superfactors as related to temperamental dimensions. In H. Nyborg (Ed.), *The Scientific Study of Human Nature: Tribute to Hans J. Eysenck at Eighty* (pp. 68–91). Oxford, UK: Pergamon Press.

Swickert, R. J., & Gilliland, K. (1998). Relationship between the brainstem auditory evoked response and extraversion, impulsivity, and sociability. *Journal of Research in Personality*, *32*(3), 314–330. doi:10.1006/jrpe.1998.2216

Tadinac, M. (1986). *Apsolutni limeni i vrijeme reakcije kao indikatori snage živčanog sustava* [Absolute limens and time reaction as indicators of the nervous system strength] (Master thesis). Faculty of Humanities and Social Sciences, University of Zagreb, Zagreb, Croatia.

Taub, J. M. (1998). Eysencks descriptive and biological theory of personality: A review of construct validity. *The International Journal of Neuroscience*, *98*(3-4), 145–198. doi:10.3109/00207459808986443

Wundt, W. (1903). *Grundzüge der Physiologischen Psychologie* (Vol. 2). Leipzig: Engelmann.

# Chapter 3
# Electrophysiology of Human Personality


## ABSTRACT

*In this section an overview on evoked brain potentials will be introduced, same as the bases of electrophysiology of the brain. The main research findings on evoked potentials and other psychological variables such as cognition, emotion, motivation and personality will be presented. The emphasis will be given to the relationship between evoked brain potentials and personality operationalized by previously presented two personality theories: Eysenck's and Strelau's theory. Even though it is possible to expect, based on arousal theory, that introverts who had higher sensory reactivity on physical stimuli of moderate intensity and higher levels of cortical arousal than extraverts, would also show higher P300-amplitudes in both modalities, audio and visual, due to other significant variables (i.e. task type, other psychological and physiological characteristics of subjects, etc.) some other results could be expected. Therefore, all complexity about the relationship between evoked brain potentials and human personality and relevant research methodology will be presented here.*


DOI: 10.4018/978-1-5225-2283-6.ch003

## EVOKED BRAIN POTENTIALS

The first application of electroencephalogram in examining brain-behavior relationships is related to the year 1929, when the Austrian psychiatrist Hans Berger published the first scientific paper in which he described in detail and interpreted the results of 73 recordings of the electrical activity of the brain of his ten-year-old son Klaus (according to Gloor, 1969). Since then, a series of electro-cortical studies have been made considering the relationship of the EEG (spontaneous electrical changes in the brain) with a series of psychological variables (Hugdahl, 1995b) with more or less success, due to the difficulty in controlling the impulses (Gale, 1987). Several decades later, in the early 1960s, due to the growing demand and interest for systematic electrophysiological studies of individual differences, and the technical improvements of the existing methodology (attempts to eliminate defects of EEG methods), there has been a method application expansion of evoked potentials of the cerebral cortex (Stelmack & Houlihan, 1995).

"Evoked potential is a by-product of electrical activity in the peripheral and central nervous pathways, which occurs as a response to external stimulation" (Dabić-Jeftić & Mikula, 1994a, p.8). The name *evoked potential* is because these resources, during the electroencephalogram recordings, are caused by certain stimulation (Polich, 1993), which represents the response of the human brain, which is the time related with given stimuli (Hugdahl, 1995b). It is the voltage change in EEG activity that is time related to sensory, motor or cognitive events. The basic difference between evoked potentials and spontaneous EEG waves is that the first appear in a specific time compared to the given stimuli, usually only in one part of the cerebral cortex. They can be used to identify and classify perceptual, memory, and linguistic operations, and in general at the time and classification labelling of specific phases in the information processing. Evoked brain potentials arise from the synchronous activity of a large number of neurons that are active in a given moment during the information processing. The parameters of evoked brain potentials, amplitudes, and latencies are obtained from the so-called signal averaging of summarizing process of time related electro cortical responses that occur at each reset the stimulation. Thereby, evoked potentials and EEG waves are separately summed, causing a gradual reduction in the amplitude of EEG noise and extraction of evoked brain activity that is otherwise difficult to distinguish from the background of EEG activity. They can be captured for each sensory modality under specific recording conditions of evoked potentials. The characteristic waveforms correspond to each modality. Components or peaks in evoked potentials usually have names of positive or negative waves depending on their polarity and latency. Their latency is typically shown in milliseconds: the earlier appearance of specific component is more likely to be determined by the physical properties of stimuli.

There are two groups of evoked brain potentials: evoked (already mentioned, which are following the physical stimuli from the environment) and emitted (those associated with processes such as preparing for cognitive or motor activity or observation of new, unusual stimuli in the environment) brain potentials (Picton, 1980), as they were defined by the original authors (Sutton, Brar, Zubin & John, 1965). Looking at the context in which the stimuli occurs (Brinar Brzović, Vukadin & Zurak, 1996), evoked (sensory or exogenous) resources, represent the brain's response to a specific sensory stimuli and event-related potentials (cognitive or endogenous) represent voltage fluctuations related to the time with some physical or psychological event, although they are not closely related to it, and can be skipped if a person is not interested in this stimulus. Sensory-evoked potentials or the so-called early components occur within the first 100 milliseconds after of stimuli and have very low amplitudes (0.1 - 20 μV). Event-related potentials or late components have a long latency (longer than 100 milliseconds) and larger amplitudes depending on the context in which the stimuli occur. Described EP-waves are shown in Figure 1.

Exogenous potentials are required answers to the stimuli, where their amplitudes and latencies depend on changes in the physical features of stimuli and the distribution on the head surface of that sensible system which is activated, not the cognitive processing of the stimuli. In these EP-studies, participants are typically passive (awake or not; relaxed or not; focused on the stimuli or not). The absence or damage of any of the components of the early ERP-components indicates some neurological damage and provides the basis for clinical testing (Donchin & Coles, 1988; Rugg, 1992).

As shown in detail in Figure 1, in a particular task, the first occurring are auditory-evoked potentials (Brainstem Auditory Evoked Potentials, BAEP) representing 7 deflections marked with Roman numerals from I to VII during the first 10-12 milliseconds after stimuli with an amplitude greater than 1μV. After them, there are components of medium latencies or MLAEP - Middle Latency Evoked Potentials: N0, P0, Na, Pa, and Nb; then exogenous components of long latencies occur or LLAEP - Long Latency Evoked Potentials): P1, N1 and P2; and the last three have just been studied in this work. These components have latencies from 50-100 to 200-300 milliseconds, and they are called transitional because they share their characteristics with the endogenous components. With auditory stimulation, P1 occurs at 50 milliseconds, negative N1 wave at 80-100 milliseconds, and the positive wave P2 at approximately

*Figure 1. EP-components in intervals from 1,000 milliseconds after an auditory stimuli of moderate intensity*
*Source: (Adapted from Hillyard & Kutas 1983 , according to Hugdahl, 1995b , p. 272)*

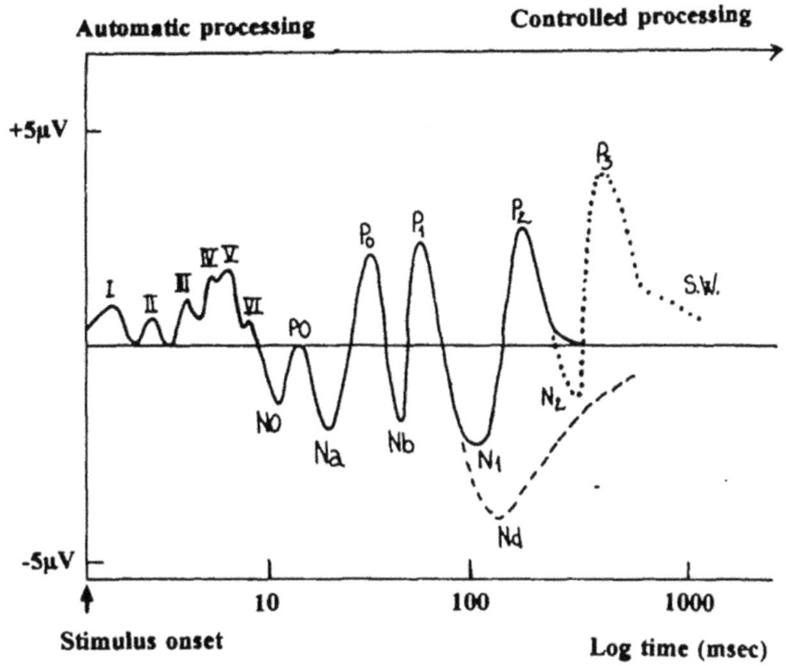


170-200 milliseconds after assigning a stimulus (Hugdahl, 1995b), and their latencies in the visual stimulation are only a bit longer.

It is considered that thcy are generated in the primary auditory cortex in the temporal lobe (Vaughn & Ritter, 1970). N1 and P2 waves share a large overlap part considering on how the stimulus is caused by external conditions, although their distribution is different. However, two waves reflect neural activity generated in the superior temporal lobe that includes the auditory cortex. The N1 component is a relatively large wave from what regularly occurs in repeated stimuli presentation. It is associated with selective attention, is thus not an exclusive exogenous component, and is associated with the endogenous component of negativity processing, PN. Hillyard, Hink, Schwent, and Picton (1973) conducted a study in which they demonstrated EP changes that reflect selective attention, accurately; they determined the increase of the N1- amplitude at selective attention. Participants were instructed to ignore the sounds that were presented to them to only one ear and to focus on counting the tones that were presented to the other ear. N1-wave recorded at the Cz-electrode showed its increase at the presentation of that stimulus which participants should count, i.e. the target stimulus. It was also found that the N1-amplitude increases with increasing inter-stimulus interval to about 10 secs (Teder, 1994). In addition, Näätänen, Alho, and Sams (1985) found that N1 consists of two sub-components: one that occurs in the auditory cortex and the other that is not specifically related either to one modality, so that it can also cause visual stimuli. Later, it was assumed that it actually consists of three sub-components (Hugdahl, 1995b).

The P2 component is associated with early treatment, and together with the N1 wave encodes the physical properties of stimuli. Unlike the N1-wave that has its maximum distribution over the vertex (Cz electrode), P2 is not as centrally localized. Most often N1 and P2 waves appear together, but can be viewed separately. After that, the MMN-component (or Mismatch Negativity) occurs, as well as visual evoked potentials (VEP), of which the most common is the P1 component, and somatosensory evoked potentials (SSEP) (Hugdahl, 1995b). Endogenous evoked potentials were induced in the absence of external stimulation in complex experiments and often require the participants' active involvement. They include higher cognitive processes such as attention and memory. If they will be triggered, depends on the type of information processing that is required of the participants, their previous experience, intentions, decisions, and only partly des it depend on the physical properties of the stimuli. The variance of the endogenous components corresponds to the variation to the task that is given (Hugdahl, 1995b).

Therefore, after the potential called Processing Negativity (PN), which occurs in distinguishing the target from non-target stimuli 50 milliseconds after issuing them (Hansen & Hillyard, 1980), there is a N2-component or negativity errors in processing, in which this research is interested. The N2 component can be recorded whenever unusual or unexpected stimuli appear and is associated with the identification of stimuli in the periphery of the participants' attention and reaction time. Its amplitude is inversely proportional to the probability of stimuli occurrence. It has latency from 200 milliseconds after the appearance of stimuli and frontally central distribution on the surface of the head. It consists of two peaks (N2a and N2b), occurs in the process of discrimination, and is associated with an unexpected stimulus (Nätäänen, 1992). Therefore, N2a reflects automatic extraction properties, i.e. the automatic processing of information, and N2b the determination of properties and indiscriminate, i.e. the controlled information processing.

Since the rare-induced changes in stimuli in a series of stimuli, no matter whether the participant pays attention to the stimuli or not, it is followed by a P3-wave if this change is relevant to the task (Donchin, Ritter and McCallum, 1978). The P3 component (Figure 2), also measured in this study, represents

*Figure 2. Graphic display of P300-wave (adapted from http://p300.scripps.edu)*

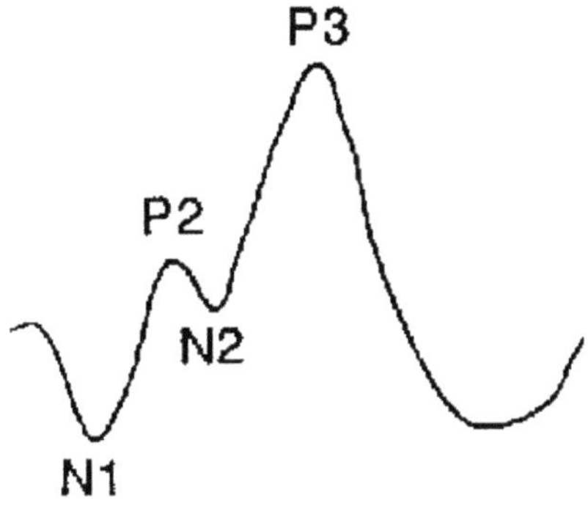


a major positive wave latency of 250-600 milliseconds and occurs while the participant is actively focused on a given stimuli and/or the occurrence of new or surprising stimuli in any modality. It is associated with drawing attention and immediate memory, and is the most commonly tested evoked potential. The P300-amplitude increases with the application of a particular type/level of cognitive involvement of participants, and also with increasing importance and relevance of certain stimuli/situations for the participants. Despite a common belief, P300-latency is independent from behavioral reaction time of participants, but represents an excellent indicator of time it takes for the participant to categorize and evaluate particular stimuli.

The P3-wave is most often caused by oddball paradigm in visual/auditory modality and consists of two sub-components: P3a and P3b. P300-wave generators are located within multiple brain regions including the frontal and parietal associative cortex, thalamus, and hippocampus, and the other limbic structures (Polich, 2002). The aforementioned oddball paradigm or a simple discrimination task of stimuli can be applied in the auditory or visual modality, wherein the two stimuli are presented in a random series with one or two, which are relatively infrequent. Hearing version of this task uses two different tones, inter-stimulus interval of few seconds, with the target stimuli, which is given less frequently that non-targeted (standard) stimuli. Participants are asked to distinguish between the two tones reacting to target stimuli (e.g. mental counting of signals in the series by pressing push buttons) and by not responding to the standard stimuli. Depending on what is to be tested, the oddball paradigm allows experimental variation by rare changes in the intensity of stimuli, tone height, tones in the context of the words, and so on. It was found that the P300 wave exists in visual, auditory, and somatosensory modalities between which there are differences in latencies and amplitudes, but not in their topographic distribution (Snyder, Hillyard & Galambos, 1980). In the oddball task, which has been incorporated in this work, the two stimuli are presented in a random series with one or two also, which are relatively infrequent. The visual oddball paradigm uses two different images, inter-stimulus intervals of few seconds, with target stimuli that are presented more rarely than non-targeted (standard) stimuli. Participants are asked to distinguish between the two images reacting to target stimuli (e.g. mental counting of the target images in series by pressing tasters) and by not responding to standard stimuli.

The most common visual stimulations are the induction of ERP components by: a) changing the brightness (luminance) using the strobe or flash pattern (only VEP); b) sampled stimuli of chessboard or bars (with constant brightness, there are two possible ways of stimulation: by changing the contrast between dark and bright parts of the sample or, inverse changes of dark and bright parts of the sample (only VEP), and for causing P300-components inversion checkerboard patterns are used that varies according to the size and slope of the chessboard, and the grid pattern, which varies in size, shape and slope of the grid), the participant has the task of counting these checkerboard patterns that are infrequent in a series of stimulation, which was the instruction in this research; c) reporting checkerboard of gray background/ disappearance of the chessboard in a gray background; d) counting towards the stimuli: colour, form, semantic category, or combined (e.g. "In a series of stimuli, drawn dogs and cats will be shown. Silently count to yourself (or press the push button) only when you see a cat" (Beijsterveldt, Molenaar, Geus & de Boomsma, 1996; Baal & Boomsma Geus, 1997).

After the measured P3-wave, the contingent negative variation, The Contingent Negative Variation, (CNV), Slow wave activity (SWA), O-wave, Readiness potential (RP), and the N4-wave can still be recorded. The N4 component is associated with the semantic evaluation of stimuli (Kutas & Hillyard, 1980) reflecting the willingness of the potential participant's willingness to provide motor responses, while the remaining waves can occur prior to the initiation of stimuli, but more often occur CNV 600-800 milliseconds after the warning and imperative stimuli (Hillyard, 1969). The duration of the interval between the two stimuli can affect the properties of the CNV-component (amplitude is higher when the reaction time is shorter, and less in fatigue), which can be separated on the sensory component, i.e. the "O-wave," and the motor component. The motor component has a somewhat longer latency of 1 sec and duration of 3-4 sec, and is called the Slow wave, and is affected by the same variables as the P3-wave, but has a different distribution on the surface of the head (Hugdahl, 1995b).

## EP-RESEARCH OF TEMPERAMENT AND BASIC PERSONALITY DIMENSIONS

Eysenck (1967) suggested that individual differences in extraversion can be understood in terms of the differences in optimal levels of arousal. This of concept is connected with ARAS (Moruzzi & Magoun, 1949), which regulates the activation of the cortex. In other words, extraverts who are inherent to higher sensory arousal thresholds in ARAS reach their optimum level of arousal on higher levels of stimulation. But Eysenck, (1990) in his view of biological basis of personality, pointed out the problems that have arisen from attempts to uncover the relation between physiological functioning, behavior, and personality. One of the most relevant problems proved to be the one related to the fact that one psychophysiological measure cannot be considered representative of the general index of cortical arousal or excitation.

It is known from individual psychophysiological studies that, for example, influencing the emotional stimulus can be reflected in different ways in different physiological systems, depending on individual differences, i.e. reaction specificity. One person may be reacted with intense increase of skin conductance activity when presented with a threatening stimulus; others turn to rapid heart rates; and some to the increased EEG activity, and so on. Therefore, Eysenck's (1990) main conclusion was that a physiological action couldn't be sufficient to describe the complexity of one's responses. A possible solution to this problem would be taking such measures that are representative of a large number of systems and identifying physiological changes in the activity of the most relevant system.

Of course, the realistic precondition of the possibility for implementing such a study should be added, i.e. in those studies in which it is possible to apply a number of different physiological measures. His thinking is almost identical to critical thinking of Zuckerman about three different arousal constructs within the theory of personality (1987). This famous personality researcher highlights the problem of the very definition of arousal, but also in the fact that our body has different forms of reacting to stimuli that depend on factors such as news, intensity, meaning, and type of cognitive processing that is required of a person at a given moment. Generalized "arousal" is a too broad construct for capturing all these different modalities that are at the disposal to the answer. Therefore, Zuckerman (1987), among others, believed that arousal should never be used in studies, without their extremely significant elaboration, as is evident in the names of: cardiovascular arousal, cortical arousal, electro dermal arousal, behavioral arousal, emotional arousal, and it is possible that even such elaboration is not enough in the interpretation of results... Therefore, this work will refer to arousal in the exactly specified period of cortical arousal.

Eysenck's conception (1967) of physiological arousal is multidimensional as it postulates two different systems: cortical and visceral arousal. While it is clear that there are a number of arousal dimensions (Vanderwolf & Robinson, 1981), it is not quite understandable how different psychophysiological measures are designed to evaluate the reactivity of different arousal systems. When observed from this perspective, the reason for an unsuccessful validation of Eysenck's theory could be found in the inadequacy of measurement methods, or in the bad choice of physiological variables. Also, what may contribute to an experimental error is the fact that each individual can be more sensitive to one and less responsive to another stimulus (Eysenck, 1990).

The famous Yerkes-Dodson Law (Yerkes & Dodson, 1908) and Pavlov's law of trans-marginal inhibition (Pavlov, 1928) also represent a challenge in relating personality, behavioral, and physiological reactions. Both laws describe the nonlinear relationship between stimulus and response. With an increased intensity of stimulation, power of responses initially increases and then decreases, thereby producing the inverted U curve. This curve seems to apply to interactional effects, which extraversion and manipulation have on performing tasks and neurophysiological functioning. Energizing or stressful events improve performance in extraverts and deteriorate in introverts (Revelle et al., 1987). The thesis used for an explanation of these findings is that introverts are usually excited and extraverts are too little excited, and in situations where there is a stronger excitation extraverts reach their optimal level, while for introverts a too powerful excitation badly affects their performance (Zuckerman, 1987).

Finally, Eysenck's theory of personality is truly exploited in terms of the extremely large number of psychophysiological researches, including those that use the method of evoked potentials. Most researched are the dimensions of extraversion and neuroticism. The differences in cortical arousal in relation to Pavlov's temperament dimensions are less studied, partly because Pavlov's theory of personality is represented in a smaller number of studies that deal with its empirical validation. Also, for similar reasons, there are very few studies of the biological basis of psychoticism operationalized in terms of the application of the evoked potentials method, which is compensated in fact by a large number of other clinical studies. They have generally demonstrated a prolonged latency and amplitude reduction of evoked potentials in a variety of diseases/disorders, and is generally considered an indication of a particular vulnerability to a disease/disorder. Therefore, EP-studies will be shown in relation to the temperament and Eysenck's personality dimensions with addition of EP-studies and control variables in this study, such as depression and giving socially desirable answers.

## Temperament and Evoked Potentials

The first connection between the method of evoked brain potentials and Pavlov's CNS properties emerged in the implementation of laboratory methods that non-Pavlovian theorists used with the aim of diagnosing the properties of the nervous system. Russian researchers strongly believe in the EEG method that allows the study of general characteristics of CNS as opposed to partial characteristics, which can detect all other psychophysiological methods (Strelau, 1983a). Nebylitsyn (1961, 1963) was the first researcher who used the EEG method the in characteristics study of CNS, and since the 1960, method has become indispensable in the study of temperament among Moscow researchers.

After the application of EEG in the research of the nervous system strength and recommendations that the variance of EEG amplitude is used as a measure of the same strength, Klyagin (1974) found that people with a strong NS have a significantly greater variance of the EEG amplitude than those with a weak NS. This author operationalized a higher variance of the EEG amplitude as the individual's ability to withstand a long time in an activity that has a high level of stored energy, which then manifests itself in the form of physical characteristics of the variance of the EEG amplitude. Furthermore, Regan (1972) found that the EP-amplitude is associated with the intensity of sensory stimuli. By applying somatosensory evoked potentials measurements of NS properties, Bazylevich (1974) found that the strength of NS is manifested when an increased stimulus intensity stops evoking an increased reaction - law of strength.

Chuprikova (1977) proposed the amplitude application of the early evoked potentials N1 and P2 in the auditory modality for causing varying intensity of the NS strength. On the other hand, a certain group of authors did not consider the relation between the evoked potentials and strength of CNS to be essential (Maryutina, 1974, 1978; Rusalov, 1974; Golubeva, Izyumovy & Pechenkov, 1977; Pasynkova, Guseva & Lipovetsky, 1980). Rusalov found that the phenomenon of asymmetry polarity and amplitude of the EP is consistently independent of variables under control, reflecting the general brain factor that can be identified as a general feature of NS. Almost to the present day, the power of inhibition has been very poorly examined in relation to not only to the electro cortical activity but also in relation to other psychophysiological measures, so that even in literature the power of CNS has been neglected.

Apart from electro cortical studies of a prior date, the researchers used a number of other psychophysiological measures as evidence for the construct validity of psychometrical surveyed dimensions of temperament. It should be specified what Strelau (1991) highlighted, and it refers to the fact that it often happens that questionnaire results of some personality characteristics do not correlate with the psychophysiological measures, which should in fact form the basis of these characteristics. The author explains it in a way that the main cause lies in theoretical properties, which are the basis of the construct of temperament.

The most common laboratory arousal measure, or in other words the strength of excitation, which was generally accepted by Russian researchers of CNS-properties, relates to the slope of the reaction time curve, has declined, which was achieved after a certain period of exposure of respondents viewing or hearing stimuli to which they should respond as quickly as possible. What was obtained in some studies (Kohn, 1987; Strelau, 1987) refers to a significant association between all psychometric characteristics measures used, including STI (Strelau Temperament Inventory), which examines Strelau's dimensions of temperament, which was expected, but without any significant correlation between all psychometric measures of personality and psychophysiological measures of excitation (Strelau, 1991). In other words, no significant correlation was found between the two laboratory measures of the strength of excitation (visual and auditory modality) and the strength of excitation as measured with the STI (Strelau, 1991). The author concludes from the results: first, the scale of strength of excitation of STI has low construct validity because it does not correlate with laboratory measures of strength of excitation. But, on the other hand, the same scale significantly correlates with other psychometric measures of personality, which takes this whole story to a slippery area. The second, the respective strength of excitation as a psychophysiological measure is not comparable with the results of psychometric properties of CNS or with the results of other questioned personality measures. It seems that the latter conclusion is much more acceptable than the other. Regardless of the confusing results that have been reached, other researchers continued with their work.

Danilova (1986) is one of the few researchers who examined the relationship Strelau's dimensions of temperament and EEG respondents. In her research, in addition to the above examined, she researched evoked potentials and heart rate in patients with strong and weak CNS (which she divided with regards to the result of Strelau's temperament questionnaire), while they learned the discrimination of light-flashing stimuli. She first established that there is a significant difference between the participants with strong and weak CNS. In other words, at the beginning of the learning task, participants with a strong CNS showed significantly lower amplitudes of N150 and P200 waves unlike the participants with a low CNS. For the group of participants with a strong CS ($N = 5$), it was found that by reducing the number of errors, heart rate increases as well as EP-amplitudes. For the group of participants with a low CNS ($N = 5$), it was found that with a decrease in the number of errors during the learning task, the heart rate slows down and EP-amplitudes decreases.

These findings coincide with the findings of De Pascalis (1993), who examined the relationship of hemispheric asymmetry, personality, and temperament. 60 participants, in whom groups of evoked potentials were measured like in this survey: N1-P2-N2-P3, but also the auditory and the visual modality, completed two personality questionnaires: Eysenck's and Strelauov's. The author's correlation analysis found a significant negative correlation between the strength of excitation and amplitude N1 posterior and P3 anterior in the auditory modality and amplitude P2 anterior in the visual modality, and the conclusion can be drawn that with an increased strength of excitation there is a decrease in EP-amplitudes. In contrast, the strength of inhibition showed a significant positive correlation with the behavioral reaction time measure in both modalities. But, as in the context of further implemented factor analysis within the same factors only strength of excitation, strength of inhibition, while positive reactions and negative errors had a significant saturation, it was concluded that these temperament dimensions are directly associated with behavioral performance, more than with the electro-cortical activity.

Considering other studies that examined the changes in evoked potentials related to personality, but that assessed some other personality characteristics such as characteristic "augmenting-reducing", it can be observed that there is a generally determined significant correlation between the EP-amplitude and the uppers (Buchsbaum, Haier & Johnson, 1983), and a negative correlation between the EP-amplitude and the downers. In other words, in situations of very high intensity stimulation it was found that the cortical response, i.e. EP-amplitude (N1-P1), decreases in people who have been assessed as downers, while the same response increased in people who have been assessed as uppers. With these personality characteristics, lowering can be conceptually related to Pavlov's construct of trans-marginal inhibition, the main characteristic that is associated with the type of person with a strong NS.

Although Petrie (1967) obtained completely opposite findings, but using a task that has a very low stimulation, Buchsbaum and colleagues (1983) pointed out that his measure is very reliable, showing a strong genetic determination and a direct measure of cortical activity. The same author (1971) for the first time related the evoked potentials and characteristic of sensation seeking and found a significant negative correlation between the EP amplitude and sensation seeking, which was later confirmed by a number of other authors (Zuckerman, Murtaugh & Siegel, 1974; Coursey, Buchsbaum & Frankel, 1975; von Knorring, 1981; Lukas, 1982; Como, Simons & Zuckerman, 1984; Orlebeke, Kok & Zeillemaker, 1984; Lukas & Mullins, 1985). However, it is important to point out that Como et al. (1984), by varying in their research the inter-stimulus variable interval (from 2 to 17 seconds), pointed out the significant impact of these variables on the relationship between evoked potentials and personality characteristics, and that it was more important to record the visual modality, therefore it is necessary for the research design itself but also for results interpretation to take these variables into consideration.

Strelau (1982, 1987) summarized a differently operationalized correlation analysis of ERP amplitudes and personality dimensions within his theories (Figure 3), which showed that: a higher level of arousal, i.e. higher amplitude measurements at the auditory EPs (moderate stimulation) has been found in people who have in the personality questionnaires been assessed either as uppers or as people looking for excitement, or people with weak CNS or as introverts, or as highly impulsive (Figure 3). Is a schematic representation of the amplitude relationship of auditory evoked potentials and different operationalized personality dimensions (Strelau, 1987).

People with reduced ERP amplitudes assessed themselves contrary to these questionnaires. What supports the obtained findings is the established significant correlation between P300-amplitudes for all categories of words and characteristics of endurance, which is measured with the personality questionnaire called Formal Characteristic of Behavior - Temperament Inventory (FCB-TI; Strelau & Zawadzki, 1993, 1995). Compared to an optimum level of arousal, under intense stimulation, not only does a person with low durability, compared to those with a high level, exhibit a lower efficiency of operation, but also experiences stronger negative emotions. Strelau and Zawadzki (1995) found that endurance characteristic significantly correlates with the strength of excitation, and also, although to a lesser extent, it correlates with mobility and the strength of inhibition. It was also found that the characteristic of endurance negatively correlates with neuroticism and emotionality. As for the findings of the relationship between evoked potentials and qualities of endurance, the study of De Pascalis, Strelau and Zawadzkie (1999), with a sample of 63 right-handed women aged 19-25, found that the group of participants with high scores on a scale of endurance that measures the ability to adequately respond to situations that require long-term and highly stimulating activity, showed significantly lower P300-amplitudes for all categories of words than the group with low scores on this scale.

*Figure 3. Schematic overview of the relationship between amplitudes of audio evoked potentials and differently operationalized personality dimensions*
*Source: ( Strelau, 1987 )*

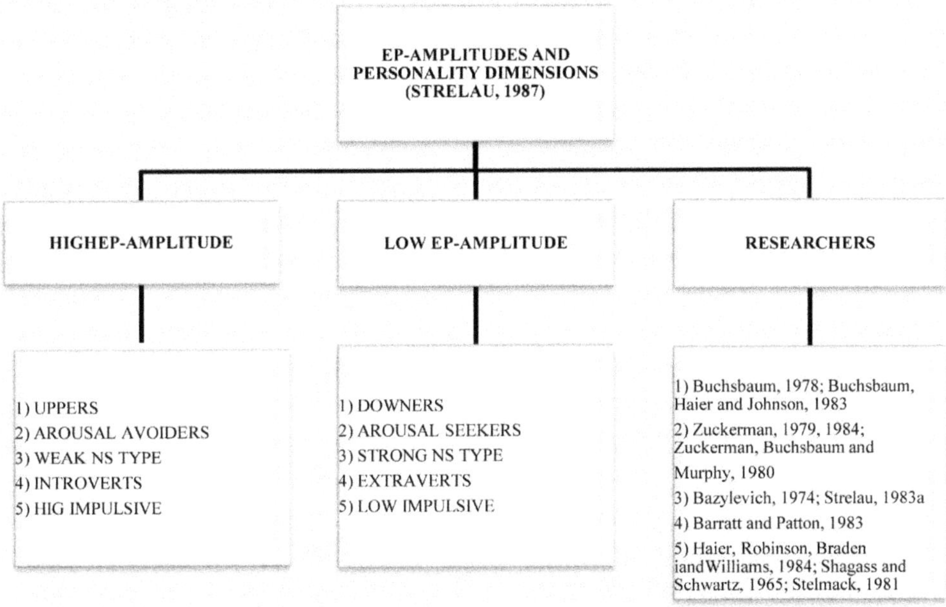


## The Basic Personality Dimensions and Evoked Potentials

The psychophysiological measure is a direct source of information on monitoring the electrical activity of the brain during the perceptual and cognitive processes. High levels of arousal are operationalized as the brain activity of low amplitude and high frequency in alpha (8-13 Hz) brain rhythm (Stelmack, 1981; De Pascalis, 2004). The first research of the psychophysiology of personality was done by Lemere (1936), who pointed out that there is a relationship between the electrical activity of the brain and personality style. After that, the discovery of ARAS has contributed to a research boom in the relation between the bioelectrical activity of the brain and personality, especially in the EEG differences between introverts and extraverts. EEG desynchronization, or the change from high amplitude and low frequency (alpha value) to a low amplitude and high frequency (beta activity) is associated with increased activity of ARAS, when attention is focused on the upcoming stimulation or formation of the reaction, and is most common among extraverts (Tran, Craig & McIsaac, 2001). Venturini and associates (1981) found no significant differences in the primary α-rhythms with extraverts and introverts, but they found them in all characteristics of measured responses to auditory stimulation in the form of a declining α-rhythm (latency, duration and instability). Extraverts habituated on the auditory startle response, and introverts did not, while introverts were more responsive to auditory stimulation, which essentially implies that introverts are generally more sensitive to stimulation. In addition, the following was found: a) in experiments of performing some activities introverts prefer quieter, less excitable environment with fewer opportunities for socializing than extraverts, and choose to study in the library with lower levels of visual and auditory stimulation (Campbell & Hawley, 1982); b) introverts are sensitive and have a lower tolerance to stimulation than extraverts (Campbell, 1983, 1992; Dornic & Ehehammar, 1990); c) extraverts set sound intensity higher than 20dB than introverts when they were offered a choice in this regard (Green, 1984).

Gale gave the first detailed overview of the literature in the field that studies the relationship between EEG and personality (1981, 1983). During the last three decades, several studies have established a positive correlation between the EEG alpha activity and extraversion (Gale et al., 1969; Marton & Urban, 1966; O'Gorman & Mallis, 1984; Savage, 1964; Zuckerman, 1991). Others have established negative correlations between the EEG alpha activity and extraversion, or the effect that contradicts the hypothesis of arousal (Broadhurst & Glass, 1969; Young et al., 1971), or that the relationship is not significant in either direction (Fenton & Scotton, 1967; Gale et al., 1971).

Gale (1981) argued that all these inconsistent results reflect a weakness in the convincing research methods and designs that characterize this research area. One of the potential factors that contributes to the formation of these inconsistent findings is the means of causing arousal in these studies. This author studied experimental conditions in experiments of high arousal, which required problem solving or time control tasks. The conditions, in which the subjects were asked not to do anything apart from keeping their eyes closed, but not falling asleep, are estimated as low arousal. He concluded that high and low arousal conditions are not suitable for studying the relationship between personality and EEG, given that the differences between introverts and extraverts are masked at the extreme poles of arousal conditions. Conditions of very low arousal will produce strong feelings of boredom with extraverts, and they will be directed how to raise their level of activation. In contrast, in situations of high stimulation levels, introverts produce paradoxical reaction of the reduced level of arousal, which is described as Pavlov's law of trans-marginal inhibition.

Gale (1983) proposed conditions that cause secondary level excitation for an evaluation of extraversion and the EEG. These are conditions in which the participants are allowed to have interaction with experimentalists, such as receiving instructions to open or close the eyes. In addition, in an attempt to confirm Gale's hypothesis (1983) on the relation between higher amplitude and low frequency of alpha brain rhythm with low levels of arousal that are present at extraverts, different researchers succeeded only in the fourth experiment (Tran et al., 2001), but with control of four factors which have been found to have a significant impact on not straightforward results: a) frontal cortical location where alpha activity is measured; b) recommendations for the use of methods of fast Fourier transformation to measure EEG; c) a questionnaire was used to measure extraversion, in this case Catell's; and d) age of participants in the study. Therefore, there was a significant positive correlation between extraversion and frontal EEG activity, where extraverts showed significantly greater amplitude in the alpha rhythm than introverts, but only on the frontal electrodes. Thus, this study has not only confirmed Gray's hypothesis and Eysenck's theory of extraversion (1967), but has also pointed to the importance of the frontal brain regions in the development of personality.

## Extraversion and Evoked Potentials

Stelmack, Achorn and Michaud (1977) found the first EP results that were in line with the hypothesis of arousal, where introverts are more susceptible to auditory stimulation than extraverts were. They run two experiments of evoked potentials with 60 participants with different degrees of extraversion, who were exposed to low- (0.5 Hz) and high frequency (8.0 Hz) tones at 3 levels of intensity (40, 55 and 85 dB). Participants were instructed to count target tones in a series of alternating high and low frequency tones in order to raise the level of attention. Introverts showed greater amplitude of N1-P2 waves than extraverts did with low-frequency tones of 55 and 85 dB. There was no difference between introverts and extraverts in high-frequency tones. The authors concluded that the use of low-frequency tones with auditory stimulation eases spotting the difference between extraverts and introverts because the individual variability of the EP at low frequency tones is higher than of high frequency tones (Rohtman, 1970). Higher EP-answers (N1-P2) are found in introverts in exposure of low frequency tones of moderate intensity.

This increase in the amplitude of the sensory stimulation ERP in simple tones in introverts is obtained in the majority of electro-cortical studies (Stelmack & Campbell, 1974; Bruneau, Roux, Lelord Percy, 1984; Stelmack

& Michaud-Achorn, 1985; Stelmack & Geen, 1992). The same results were obtained when recording visual ERP (Stenberg et al., 1988, 1990). Although the work of Rust (1975) found no significant correlation between cortical evoked potentials with variables of personality and intelligence, finding that those participants who were more bored had significantly more EP-amplitude, it implies a relation of evoked potentials with one aspect of the dimensions of extraversion - adventurousness. However, comparing the research of Rust (1975) with those of Stelmack and associates (1977), it is evident that the attention of participants in the second study reinforced the instruction to count series of alternating high and low frequency tones, while in the first survey the participants were simply exposed to receiving series of stimulation at one frequency of every 33 seconds.

Bruneau and colleagues (1984) showed that when tones are presented in alternating low and high frequency tones or a variety of sound intensities in a series of recording, it is more likely that differences between extraverts and introverts will be noticeable than when tones are presented in a repetitive manner. Stelmack and Michaud-Achorn (1985) found that repetitive series of stimuli with short inter-stimulus intervals are higher in N1-P2 amplitudes among introverts, mostly in the central electrode positions, but only for the first presentation of stimuli in this series. After the initial stimulus for all subsequent stimuli, there was a significant reduction in the EP-amplitude, suggesting the effect that shows that the circle of recovery until answering was not completed.

De Pascalis and Monitorosso (1988) used the Tone probe paradigm to cause evoked potentials, while the participants should identify the target word in meaningful and meaningless fragments of texts. It was found that introverts have a higher N2-amplitude in meaningless than in meaningful stimuli, and for extraverts it was the reverse. This finding was accompanied by the introverts' estimation of their significantly longer subjective involvement in the experimental situation with meaningless text, and extraverts estimated a significantly higher personal involvement in the condition with meaningful text. The authors interpret this finding as being indicative of individual differences in sensory discrimination among extraverts and introverts. But the difference between the recorded EP amplitude for meaningful and meaningless material in introverts was lower than in extraverts. This was the expected result due to the authors' predictions that meaningful material will be more interesting and thus have a greater potential for generating, and that the differential effects of excitation of meaningful and meaningless tasks will be higher in extraverts than in introverts, who were expected to take a relatively high level of arousal or involvement in the task in both experimental conditions.

In addition, extraverts generally showed a lower P2 amplitude in the left hemisphere than introverts, while there were no such differences between them in the right hemisphere. However, overall, these findings are consistent with the increased N1-P2 amplitudes in introverts compared to extraverts, which was first determined by Stelmack et al. (1977). Also, using a 40-minute task to maintain focus in their study, Beauducel, Brocke, and Leue (2006) found significantly a lower P300-amplitude, a significantly lower level of arousal and a significantly worse performance in tasks in extraverts than in introverts. Some studies (according to Sternberg, 1994) showed that impulsivity, which forms most of the extraversion dimensions, shows a stronger association with low excitation than extraversion, when it is considered in its entirely. Similarly, in other paradigms of selective attention, it which was expected that introverts will perceive more seldom signals from extraverts, introverts actually showed greater amplitudes with response clusters of exogenous ERP components N1-P2, recorded in central electrode positions (Geen, McCown & Broyles, 1985), and generally significantly higher N1-amplitudes than extraverts (Rammsayer & Stahl, 2004).

In the studies of recording of somatosensory evoked brain potentials, some of the results have been very inconsistent and difficult to interpret (according Stelmack & Geen, 1992). In studies that recorded auditory brainstem potentials, extraverts showed a significantly longer latency response in BAEP-components than introverts (Stelmack & Wilson, 1982; Szelenberger, 1983; Bullock & Gilliland, 1993; Swickert & Gilliland, 1998; Cox, Luz, Gilliland & Swickert, 2001), even when the participants slept (Stelmack et al., 1993). This produced faster latency of BAEP components means, greater auditory sensitivity or reactivity to stimulation for introverts, which is visible on the level of the auditory nerve. Finally, studies of contingent negative variation recording that represents the EP-indicator of preparations for a certain motor response, showed a mostly smaller KNV amplitudes in introverts, pointing to a less effective preparation for reaction and a smaller submissiveness to distraction than it is the case with extraverts (Stelmack, 1997). In conclusion, this EP study of personality indicates that increased N1 and P2 amplitudes are characteristic for introverts and not extraverts, which is consistent with the hypothesis of arousal, respectively greater arousal in introverts unlike extraverts (De Pascalis, 2004). In other words, a strong proof of the thesis is provided that introverts inherent higher reactivity of prominent physical stimuli than extraverts do, and that this effect should be set as a basic fact at the causal extraversion base (Stelmack, 1997). It is evident that components N1 and P2 are under the influence of exogenous, physical properties of stimuli, and therefore reflect the differences in the sensory reactivity between the groups. When a task is complex, late EP components are also included, e.g., N2 and P3, where the differences in extraverts and introverts are interpreted in terms of the subject's capacity to process information.

There is a high number of studies that have attempted to relate attention and cognitive evoked potentials with extraversion. Representations of such surveys indicate similar problems as those related to EEG studies of personality (Eysenck, 1990, 1994; Stelmack & Geen, 1992; Zuckerman, 1991), but with a significant degree of variation of experimental conditions, characteristics of stimuli, and choices of participants. It seems that the P300-wave is a promising measure to distinguish between extraverts and introverts. It is known that the P300-wave reflects cognitive processes and processes of attention. Eysenck pointed out (1994) that habituation, orienting process, and classification processes of stimuli are associated with P300 and the concept of cortical arousal, and P300 may have an advantage in the application in testing the hypothesis of arousal.

Daruna and colleagues (1985) were the first to identify a significant association between P300 amplitude and extraversion. They compared extraverts and introverts using the paradigm of selective attention. Participants were instructed to predict the occurrence of high and low frequency tones. Introverts showed a larger-P300 amplitude over the frontal, central, and parietal electrodes, unlike extraverts. Execution of the task did not discriminate the groups. The authors interpreted the findings indicative of the fact that introverts use more power to focus attention on a task than extraverts do (Kramer, Siveraag & Braune, 1987; Polich, 1987). O'Connor (1983) also found higher P300 amplitude among introverts than in extraverts using a paradigm of vary reaction time.

Pritchard (1989) examined the association between P300 amplitude and extraversion using the auditory oddball paradigm in which P300 causes a random appearance of target tones in a series of standard tones. He found an inverse association between the P300 amplitude and extraversion. Differences in the selection of participants and conditions of issuing stimulus made it difficult to compare the results between studies. Moreover, a higher P300 amplitude recorded in introverts was not evident in the initial series of recordings or in those series of recordings, which had a small number of recordings. This is explained by the fact that these differences are a result of higher habituation in extraverts and therefore are more likely to occur only after the participants spend enough time with the task to even come to habituation. Ditraglia and Polich (1991) studied the effect of habituation. They caused EPs using a simple two-tone auditory discrimination task with two record blocks. The P300-amplitude related to the target stimuli significantly fell between two blocks among extraverts, but did not change during recording among introverts. These results are consistent with Eysenck's assumption of faster habituation in extraverts. This finding also matches with the greater attention that is usually showed among introverts (Eysenck and Eysenck, 1985), and with a weakened EEG alpha response as it was found before in the laboratory of Venturini and associates (1981). In this case, extraverts habituated to auditory clicks and introverts did not.

Cahill and Polich (1992) manipulated the likelihood of target stimuli while adjusting the time on a mission to a minimum to avoid the effect of habituation. Under these conditions, extraverts produced a greater P300 amplitude than introverts did. They also showed a significant effect of probability of stimuli occurrence by producing a rapid increase in the amplitude tip with a dropping of the probability of target stimuli occurrence. In a later study, Polich and Martin (1992) recorded a P300 wave with both male and female participants when they were active in the three-tone task of detection, which varied the probability of target stimuli occurrence. P300, which is caused by target tones, gave results, which support previous findings. In male participants, introverts showed larger P300 amplitude than extraverts did, while the trend was not found in female participants. These results have the same direction as P300 findings of previous studies (Daruna et al., 1985; Ditraglia & Polich, 1991), but also some differences (Cahill & Polich, 1992; Pritchard 1989). The reason for this discrepancy is not clear. It is possible that Polich and Martin (1992) used more complex tasks than simple detection of the target tone or the reason can be attributed to the different impact of habituation to P300 for different types of personalities (Ditraglia & Polich, 1991; O'Gorman, 1977).

Like other electro-cortical measures, the relation between the P300-wave and E-dimensions is not simple. However, this does not imply that the P300 is not a valuable tool in testing theories. Ortiz and Maojo (1993) recorded the EPs in patients with extreme scores on extraversion scale as they were engaged in the auditory oddball task. Latency and amplitude of the P300-wave were measured. Introverts showed larger P300 amplitude than extraverts did over Fz, Cz, and Pz. There were no significant differences between the groups in the P300 latency. The P300 amplitude for introverts was three times higher than the P300 amplitude for extraverts. These findings are contrary to the findings of Pritchard (1989), but confirm previous findings of O'Connor (1983) and Daruna et al. (1985).

Stenberg's (1994) presentation of research indicates that the P300 is higher in extraverts when the task is cognitively demanding. Brocke and colleagues (1996) showed their two studies, one in which they used an auditory attention task and another in which they used a visual attention task with a high-level task difficulty. They managed to prove that the differences between extraverts and introverts could better identify situations that require strenuous response. In both studies, a higher P300 amplitude was discovered, mainly by means of frontal electrodes for introverts than for extraverts under highly demanding conditions of attention tasks. There were no group differences when the task requirements were low.

Similarly, Brocke et al. (1997) recorded the EP of introverts and extraverts during a 32-minute visual task attention in three experimental conditions: 1) without acoustic stimulation; 2) the stimulation of sound of 40 dB; and 3) the stimulation of sound by 60dB white noise. Introverts showed larger P300 amplitude in the first and second experimental situation, while extraverts showed a greater P300 amplitude only in the third situation. These results were explained by the authors in terms of the theory of control arousal. In other words, in monotonous situations, extraverts are increasing investment effort that is reflected in the increase of reliable P300 amplitudes. For these participants, the continuing decline in the stressful situation that is the consequence of further stimulation (60 dB white noise) is reflected as a safe increase of P300 amplitudes. By contrast, the situation with low levels of stimulation is better suited for introverts and requires a low level of compensation effort, which is then reflected as a reduction in P300 amplitudes. An alternative explanation of these results is that introverts are more sensitive to stimulation than extraverts, and that, figuratively speaking, high intensity stimulation is "competing" with the visual stimuli from attention task in "favor" of those capabilities that are included in the attention tasks.

A significant relationship between E-dimensions and EP-response in low and high demanding tasks is found in the study of De Pascalis (1993). The subjects participated in two visible and auditory stimuli recognition tasks in which the weight varied between very heavy and light tasks. A significant positive correlation between extraversion and EP-response was found in heavy tasks of identifying and for visible and auditory modality. The easy task of recognition did not allow for an establishment of a significant correlation between extraversion and EP-response. During the difficult task of identifying, a positive correlation was established between extraversion and the frontal 40 Hz EP-response, as index of focused excitation. This effect is specified in the left hemisphere and for visible and auditory modality. A similar positive association between extraversion and frontal N2-amplitude is determined for the hearing stimulation. These results are contrary to the results of later studies (De Pascalis, 1994) that used the visual task of identifying conditions with and without stress. A significant negative correlation was obtained between extraversion and frontal P2 and N2 amplitudes in stressful and non-stressful situations. These results also suggest that the frontal cortex plays a leading role in the differentiation of extraverts and introverts regarding EP-waves as indexes of attention and discrimination during the process of stimuli recognition.

In recent Gurrerae and colleagues (2001) extraversion study, the P300 wave was caused by a new auditory task during an auditory discrimination paradigm. Three types of stimuli were used: frequent (70%) of non-target tones, rarely (15%) target tones, and rare non-target new tones. Frequent tones (1 kHz) and target tones (1.5 kHz) have 97 dB and a short duration (50 milliseconds). New tones last from 50 to 150 milliseconds and have complex spectrum of sinusoidal tones or the comparable average intensity. There was a positive correlation between extraversion and frontal P300 amplitudes in these high-intensity new tones. Finally, in contrast to a series of researches and EP amplitudes, very little experimental evidence was found for any consistent difference in the P300 latency between introverts and extraverts.

The study of Doucet and Stelmack (2000) examined individual differences in processing speed and reaction response with regards to the degree of extraversion. Starting theoretical background in this study was based on whether introverts are more cortically excited than extraverts, then if this difference would manifest itself in their faster cognitive processing, and shorter P300 latencies. This hypothesis was confirmed by Brebner (1990), who used the experimental manipulation compatibility stimuli and task responses, wherein introverts showed significantly shorter P300 latencies and prolonged response time than extraverts. The finding is explained by the introverts' nature as being "focused on inspect" and that they draw excitement from the stimuli analysis that leads them to a continuation or expansion of activities that involve the stimuli analysis (Brebner, 1983), as opposed to extraverts who are focused more on organizing the stimuli than analyzing information about the stimuli, or "focused to react".

In addition to the P300 wave, reaction and movement time measures were used within 67 participants aged 18 to 30 years, and various types of assignments. During the reaction time task, participants should respond by pressing the target tone of 500 Hz and 70 or 85 dB, and in four different conditions: in the first condition they should just simply lift their finger from the button (0 cm), while in the other three conditions they were supposed to push buttons placed at different distances of 7, 15 and 23 cm. During the time movement task, participants were given two types of tasks: congruent and incongruent arrow keys. Focusing their attention on the middle arrow, participants should press the key that matched the direction that was given to the shown instructional word of compatible or incompatible response. P300 waves were recorded during the measurement of reaction time and movement time. During the reaction time task, it was found that the P300-amplitude significantly increased with increasing distance keys (expected increase in the P300 amplitude due to the increase in requirements in the type of giving answers), while the P300 latency was significantly prolonged during an increase of the auditory stimuli intensity. Despite these, there were no other significant findings related to the variable extraversion. On the other hand, in the task of time of movement, there were different findings in terms of the P300 latency, since it was found that there were no differences between extraverts, ambiverts, and introverts although a significant increase was found in the P300 amplitude by making the given task harder. In contrast, shorter P300 latencies were found in a congruent-compatible (easiest) task in extraverts and ambiverts, unlike introverts ($F_{(1, 56)} = 3.9, p <.052$), and in total of all three other types of tasks the P300 latency was significantly positively correlated with extraversion ($r =.29,.26,.17, p <.05$). In other words, in the three conditions, the P300 latency was significantly longer among extraverts than introverts, whereas introverts showed significantly faster cognitive processing than extraverts, but in the congruent-compatible condition the P300 latency was shorter for extraverts than for introverts.

In the end, the authors concluded that the P300-latency is sensitive to the very requirements of the task and is independent on the application selection type of response to the task in cognitive processing, and under some conditions it is sensitive to group differences in cognitive processing speed, which is attributed to personality variables, more precisely, to the differently represented dimension of extraversion among the participants. Based on this, it is considered that in the conditions of a specified simple visual or auditory task, discrimination of the target stimuli, such as a task to measure reaction time, with minimal requirements of evaluation stimuli, does not cause any differences between extravert and introvert participants in the speed of cognitive processing or in the P300 latency. When these requirements are increased or the evaluation and selection of the stimulus response are in conflict, there is a significant prolongation of the P300 latency in extraverts, unlike in introverts. In the study by Pritchard (1989), with a sample of 47 paid volunteers (24 male and 23 female) ranging in age from 18 to 31 years, the relationship was analyzed between Eysencks' personality dimensions and the P300 wave with the use of the auditory oddball paradigm. A borderline significant positive correlation ($r =.470$) was found between the P300-latency and the degree of extraversion, but only among male participants.

In other words, it was found that male extraverts evaluate auditory stimuli significantly slower than to male introverts (for women this relationship was not significant), which has been attributed to a very high and significant negative correlation degree of extraversion and neuroticism among male participants ($r$ = -. 439). This explanation is based on the results of the implementation of a partial correlation analysis, where it is found that the correlation between the P300 latency and neuroticism, after the separation of the partial portion of the impact of extraversion, remains significant ($r$ =.-. 480), while the correlation between the degree of extraversion and P300 latency after separating a partial degree of neuroticism is significantly reduced to $r$ =.290, and was statistically insignificant. On this basis, but also on the basis of the obtained significant negative correlation between the degree of neuroticism and P300 latency ($r$ = -. 588) in male but not in female participants (Pritchard, 1989), which is usually found in previous researches (Plooij-van Gorsel, 1981; Stelmack et al., 1993) that are are explained on the basis of higher and faster reactivity of higher neurotic people unlike low neurotic ones, it is suggested that future studies of the relationship between extraversion and P300 latency should research groups with high scores on the neuroticism scale, or that only those studies should be conducted in which the results of the extraversion scales and neuroticism do not correlate. Pritchard (1989) explained why the same results are not obtained on the female sample with the fact that a major emotional component of inverse relationship between neuroticism and P300 latency is anger, among men, as opposed to anxiety, which is very closely related to the male gender role unlike the female role, and based on the mentioned intermediary it is clear that this type of relation is not to be expected in the sample of female participants.

In conclusion, there is a large number of findings on different levels of the brain process that relate extraversion with individual differences in information processing and motor behavior. Introverts, when compared to extraverts, are characterized by greater electro-dermal and electro-cortical reactivity to sensory stimulation. There is not a lot of evidence that introverts and extraverts differ in tonic or basic levels of electro-cortical and autonomous activities. This conclusion stems from the fact that there are no extraversion-related differences in the levels of skin conductance in situations which are induced by a low level of arousal in those levels of conductivity of the skin prior to any stimulation. Similarly, in low arousal or sleepiness, differences in the EEG, which are associated with extraversion, are rarely spotted. When physiological arousal is manipulated by using CNS stimuli (e.g. caffeine, nicotine) or depressants (e.g., chlordiazepoxide), systematic effects of electro-dermal responses and EP-measures are determined that are consistent with the predictions of the theory of arousal (Eysenck, 1967). These effects support the view that introverts have more excitation than extraverts do, i.e. their increased reactivity to stimulation is inherent.

They do not support the hypothesis that individual differences in extraversion are characterized by individual differences in tonic excitation. Yet it is not clear whether an increased sensitivity to stimulation in introverts reflects differences in the central or peripheral nervous system, or both? Extraversion-related effects during auditory stimulation indicate that the higher the introverts' sensitivity could be related to differences in axonic or synaptic transmission on the level of the auditory nerve. Experimental evidence supports the thesis that the construct of excitation cannot be generalized. The main reason for this lies in the fact that extraversion-related differences are more related to arousal than with a basic level of tonic arousal. Moreover, EP differences in extraversion are not apparent throughout the continuum intensity levels, but mainly in the stimulation of moderate intensity. Another limiting aspect of the hypothesis of excitation is that psychophysiological measures of arousal responses are not equally effective in determining individual differences in extraversion. Significant effects also depend on the specific requirements of the task. The inconsistency of findings in the relationship between the P300 wave and extraversion indicate greater P300 amplitudes among extraverts in cases of high demanding tasks, while the results were reversed or with no differences in experiments when the variable of sustaining attention was not controlled (Sternberg, 1994). Considering other evoked potentials and extraversion, higher amplitudes of ERP waves were found in introverts, but only considering the tasks with moderate sensory stimulation of either an auditory or visual modality. Such difference was not found in the experiments with high intensity stimulation.

Considering that, there was significant less distractibility and a significantly greater focus on the task among introverts than extraverts (Blumenthal, 2001), attention is a variable that should be first on the list of control variables in extraversion ERP research. In addition, the hypothesis of arousal has received significant support by applying measures of skin arousal and EP auditory stimulation, and a somewhat less significant application of EP visual stimulation. Measures of heart rate, on the other hand, resulted in unambiguous findings. Finally, the latest EP studies of biological determinants of extraversion applied experimental evidence of individual differences in moto-neural excitability. By using a very large number of different tasks that require a motor response, there is a lot of proof that extraverts are different from introverts in expressing their motor behavior. Studies have shown that this difference is present in the execution process of the peripheral response and the central analysis of stimuli and responses in the process of response selection (Brebner & Cooper, 1974; Rammsayer & Stahl, 2002Houlihan, Pritchard, Guy & Robinson, 2002). Measurements of latency potential for readiness showed faster movement and earlier latency repetition in extraverts than in introverts.

## Neuroticism and Evoked Potentials

There is almost universal agreement that neuroticism is one of the most significant human personality characteristics (Mathews, 2004). As previously noted, a person who has a high degree of expressed neuroticism has a tendency towards anxiety, depression, and other negative emotions along with concern, frequent and sudden mood changes, and vulnerability to stress. In contrast, low levels of neuroticism are characteristic for an emotionally stable person that is calm and unconcerned. These are personality characteristics that are associated with individual differences in excitability and emotional reactivity, which is reflected in autonomous activation (Eysenck and Eysenck, 1985).

It is therefore understandable that a large number of studies of this personality dimension is, among other things, focused on exploring its biological background. It has been found that neuroticism is largely inherited, and Zuckerman (1991) estimated that it possesses a broad heritability of about 0.40-0.60. Therefore, it is certain that neuroticism significantly affects brain development, so that all significant differences between people with low and high neuroticism may be included with various psychophysiological paradigms. From initial neuroticism researches until today, it can be stated that psychology as a science hosts a large number of theories and theorists, as well as empirical confirmations of these same theories regarding efforts in understanding neuroticism. Keeping in mind each of these, it can be observed that they are grouped into three main theory groups or models: the bottom-up model, Zuckerman's psychobiological model (1991), and the cognitive-adaptive model or the top-down model (Mathews, 1999). The first theory group which was led, on the one hand, by Eysenck (1967), who related neuroticism with the excitation of the reticular-limbic-cortical system for controlling emotions, and, on the other hand, by Gray (1991), who related these personality traits to the sensitivity of brain systems to punishment or award. This model has been attractive to researchers for many years now and the reason for this lies in the fact that it provides a simple, unified theory of neuroticism, which potentially explains the significantly large number of correlations of personality characteristics ranging from psychophysiological responses to complex social situations.

Therefore, it was sufficiently seductive to begin this study with it, which certainly points to some limitations in interpreting the results, which will be tackled in the discussion paper. Zuckerman's model (1991), on the other hand, begins from highlighting the lacks of the first model that applies to isomorphism of the dimensions of neuroticism, and emphasizes and confirms in his empirical findings (Zuckerman, Kuhlman, Joireman, Teta & Kraft, 1993) that neurotic emotionality has several sources, including biochemical effects on emotions, subcortical structures such as the amygdala, cortical emotional-control systems such as the orbitofrontal cortex, and the various cognitive processes of higher order, while its relationship with these sources is not linear and single. Finally, the latest model in the framework of the three-stage cognitive paradigm (Pylyshyn, 1999) proposes a systematic approach to understanding different empirical correlates of neuroticism and other personality dimensions in which it is highlighted that psychophysiological and neurochemical studies represent multiple attributes of neural functioning that contribute to this personality characteristic, but do not fully explain its behavioral expression.

Therefore, Matthews (1997, 2000) suggests that neuroticism should be related and analyzed in reference to a series of operations that underlie information processing. In any case, no matter which theoretical model is discussed, to this day it has been noticed that the psychophysiological studies of neuroticism, no matter what the psychophysiological measure is used, have resulted in a series of inconsistent and vague, hard-to-explain results, which is mainly attributed to the fact that characteristic of neuroticism is tested in stressful conditions, but there has never been a consensus among researchers as to what is sufficiently stressful or less stressful for a particular person or group of participants (Eysenck & Eysenck, 1985). Also, in all these studies a question was raised considering the significant interaction between extraversion and neuroticism, whose effects have been controlled by only few researchers in their psychophysiological personality studies (Stelmack, 1981).

In relation to the objective and theoretical starting point of this research, it is necessary to show significant EP-researches of neuroticism within the bottom-up model. Eysenck (1967) related neuroticism with excitation of the emotional system, which is located in the limbic system. Therefore, the primary assumption is that under stressful conditions, neuroticism can be positively correlated with autonomic and cortical arousal, but empirical findings did not significantly support this assumption (Matthews & Gilliland, 1999, 2001). Although some authors (Winter, Broadhurst & Glass, 1972; Gale, Edwards, Morris, Moore & Forrester, 2001) found a certain trend towards high cortical arousal in the EEG data with highly neurotic people, a large number of well-designed studies failed to establish such findings or to achieve complex interactions in which the effect of neuroticism and extraversion depends on situational factors, as it has already been mentioned, and some studies have shown a significant association of high neuroticism with lower levels of arousal (Coles, Gale & Kline, 1971).

Also, a correlation between neuroticism and sensory evoked potentials, which are expected to reflect arousal and cognitive potential, has not been established (Rust, 1975; Golding, Ashton, Marsh & Thompson, 1986; De Pascalis & Montirosso, 1988; De Pascalis, 1993 Lolas, Camposano & Etcheberrigaray, 1989; Fjell, Walhovd, Meling & Johansen, 2005), although some other studies have found that neuroticism is negatively correlated with P3-latency (Plooij-van Gorsel, 1981; Pritchard, 1989; Stelmack et al., 1993; Stelmack & Houlihan, 1995) considering the increased and faster reactivity due to the anticipation of high neurotic person as opposed to a low neurotic one. By using simple oddball paradigm, Pritchard's' study (1989) established a negative correlation between P3-latency and neuroticism on a small sample of participants, but only in male participants, as it was a common finding in other studies that used simple cognitive tasks (Stelmack & Houlihan, 1995). The abovementioned Plooij-van Gorsel (1981) measured the reaction time in the task of selecting some goal on participants who were categorized as neurotic and anxious according to DSM-III criteria, and he also found a significant negative relation between P3-latency and neuroticism. Stelmack and colleagues (1993) established a consistent finding of a faster P3-latency and slower reaction time at high neurotic participants and in the implementation of the "YES" and "NO" answer categories with 6 simple cognitive tasks. They examined the relation between intelligence and the P3-wave, and found that although high levels of neuroticism and high levels of intelligence show a rapid stimuli evaluation (which is operationalized with the P3-latency), initiating the participants' reaction (which is operationalized as reaction time) is facilitated due to a more intellectual capacity, but also inhibited because of high neuroticism. This finding is very interesting and the authors pointed out that future research should be directed toward the analysis of P3-latency and reaction time, as the factors that would contribute to the understanding of the component structure of information processing in the context of the interrelationship between intelligence and neuroticism.

In addition, several studies have found a significant negative correlation between neuroticism and P3-amplitudes, as well as a positive correlation between neuroticism and P3-latency (Polich & Martin, 1992; Gurrera et al., 2001; Momirović, 2008). It is interesting that all these studies used complex tasks for evoking brain potentials and all in the auditory modality - Gurrera and colleagues (2001) applied new tones in addition to the standard ones. Polich and Martin (1992) tended to interpret the observed findings in relation to Pritchard's (1989) findings, and explained the opposite results with different patterns and EP-recording conditions, while Gurrera et al. (2001) and Momirović (2008) explained the obtained findings with a clinical sample, which participated in the survey highlighting that, in general, a reduced EP amplitude of a particular P3-amplitudes may not be specific for some mental disorders, but certainly indicates the vulnerability to some psychological dysfunction. A large number of clinical studies that used the method of evoked potentials, in order to analyze their diagnostic power, have precisely shown the presence of prolonged latency and reduced amplitudes of evoked potentials, especially those in the cognitive domain with a series of psychological (alcoholism, depression, obsessive-compulsive disorder, schizophrenia), neurological (Alzheimer's disease, HIV dementia, Parkinson's disease, supranuclear paralysis), and other (normal aging, dyslexia, head injury, narcolepsy) disorders (Polich, 1999).

It is interesting to mention the work of Criado and Ehlers (2007) in which, among other things, a significant correlation was found between the P45-amplitude and neuroticism after the participants observed happy and sad faces. They compared their findings with other research findings in which it was found that auditory P3-amplitudes were higher in people with an anxiety disorder (Enoch, White, Harris, Rohrbaugh & Goldman, 2001), which is relevant considering that anxiety is the basic line of neuroticism as a personality dimension (Otten, Gaillard & Wientjes, 1995), although other studies have not confirmed this (Bauer, Costa & Hesselbrock, 2001). Thus, they interpreted the obtained results in relation to the task they used in their research, which relates to stimuli with a varied emotional content, and concluded that neuroticism increases the electrophysiological response to affective stimuli such as emotional expressions of human faces, especially in women (Criado & Ehlers, 2007). For an interesting comparison, studies that used other psychophysiological measures, such as the degree of habituation of the orienting response, showed inconsistent results in all directions, some of which have been important and some not (Eysenck & Eysenck, 1985), when exposed to the task of repeating stimuli, which is often criticized with regard to the operationalization (as a response to the volume of a finger or electro dermal response).

Similarly, studies that used indicators of the autonomic nervous system, such as electro-dermal activity and electro-cardiac answer, usually found stronger responses in highly neurotic people, but there are also studies that have failed to confirm this hypothesis (Fahrenberg, 1991). Furthermore, the previously mentioned Gray's theory (1991) assumes that anxiety instead of neuroticism represents the causal effect on the physiology and behavior, so that neuroticism is an amalgam of high anxiety and high impulsivity. But in the most famous version of this theory, the anxiety trait is based on the sensitivity of the behavioral inhibition system (BIS), which reacts to threats signals that initiate behavioral "freezing," which is oriented to the source of the threat and to an increase of noradrenergic arousal.

Again, as it has already been mentioned, attempts to confirm this theory have resulted in ambiguous findings (Matthews & Gilliland, 1999). For example, Stenberg (1992) found that the anxiety trait, but not neuroticism, is associated with an increased EEG beta activity in response to a situation with a negative emotional imagining, which is consistent with Grays' theory. Other studies have failed to confirm that neuroticism and/or an anxiety trait moderate the response to negative stimuli (De Pascalis & Speranza, 2000). Therefore, it was concluded that Eysenck's and Grays' theories fail to fully solve the so-called neurotic paradox, mostly for the reason that they did not take into consideration that this strong relationship between neuroticism and negative emotions is moderated by situational stress (Suls, 2001). Although some researches determinate the correlation between neuroticism and psychophysiological response, this connection was weak and it was very difficult to isolate reliable moderator factors. It remains a possibility that this bottom-up model may be more supportive for the application of brain imaging techniques that could isolate the key structures that control the increased emotionality in a highly neurotic person. For example, Canli and colleagues (2001) found that neuroticism is positively associated with brain activation in situations with a negative emotional stimulus in the middle frontal gyrus and middle temporal gyrus.

## Types of Temperament and Evoked Potentials: EP-Studies E-N Interactions

Even though this interaction is not the focus of this study, it is interesting to provide a short overview. One of the major issues relevant to the ontogenesis of neuroticism, which is researched in several studies, relates to the fact if the established psychometric independence of extraversion and neuroticism simultaneously monitored by equally separate physiological processes, as Eysenck (1967) suggested. This research area, otherwise quite confusing and ambiguous, occurred as a result of certain findings related to those psychophysiological measures which correlate with neuroticism and extraversion. Claridge and Herrington (1963) were the first researchers who, after studying individual differences in thresholds of sedation, spiral after-effects and blood pressure, studied the question of separate neurological processes. As has already been stated, EEG indicators of cortical arousal found that neuroticism was associated with higher levels of cortical arousal (Winter et al., 1972) and with lower levels of arousal (Coles et al., 1971).

Besides that, where here was no significant association between neuroticism and EEG indicators of cortical arousal, there was psychometric independence between extraversion and neuroticism. Therefore, if a certain level of correlation between these two dimensions of personality is determined, the connection between the used indicator of brain activity and neuroticism can be expected (Stelmack, 1981). This is one of the most important aspects within Eysenck's theory of personality, given that he himself claimed a few times that in fact the analysis of extraversion in any context does not make much sense if studied in isolation from neuroticism, and that an interpretation of the results related to extraversion should be carried out in relation to the dimension of neuroticism (Eysenck, 1967; Eysenck & Eysenck, 1985). In other words, when considered in the context of Eysenck's personality theories and hypotheses of arousal, it is expected that introverts will have larger cortical arousal, unlike extraverts, and under Pavlov's hypothesis of excitation-inhibition melancholic (IN) will have the highest so-called maximum natural frequency and predominance of excitation, and sanguine (ES) will have the lowest natural frequency and predominance of inhibition (Robinson, 1982).

The system that has an increased natural frequency indicates a faster "transmission time," a higher "reactivity," a short "latency response," and generally a higher excitation level (Robinson, 2001). In relation to this, in an effort to improve Pavlov's hypothesis, three categories are obtained by measuring auditory evoked potentials (N2 and P2) and through factorization of the obtained values: waves of 4 Hz, 7 Hz and 10 Hz, which, according to Robinson (1999, 2000) correspond to the characteristic frequencies of the brain stem, the limbic and thalamocortical systems, the same author (2001) found that the maximum level of balance between the excitatory and inhibitory effect is present in sanguine ($N = 41$) and phlegmatic ($N = 28$), that the assumed predominance of excitation is significantly determined in choleric ($N = 16$) and the predominance of the inhibition in melancholic ($N = 8$).

Following this finding, the survey of Buckingham (2002) examined the relationship between temperament and evoked potentials (P1N1 and N1P2), and precisely for this reason that emphasizes automatic familiarity of extraversion towards neuroticism and vice versa in researches. In this study, subjects were divided into 4 groups according to their scores in EPQ: ES/sanguine ($N = 16$); EN/choleric ($N = 16$); IS/phlegmatic ($N = 8$), and IN/melancholic

($N = 16$). Two different EP-responses were induced with the tasks in which they had to respond to three different tone intensities (auditory modality) and light flashes (visual modality). The results showed a statistically significant difference between the IN and ES groups. The melancholic group showed significantly steeper and significantly higher amplitudes P1N1 and N1P2 of groups of evoked potentials, but only in the auditory modality, which is consistent with the hypothesis about the optimal level of arousal and previous results, as well as the assumed elevated cortical arousal and reactivity in this group of participants; in the visual modality there were no significant differences. The author concluded that the auditory EP-amplitudes are a much more suitable index for cerebral activity as opposed to the visual EP-amplitude (Buckingham, 2002).

In this study, opposite results were determined from the expected when it comes to EP-amplitudes (Tatalović Vorkapić, 2011). The lowest EP-amplitudes were determined in phlegmatic and the highest in choleric, while mean values of the EP-amplitude in sanguine and melancholic. The longest-N2 latency was found in the group of phlegmatic, and longest P2-latency and SW-latency in melancholic, as was to be expected given their low positioning in relation to the level of extraversion. Thus, the research clearly defined the statistically significant electrophysiological differences between different types of temperament, which are explained by the mediating role of attention and the habituation effect in the visual oddball paradigm.

## Psychoticism and Evoked Potentials

Most often on the nature of psychoticism is concluded based on the content of a particle scale that measures it on the basis of experimental studies, and on the basis of studies that have been conducted on relevant clinical samples (schizophrenic individuals, psychotic people, people with antisocial personality disorder, prisoners, etc.). However, it is important to note that this is a trait which is part of the normal personality and normal behavior, although in extreme cases and extremely stressful situations this variable figures can turn into pathological behavior, as is the case with neuroticism. In any case, it is the individuals who achieve a high score on the scale of psychoticism. Their main characteristics are loneliness, inhumanity, cruelty, insensitivity, neglect of other people, they are often unpleasant, and they seem like they di not belong anywhere. They are characterized by stubbornness in thinking and behavior, their socialization is very weak as are their feelings for others – they are poor, without empathy and understanding for others, without feelings of guilt. During the validation of the P-subscale of Eysenck's Personality

Questionnaire (Eysenck & Eysenck, 1994), it was found, in addition to the aforementioned clinical group participants who achieve high results, that there exists a significant association between the degree of masculinity and psychoticism, and that gender differences consistently occur in psychosis in favor of men, which is logical given its close relationship with aggression and hostility. In addition, it appears that the biological basis is closely related to male sex hormones.

Furthermore, it is important to mention that there are complaints about all those studies in which the results on a scale of psychoticism were interpreted independently, that is, independently of the other personality dimensions, which then affect the overall interpretation of the findings in this study. It is known that if researchers are interested in the level of psychoticism in a sample, it is required to analyze the level of socially desirable answers or lying by the same pattern shown in this study (both subscales are in EPQ). A high P-result can be interpreted independently and there is a very high probability that it actually is the way it has been obtained, but low-P results may be questionable, since a common high negative correlation between psychoticism and lying is expected, of about $r$ = -0.4. In order to clarify the resulting P-score it is necessary to examine the L-results of the persons achieved a low P-result in order to test the authenticity of the high result ton he L-scale in individuals with a low P-result.

Similarly, an extravert person who achieves a high P-result has quite different characteristics than an introverted person. People with high scores of a PE-combination can be very adventurous, often entering a high-risk situation; they are impulsive, fun-loving, and looking for excitement. However, again, when to such a combination we add varying degrees of neuroticism, the whole picture of personality can change once again. People with a high degree of PE combinations that also have a high degree of neuroticism can be quite anti-social and do not accept social norms, while the present low but sufficient degree of neuroticism show a very desirable "brake" in dangerous situations, restraint in the search for excitement, as well as carefulness in adventurous situations. A characteristic profile of heavy opiate addicts is highly represented by a combination of PN and low EL. In other words, pathological points are elevated in introverted low L-results resulting in the attitude: "I do not care what others think." A more reliable and a more valid interpretation of the results achieved in the EPQ-psychoticism subscale is achieved with a parallel analysis of the results achieved in other Eysenck's personality dimensions, in particular on the scale that, on the one hand, measures social desirability/lying and, on the other, conformity.

In addition, it was found that psychoticism is strongly dependent on genetic factors (Eaves, Eysenck & Martin, 1989), and Zuckerman (1991) widely discussed its biological roots. It is important to mention the various groups of variables; whose purpose was to try to get into the best possible explanation of the nature of psychoticism. The first of this group refers to the biological variables (HLA-B27: subsystem of the human leukocyte antigen; MAO: mono-amine oxydase, serotonin, and dopamine D2), the second to the study of laboratory behavior (eye movements, dichotic shadowing, sensory thresholds), the third variable to learning conditioning (latent inhibition), the fourth to the psychological variables (creativity, hallucinations, associations words), and the fifth to the physiological variables (EMG, autonomously-perceptual inversion). It is quite important to note that psychoticism is significantly associated with dopamine D2, which is also closely related to all theories of schizophrenia (Gray, Pickering & Gray, 1994), while a similar correlation was not found with psychopathy, which would then in the same way link psychopathy and psychoticism. Eysenck (1997) explains this fact in the way that psychopathy includes psychoticism and can be linked to psychosis.

One part of this research relates to the interesting relationship between psychophysiological measures such as evoked brain potentials and psychoticism. All EP research could be divided into three main categories: a) EP studies of schizophrenia; b) EP studies of alcoholism and antisocial personality disorders; and c) EP research personalities that, in addition to other personality dimensions, check the relationship of psychoticism and evoked potentials.

Concerning the first category, it is interesting because, as is was stated above, higher levels of psychoticism are associated with the occurrence of schizophrenia. It was found that the P3- amplitude is reliably reduced in schizophrenia (Ford, Pfefferbaum & Roth, 1992), even when patients are stabilized on medication (Pass, Klorman, Salzman & Kaskey Klein, 1980; Pfefferbaum, Ford, White & Roth, 1989) in patients with a first psychotic episode (Salisbury, Shenton & Sherwood, 1998) and in retesting patients after one year (Turetsky, Colbath & Gur, 1998). Findings suggest that the P3-amplitude is an important marker of the neurobiological nature of disease progression (Ford, Mathalon, Marsh, Faustman, Harris, Hoff, Beal & Pfefferbaum, 1999). Neurophysiological analyses of sensory information processing have shown in schizophrenia the existence of a number of abnormalities, such as changes in excitability, and temporal limitations in the collection of sensory information (Coquery, 1979) can be quite dysfunctional in a group of schizophrenic patients, and is reflected in their inability to filter external information, which ultimately leads to a deficit of attention.

Focusing and filtering irrelevant information are two major problems with most schizophrenic patients (Cornblatt & Keilp, 1994), although their anatomical origin is still unknown (Nieman, Ongerboer de Visser, Koelman, Hofman & Linszen, 1998). EP studies of schizophrenia have identified three groups of relatively consistent findings (Grebb, Weinberger & Morihis, 1986). First, early EP components tend to increase in amplitude (Callaway & Naghdi, 1981; Kaplan, Sadock & Grebb, 1994). Second, the amplitude of the transitional EP-components is usually reduced due to the impact of stimulus patterns. Third, late EP-components, in particular the P3- wave as noted above, also exhibit a reduced amplitude (Grebb et al., 1986).

In addition, several studies (Pfefferbaum, Wenegrat, Ford, Roth & Kopell, 1984; Blackwood, Erbmeier & Muir, 1994; Souza, Muir & Walker, 1995) have found a significantly prolonged P3-latency in people diagnosed with schizophrenia. The causality of some types of schizophrenia is attributed to the dopamine hyperactivity in different parts of the limbic system, including increased dopaminergic inflows into amygdala (Lloyd, 1978; Reynolds, 1983, 1987). This effect is interpreted as an overaroused condition.

This hypothesis is consistent with data that dopaminergic agonists, such as L-dopa and amphetamines, can produce a behavioral syndrome, which is compared with schizophrenia (Stevens, 1993), although it was found that L-dopa improves the negative symptoms of schizophrenia (Albert & Rush, 1983). In the opposite direction, different antipsychotic drugs that block dopamine receptors in sufficient quantities can lead to catalepsy resembling Parkinson's disease (Hornykiewicz, 1975). Therefore, this model assumes that some schizophrenic individuals and people with Parkinson's disease are at opposite ends of the same dopaminergic continuum: one end indicates a too aroused state and the other too low aroused state where both ends represent some form of abnormal behavior, and overall arousal works on the principle of a reverse U-curve as well as in the depressive syndrome. At the ends of the inverted U-curve in the function of the level of arousal, are the too high and too low levels of arousal, which can be seen in the same behavioral patterns. An insufficiently aroused end of the continuum has an insufficient amount of arousal tat serves to initiate the process of learning, as well as short- and long-term memory.

On the other hand, however, a too aroused end of the continuum is even harder to understand because it actually has the exact amount of energy required to run the before mentioned cognitive, emotional-motivational, and motor processes, and yet eventually it badly damages learning and performance in a person, which has been mathematically proven (Grossberg, 1982). In other words, the neural network loses its ability to represent its plans and other contextual representations of a higher order that depend on sequential information. The resulting contextual collapse, confused response categories, and word play that are based on the associations of a lower order are also the core features of schizophrenia (Maher, 1977).

Remaining within the framework of arousal, EP-research on antisocial personality disorder and the like, and even alcohol, reduced EP-amplitudes, in particular the P3-wave and prolonged latency explained with the so-called underarousal hypothesis (Coren, 1999). This hypothesis states that individuals who exhibit criminal tendencies also tendencies of reduced autonomous and cortical excitation as opposed to people who have no history of antisocial activities (Hare, 1978; Zahn, 1986). Some studies have found reduced levels of arousal in 15-year-olds on the physiological measures such as skin conductance, heart rate and slower brain wave frequencies, who until the age of 24 had committed some criminal act (Raine, Venables & Williams, 1990). The same authors based on this suggested that high levels of arousal actually protect individuals from engaging in some antisocial act.

Low levels of arousal in individuals lead to the establishment of the need to engage in some of the activities that bring them excitement (which often includes crime, risk, and even violent behavior) in order to raise their arousal to the optimum level. This is consistent with the statements of criminals who explained their involvement in a crime and created risky situations in which they had a need for excitement (Hare, 1993). Precisely by starting from the described hypothesis, EP-research of antisocial behavior and alcoholism found significantly lower levels of EP-amplitudes (Golding et al., 1986), especially the P3-amplitudes, which also confirmed the hypothesis of too low arousal (Porjesz & Begleiter, 1990; O'Connor et al., 1994; Polich, Pollock & Bloom, 1994; Bauer & Hesselbrock, 1999a,b; Costa, Bauer, Kuperman, Porjesz, O'Connor, Hesselbrock, Rohrbaugh & Begleiter, 2000), whether these are prisoners (Barrat, Stanford, Kent & Felthous, 1997) or adolescents with conduct disorder (Porjesz & Begleiter, 1998).

Finally, a few EP- personality researches also checked the relationship between psychoticism and evoked potentials, and some of them analyzed this relationship on healty and some on sick participants. Their findings are not unambiguous, but they are all similar studies in that none of them paid attention to these obtained results nor tried to explain in some way. As far as the findings are concerned, a number of studies identified a significant relationship between psychoticism and measured parameters, either of earlier or later EP-components (Rust, 1975; Pritchard, 1989; Lolas et al., 1989; De Pascalis, 1993; Robinson, 2001), which was simply not even explained then since it was not the aim of these studies. Stelmack and Houlihan (1995) in their study on healthy participants only mention a significant negative correlation between the levels of the measured psychoticism among participants and their P3-amplitude, while Polich and Martin (1992) found a lower but still significant positive correlation between the P3-amplitude and psychoticism ($r$ =.34), and only in female participants. In male participants, it was in the same direction but at a significant level.

Golding et al. (1986), in testing the relationship of personality traits and early and late somatosensory evoked potentials, found a significant negative correlation ($r$ = -.41) between psychoticism and early somatosensory evoked potentials (N21-P27), and it is interesting that in calculating partial correlations, where impact of the varied intensity of stimuli was exempted, they found a significant negative correlation of the same order of magnitude both in early and late somatosensory evoked potentials, and also in relation to the amplitude with respect to latency. Finally, Momirović (2008) found symptoms of psychotic dissociation and psychotic regression and low ego strength compared to the P3-wave in a mixed sample of healthy ($N$ = 15) and sick ($N$ = 21) participants, a positive correlation between variables that were significantly related to the psychosis and P3-latency but not at significant levels, and a significant negative correlation between P3-amplitudes and the aforementioned variables in the domain of psychoticism by analyzing the tendency to aggressive and impulsive reactions, confirming thereby the assumptions about the reduced P3amplitude and prolonged P3-latency as general indicators of vulnerability to a psychological dysfunction (Gurrera et al., 1991).

## Social Desirability and Evoked Potentials

With the Social desirability subscale from the revised Eysenck's Personality Questionnaire (EPQ/R; Eysenck & Eysenck, 1994) it is attempted to measure the tendency of some participants to "act good," which is especially pronounced when it seems that this is desirable. Although he conducted a series of factor and experimental researches in order to further investigate the nature of this scale (Eysenck & Eysenck, 1970; Michaelis & Eysenck, 1971; Eysenck, Nias & Eysenck, 1971), there are certain difficulties in the interpretation of results as the sole factor of dissimulation, because in addition to this, the scale also measures the stable personality factor, which to some extent indicates naiveté or conformity. Since the degree of reliability of the scale of lies did not change due to the change in the variance of the results on the scale depending on the greater or lesser degree of dissimulation, as it could have been expected, Michaelis and Eysenck (1971) concluded that the scale must measure a stable personality trait. The same authors also proved that situations that encourage dissimulation could be quite clearly distinguishable from the situation that does not encourage it on the basis of high or low correlation between neuroticism and social desirability. In other words, recommendations by the original authors are that if the association between neuroticism and social desirability is large, and is approaching or is above $r = -0.50$, it is a situation that greatly encourages dissimulation and the results of the scale should be used for the purpose of extracting the dissimulator, i.e. 5% of the highest scores on the L-scale.

Otherwise, the results on this scale are interpreted in terms of the personality trait of conformism and social desirability. In any case, the same properties (measured either within the Eysenck's Personality Questionnaire or some other measuring device) are rarely studied specifically in relation to the evoked brain potentials. Most often this happened in such a way that the main focus of the study was the relationship between Eysenck's other dimensions and evoked potentials, and the relationship between personality traits and evoked potentials was additionally checked, so that the number of relevant researches is rather small. But despite that, most EP-research figures have not find a significant association between the level of social desirability or the tendency to reveal themselves in a socially desirable light and evoked potentials (Pritchard, 1989; Golding et al., 1986; Polich & Martin, 1992; de Pascalis, 1994).

However, de Pascalis (1993) found in his research, while measuring the early and late EP components in visual and auditory modality, a significant relationship between the evoked potentials and results which participants ($N = 60$) achieved on the EPQ-scale of lying. The findings are interesting and definitely "cry" for deeper analyses: There was a significant negative correlation between the amplitude of the visual N1-wave and lying ($r = -.32$), a significant positive correlation between the amplitude of the auditory N2-wave and lying ($r = .30$), and a significant negative correlation between the amplitude of the visual P3-wave and lying ($r = -.26$). Although the author did not elaborate in detail the obtained results, it is evident that the relationship of this personality variable and evoked potentials certainly affects the modality in which the potential is caused, and whether this refers to early and late EP components.

On the other hand, Robinson (2001) found a significantly negative correlation between the P3-amplitude in the auditory modality and the results on the EPQ-scale of lying ($r = -.25$), which is consistent with previous findings, but as it was the case with de Pascalis, he also did not engage in a detailed interpretation of the findings. Although due to the very nature of the definition of preferences for presenting oneself in a socially preferred light or the inclination to conformism it would be logical to expect that maybe the EP-latency of particularly late components would be extended because of the responses that are adapted to social expectations and not to accurate ones, and therefore to automatic (faster) responses, currently there is no research that examines the relationship between the EP- latency and the level of conformism, which this work attempts to change.

## Depression and Evoked Potentials

In everyday life, depression usually means a certain fleeting sadness that disappears with the change of a situation or immediate circumstances. Therefore, it is very often associated with disappointment, the loss of a close person, break up of a meaningful relationship, fatigue or some sort of trouble the individual or his immediate is experiencing. Nevertheless, usually with the passing of time or during mourning all these types of depression go away without professional assistance. Surely, there is no human being that has not experienced at least once during their lives (and usually more than once) depressive emotions, and they as such are not considered to be signs of emotional disorders (Krizmanić & Kolesarić, 1994). In contrast, clinical depression is much less likely to occur and a significantly more serious problem than dismal situations in which people sometimes find themselves in. Many researchers believe that normal and pathological depression on the same continuum (Krizmanić & Kolesarić, 1994).

Although in most cases, the extreme ends of this continuum are quite clear, it is very difficult to determine where in fact normal depression stops and pathological begins. However, today's expert application of diagnostic criteria in determining psychological disorders with a quality differential diagnosis manages to find this border. Deficits in cognitive processing consistently occur in persons who have been diagnosed with a depressive disorder (Austin, Mitchell & Goodwin, 2001; Ottowitz, Dougherty & Savage, 2002). In addition to a large number of other neurophysiological studies of depression, the researchers often sought to examine the biological basis of depression using the method of evoked potentials, specifically the P3-wave. A significant number of previous works did not produce consistent findings (Houston, Bauer & Hesselbrock, 2004).

Although the thesis that starts from a supposed vulnerability to a psychological dysfunction in the form of a prolonged latency and reduced amplitude in depressed individuals is logical, a number of studies have found no significant association between depression and the EP-amplitude (Giedke, Thier & Bolz, 1981; Roth, Pfefferbaum, Kelly, Berger & Kopell, 1981; Plooij-van Gorsel, 1984; Patterson, Michalewski & Starr, 1988; Bruder, Towey, Stewart, Friedman, Tenke & Quitkin, 1991; Bruder, Tenke, Towey, Leite, Fonk, Stewart, McGrath & Quitkin, 1998; Sarah Gordon, Kraiuhin, Coyle, Howson & Meares, 1994; Bange & Bathie, 1998), while a number of works resulted in ambiguous findings concerning the relationship of depression and the EP-latency (Bruder et al., 1991; Bange & Bathie, 1998; Vandoolaeghe, van Hunsel, Nuyten, & Maes, 1998; Giedke, Thier & Bolz, 1981; Diner, Holcomb & Dykman, 1985; Gordon, Kraiuhin, Harris, Meares & Howson, 1986; Blackwood, Whalley, Christie, Blackburn, St Clair & McInnes, 1987; Muir, St. Clair & Blackwood, 1991; Gangadhar, Ancy, Janakiramaiah and Umapathy, 1993).

On the other hand, however, most works have confirmed the above-mentioned assumptions, and significantly lower P3-amplitudes have been found in depressed participants with different forms and levels of depression (Baribeau-Braun & Leserve, 1983; Pfefferbaum et al., 1984; Diner et al., 1985; Thier, Axmann & Giedke, 1986Blackwood et al., 1987; Muir et al., 1991; Gangadhar et al., 1993; Santosh, Malhotra, Raghunathan & Mehra, 1994; Bruder, Tenke, Stewart, Towey, Leite, Voglmaier & Quitkin, 1995; Defrance, Ginsber, Rosenber & Sharma, 1996; Yanai, Fujikawa, Osada, Yamawaki & Touhouda, 1997; Kaustio, Partanen, Valkonen-Korhonen, Viinamäki & Lehtonen, 2002 Roschke & Wagner, 2003 ; Houston, Bauer & Hesselbrock, 2003; Urretavizcaya, Moreno, Benlloch, Cardoner, Serrallonga Menchón & Valley, 2003).

One possible explanation for this heterogeneity of P3-findings in relation to depression should be sought in the possible heterogeneity of the sample. Many people with depression use various medicine throughout the course of the disorder, have comorbid psychiatric disorders and complex family relationships. In addition, the severity of this disorder can vary considerably from one study to another, e.g. from a sample of clinically depressed patients to a sample of depressed students. In addition, there is still a problem with the distinction of depression as a state and personality trait that researchers ignore. In addition, the studies used very different measuring instruments for which the researchers did not specify what kind and to what extent the same instrument measures depression. It is therefore possible that some samples in these studies are mixed with regard to their depression status at the time of testing.

Other possible cause can of course apply, as it was the case in the examination of other relationships of the P300-wave, on the nature and gravity of the task that causes evoked potential. Several researchers have emphasized that a significant decline in the P3-amplitudes in depressed people can be expected only in the context of a difficult task (Roth et al., 1986; Bruder et al., 1991; Houston et al., 2003), although they obtained the opposite is (Kaustio, Partanen, Valkonen-Korhonen, Viinamäki & Lehtonen, 2002 Roschke & Wagner, 2003; Urretavizcaya et al., 2003). The third possible cause lies in the development phase in which the research participant is currently in. Most EP-depression research has been conducted on adult participants whose cognitive function is significantly influenced by the application of various drugs, reduced positive expectations toward their cognitive efficiency or a greater severity than it was the case in adolescents. In any case, it is important for the interpretation of the findings of any research to keep in mind how depression was initially defined, on which sample it was tested, and what kind of task caused the evoked potentials that we measured.

## Relationship Between Behavioral Variables and Evoked Brain Potentials

As can be seen from the previous chapter, a truly significant number of variables, whether situationally conditioned, by the single task or some characteristics of participants, affect the latency and amplitude of evoked potentials, and then the ratio of evoked potentials and personalities (Hugdahl, 1995b; & Polich Kok, 1995). EP-studies have generally shown that exogenous evoked potentials, or early EP-components, are more affected by changes in the physical characteristics of the stimulus, the recording conditions that affect the perception of the participants and inter-stimulus interval, while the endogenous evoked potentials affect more different biological determinants (Huhdahl, 1995b). However, it was concluded that the majority of impacts of external variables are visible and can be linked to changes in the latencies and amplitudes of later EP-waves, and therefore the research has mainly dealt with the influence of biological determinants of the late EP-component, mostly on the P3-wave (Polich & Kok, 1995).

Since the focus of this work is on the components N1-N2-P2-P3-Sw, who share the same neurophysiological basis in the cortex, and also in addition to the processing of stimuli characteristics they reflect one or more cognitive processes, those research results will be mentioned that indicate a significant influence of certain external, behavioral variables either on the evoked potentials or their relationship with the personalities of the participants. Prior to the review of relevant works, it is important to recall that the N1-P2-N2-latencies increases when it comes to the target stimulus to which the attention is directed (Hugdahl, 1995b).

Also, in EP-studies in which specific characteristics of the task varied, such as: type of response, kind of stimulus material, difficulty of the task, and perceptual weight on the P300-wave, it was found that each of these variables has a considerable impact on the latency and amplitude of the P3-wave. As for the difficulty of the task and perceptual difficulty, it was found that the variation in the difficulty of the task was not significantly associated with changes in the P300-latency, but it was with a change in the P300-amplitude: a significant reduction in the P300-amplitude was followed by a higher difficulty of the task (Mecklinger & Ullsperger, 1993), and, on the other hand, the perceptual difficulty and auditory and visual modality significantly affect the morphology of the P300-wave (Comechero & Polich, 1998). With regards to the type of stimulus material, in the auditory oddball task early P3-wave had a significantly different topography unlike late P3/N3-wave (Kayser, Tenke & Bruder, 1998)

## Changes in the Metabolism and Food Intake

Several studies have shown that the N1-N2-P2-P3 waves are responsive to the metabolic status of the individual (Polich & Hoffman, 1998). When glucose levels are reduced to the criteria that apply to hypoglycemia in normal persons, an obvious extension of the P3-latency was determined (De Feo, Gallai, Mazzotta, Grispino, Torlon, Perriello, Ventura, Santeusianio, Brunetti & Bolli, 1988; Gallai, Mazzotta, Firenze, Del Gatto, 1988; Blackman, Towle Lewis, Spire & Polonsky, 1990; Jones, McCarthy, Tamborlane, Caprio, Roessler, Kraemer, Starick-Zych, Allison, Boulware, & Serwin, 1990), which is present with diabetics (Kern, Wells, Stephens, Elton, Friedman, Tapscott, Pekala & Dohm, 1990; Pozzessere et al., 1991).

In addition, significant reductions in the EP-amplitude were determined in different variations and changes in the level of glucose (Gallai et al., 1988; Jones et al., 1990). However, the general conclusion is that both the sensory and cognitive evoked potentials are under the influence of metabolic processes, particularly with the declining neuropeptide-glycemic level (Hoffman & Polich, 1998). In addition, Geisler and Polich (1990) found that the P3-amplitude is lower and the P3-latency longer in participants who did not eat during the last 6 hours than it is the case with the participants who did not eat during the last 3 hours. With direct manipulation it has been established that a significant increase occurs in the P3-amplitude immediately after eating, and when the variable is further analyzed and the time variable is provided, it was found that the P3-amplitude is significantly higher in fed as compared to hungry participants, particularly when tested during that part of the day for which they declared that they do not like it (Geisler & Polich, 1990).

In contrast to these findings, one study found that the association between the P3-wave and recency of taking food is not significant, and in another study that same finding was confirmed in addition to that there was a change in the N1-amplitude, which was significantly lower in the group of participants the night before had begun taking special nutritious food as opposed to the control group, which started with the EP-recording after their usual breakfast, and it was concluded that there exists a relationship between EP and food, but not a direct one (Hoffman, Friedmann, Saltman & Polich, 1999). Thus the main recommendations in EP-research is conducting EP-recording after at least 60 minutes have passed since the last meal, and that the recording evoked potentials cannot be accessed immediately after consuming a meal, of course, unless consuming food as a variable is not the subject of research.

## Circadian and Ultradian Biological Rhythms

What the variable of the time of day is concerned when trials are conducted, some studies have shown that there are daily variations in the N1-P2 amplitude for auditory, visual, and somatosensory stimuli, while some others do not have them, which some authors explain with different methodological approaches to research and relatively small samples (Browman, 1979; Browman & Sullivan, 1980; Davis, Buchsbaum & Bunney, 1978, Henninger, McDonald, Goff & Sollberger, 1969). As for the P3-wave, it has been found that, although no statistically significant associations were obtained between a particular part of the day (morning/evening) and the P300-wave, circadian body changes indirectly affect P300 through physiological measures, given the existence of significant physiological/circadian changes (during the day a slight increase in body temperature and heart rate was determined, as well as a slight drop in the evening). The P300-latency is shorter in participants with an increased body temperature and in those with faster heart rate (Polich & Kok, 1995).

Some other authors in turn explained the inconsistencies in EP-research and time of day with their individual differences in the preference of a certain time of day for some activity. And so the classifications of participants into those who prefer morning or evening for an activity (Horne & Östberg, 1976) revealed different patterns of effects in behavioral tasks that are interpreted as indicators of differences between these groups in their fundamental levels of arousal (Fröberg 1977; Horne, Brass & Pettit, 1980; Åkerstedt & Fröberg, 1976). When this factor was taken into account, the series of EP-studies that were conducted by Kerkhof and colleagues (Kerkhof, 1980; Kerkhof, Koving,

Willemse, Geest & Rietveld, 1980) revealed consistent patterns of daily changes in N1-P2 waves between those participants who prefer morning or evening, but not in the P3-wave, which was explained with the possible influence of a third factor, which then significantly modulates the researched circadian changes of the P3-wave. Therefore, the main recommendation of researchers was that, whenever possible, EP-recording should always be carried out at the same or at least similar time of day so as to avoid potential variation findings. Other research has shown that there are so-called 90 minutes ultradian fluctuations in the P300-latency (Lew & Polich, 1993), which also occur in the entire EEG activity as an index of ultradian fluctuations in the general level of arousal (Tsuji & Kobayashi, 1988). These repeated applications of the auditory oddball paradigm caused a reduction in the P300- amplitude and an extension in the P300-latency (Polich, 1989; Kenemans, Verbatim, Melis & Slangen, 1992), as well as in the visual oddball paradigm where the determined habituation of the P300-wave lwas ocalized in the temporal cortex (Bruin, Kenemans, Verbaten & Van der Heijden, 2000).

Lin and Polich (1999) hypothesized that some participant would produce an increase, while other would produce a reduction in the P300-amplitude depending on when the recording of the entire EEG-cycle was started, which was confirmed. It was found that 90-minute ultradian fluctuations in the P300-wave have reversed phases with two different groups of participants: the so-called "uppers" (since they start from the stage of increase in EEG-activity and the P300-wave) and "downers" (since they start from the phase of reduction in the P300-wave). Therefore, the basic recommendations for the implementation of EP-research is that recording is conducted within the stipulated 90-minute cycle. Finally, given that it was established that the P300-amplitude grows in spring and summer when there is more light (Polich & Geisler, 1990; Deldin, Duncan & Miller, 1994), and that these changes are more expressed in women than in men (Kosmidis Duncan & Mirsky, 1998), it is essential that EP-research is carried out within the same season. Also, if the study involved female participants, it is significant to keep in mind in what stage of their ovulatory cycles they are. In a study that used the so-called "emotional" stimuli (e.g. pictures of naked women, infants, etc.) that cause the evoked potential in women, a significant increase was found in the P300-amplitude during ovulation in women (Johnston & Wang, 1991).

## Physical Activity, Exercise and Fatigue

Studies have shown that as a result of temporary or permanent forms of exercise changes occur in the amplitude and latency of the P300-wave (Polich & Lardon,

1997; Yagi, Estes & Coburn, 1997; Yagi et al., 1999). The P300-amplitude was significantly increased in people who were engaged in long-term sports activities, and more for visible stimuli, and during the exercise, a decrease of the P300-amplitude was recorded, shortening of the P300-latency, as well as shortened reaction times in tasks of pushing the button. As for fatigue, it was found that with its appearance there is also a significant decrease of the P300-amplitude and extension of the P300-latency (Polich & Kok, 1995). It is therefore very important for EP-recording that participants are well rested.

## Drinking Alcoholic Beverages, Coffee and Smoking

Research on the current impact of drinking alcoholic beverages on P300 has shown that there is a reduction of the P300-amplitude and extension of the P300-latency, while tin he so-called social drinking there are no permanent and long-term effects on the P300 (Polich & Kok, 1995). As for the caffeine variables, several studies have found that drinking coffee, or other caffeinated drinks, affects a slight increase in the P300-amplitude, and a significant shortening of the P300-latency (Lorist, Snel & Kok, 1994a; Lorist, Snel, Kok & Mulder, 1994b), since it acts as a stressor (Revelle, Humphreys, Simon & Gilliland, 1980). However, the same authors, while experimentally varying the factor of fatigue and arousal, found that the ratio of caffeine and the P300-wave significantly influenced the level of arousal (Lorist et al., 1994a,b). In other words, EP-changes associated with caffeine consumption are more pronounced when the participant is tired.

In addition, the same authors found that moderate doses of caffeine affect the deterioration of performance on cognitive tasks in introverts, while enhancing performance in extraverts. Starting from the established results, it seems that coffee drinking affects the achievement of significant differences in the rate of cognitive processing between extraverts and introverts, which makes it faster in extraverts and slower in introverts. Finally, EP-studies on smoking have shown that nicotine causes short term (after only smoked two cigarettes in smokers) an increase in latency and amplitude of the P300-wave (Houlihan, Pritchard & Robinson, 2001) and long term (comparisons between smokers and non-smokers) shortening of the P300-latency (Lindgren, Stenberg & Rosen, 1999), and a reduction in its amplitude (Anokhin, Vedeniapin, Sirevaag, Bauer, O'Connor, Kuperman, Porsejz, Reich, Begleiter, Polich & Rohrbaugh, 2000), but only in older smokers. Young smokers have demonstrated the extension of the P300-latency as opposed to older non-smokers (Knott, Harr & Mahoney, 1999).

The usual finding of a better performance of various types of cognitive tasks after smoking was attributed to the nicotine induction of increased arousal (Wesnes & Warburton, 1983; Lindgren et al., 1999), as well as those obtained in electrophysiological studies which included EEG measures (Pritchard, 1991; Knott, 1991), where cigarette abstinence caused a slowing-down of the alpha brain frequencies and simultaneously an increase in the theta brain activity - biological condition that is consistent with the conditions of fatigue or sleepiness.

Finally, a study, in which a visual oddball paradigm was applied in participants ranging in age from 17 to 74 years, compared the measured the P300- amplitude between current smokers ($N = 905$), the so-called former smokers ($N = 463$), and non-smokers, i.e. those who had never smoked ($N = 979$). It showed that the P300-amplitude was significantly lower in current smokers when compared to non-smokers, while among non-smokers and former smokers there were no differences in the measured P300- amplitude (Anokhin et al., 2000). It is indisputable that there is a significant correlation between changes in evoked potentials and smoking, so the recommendations for EP-experts is important that this variable should be controlled in future research if it is not the very subject of research.

## Medicine, Drugs, and Evoked Potentials

While examining the impact of aspirin (acetylsalicylic acid) on the P300-latency by applying the visual oddball paradigm, Austermann and colleagues (1998) found a significant reduction in the P300-latency in the group that received aspirin in the time interval of 20-40 minutes after consumption when compared to the placebo group. The resulting finding was attributed to the effect of aspirin on the serotonergic system. As far as the consumption of illegal drugs and evoked potentials is concerned, it was found that a decrease in the P300-amplitude occurs with the occasional consumption of Cannabis, while there were no changes in the P300-amplitude in frequent consumers (Polich, 2004). Significant differences were also found among opiate addicts in the recorded latencies and amplitudes of auditory evoked potentials of individual deflection from the corresponding seven (Dabić-Jeftić & Mikula, 1994b). In the second study using the same participants, the P300-latency was significantly shortened for non-target stimuli in relation to the target stimuli, which is reverse from the findings in the control group of participants: P300-latency are regularly significantly shorter for target than for non-target stimuli (Dabić-Jeftić, Mikula & Martinjak, 1991).

## Age and Gender Differences

It was found that the morphology of evoked potentials, and in particular of cognitive components changes in the function of age, i.e. in parallel with the changes in the nervous system maturation. Due to the development characteristics of the nervous system and the cognitive development of children, a linear shortening was observed in the latency and an increase in the amplitude of the P300-component in the function of age (Dustman, Schena-Kenberg, Lewis & Beck, 1977; Dabić-Jeftić & Mikula, 1994a; Johnstone, Barry, Anderson & Coyle, 1996; Pitzer & Polich, 1997; Polich, 1998, 1999; Hirayasu, Samura, Ohta & Ogura, 2000) for the age range 6-25 years. In subjects in the age range from 20-80 years, within the ERP-studies connected to normal aging processes, it was found that the P300-latency increases and the P300-amplitude reduces with age (Dabić-Jeftić & Mikula, 1994a; Polich, 1996, 1997, 1998, 1999; Gaeta, Friedman, Ritter & Cheng, 1998; Squires & Ollo, 1999; Hirayasu et al., 2000; Kok, 2000). In connection with this, the aforementioned work of Hirayasu and colleagues (2000) it was found that, among men aged over 30 years there is a more rapid extension of the P300-latency (without similar changes in the P300-amplitude) than it is the case with women of the same age, i.e. that in these age-related changes in the P300-wave there are significant gender differences.

In addition to this study, which analyzed the interactive effect of variables of age and gender in the study of changes in the P300-wave (Hirayasu et al., 2000), studies of gender differences in seasonal variations of P300 that have already been mentioned, showed a trend of greater vulnerability of women than men when it comes to seasonal influences on the P300 component. In addition, in the classical auditory and visual oddball task, men showed a lower P300-amplitude than women (Deldin et al., 1994; Polich & Hoffman, 1998; Hoffman & Polich, 1999), which is explained on the basis of neuroanatomic findings that men have a proportionally smaller area of the corpus callosum than women (Driesen & Raz, 1995). In the studies of gender differences in the change of the P300-wave, which is evoked by displaying visual stimuli of human faces, reverse results have been obtained: significantly higher P300-amplitudes were found in male participants (Oliver-Rodriguez, Guan & Johnston, 1999).

In any case, nearly every EP-research, especially one that examines personality, treats groups of male and female participants separately, on the basis of which the interpretation of findings is clearer, which then serves as a recommendation for all other EP research. In connection with this, separate analyses were also conducted in this study, that relate to the relationship of biological determinations and the P300-wave with respect to its relationship with extraversion (Tatalović Vorkapić, 2009). It was found that a significant negative correlation between the P300-letancy and extraversion occurs only in certain, specific situations that are dependent on biological factors, such as wearing glasses, drinking coffee, and taking medicine. Thus, this connection is identified as significant for those women who wear glasses, drink coffee, and do not take any medication. In connection with this, a significant negative correlation between P300-amplitude and extraversion was found only in those female students who wear glasses. In addition, it was shown that there are significant differences in these differences with respect to a series of recording. In conclusion, the determined results are discussed based on a significantly high sensitivity and variability of the P3-wave, which cannot be ignored as they have a significant mediating role in relation to this cognitive EP-wave and extraversion.

## CONCLUSION

Finally, it is important to point out that this book was written with the aim of studying the relationship evoked potentials with Eysenck's personality dimensions and Strelau's dimensions of temperament, for the simple reason that a parallel EP-comparative analysis of the two models of personality provides a detailed insight into possible changes in evoked potentials in relation to the different operationalized individual differences among participants. So far, there has been an extremely large number of ERP-research on extraversion, and, which is extremely restrictive for the overall psychological science, too much emphasis has been placed on the study of psychophysiology of extraversion. On the one hand, this research has provided important answers and guidance in the field of psychophysiology and biological determination of extraversion, but they also show a number of shortcomings. For example, research of the P300-component with the classic oddball task of simple discrimination has shown that it is a reliable index of endogenous cognitive activities. Several authors have constantly studied individual differences in extraversion using the oddball paradigm. A review of most of these works imposes one characteristic obtained in relation to extraversion and the P300 component: inconsistency. If we take into account earlier works which have generally been applied in the auditory oddball paradigm in the study of this relationship, it is evident that significantly larger P300-amplitude have been received for introverts than for extraverts (O'Connor, 1980, 1983; Daruna et al., 1985; Orlebeke, Kok & Zeillemaker, 1984; Wilson & Languis, 1990;

Polich & Martin, 1992 (only male participants); Ortiz & Maojo, 1993; Brocke, Tasche & Beauducel, 1996, 1997).

None of these studies have established a correlation between the P300-latency and extraversion. The basic objections to the methodology of those studies are: a) a small number of participants (e.g. $N = 6$); b) division of participants due to the extreme results on the questionnaire EPQ/EPI; c) uneven operational definitions of the dimensions of extraversion/introversion and thus the initial theoretical basis (each authors started from Eysenck's definition, others from Gray's settings of inhibition/disinhibition); d) oversimplified requirements of the oddball task that was applied in the study, which tends to cause habituation to which introverts and extraverts react differently - extraverts habituate faster and have a more rapid decline in performance on tasks that require attention and concentration (Keister & McLaughlin, 1972), which is further coupled with other factors of the oddball task: probability of a target excitation and length of the interval between stimuli, number of recording sets, level of complexity and type of the target stimulus; e) lack of control over natural factors: circadian variation (food intake, heart rate, body temperature, time preference activities), ultradial rhythms, seasonal rhythms, electrodermal response, current frequency of cerebral activities; f) lack of control over induced factors: physical exercise (current, continuous), fatigue, intake of aspirin, caffeine, nicotine, alcohol, drugs; and g) lack of control over the specific constituent factors: age, intelligence, hand dominance, gender, personality, and genetic factors.

Although the aforementioned studies abound in significant methodological shortcomings, they have set a significant and important theoretical and methodological framework for the study of psychophysiology of individual differences in human personality. But simultaneously, EP-personality research has been largely denied a variety of information regarding psychophysiology of personality that is operationalized in a different way (e.g. Strelau's theory of temperament), and the information that deal with the mutual relationship between individual personality theory in psychophysiological terms, in this case electrocortical parameters. This research seeks to change that. In addition, a large number of studies have shown a non-correlation relationship between psycho-radiological measures of power excitation to the questionnaire, such as the STI, which is intriguing and requires empirical verification. Furthermore, overlapping and significant correlation between Eysenck's and Strelau's dimensions of temperament indicate a significant possibility of connectedness between the dimensions of temperament and EP-components. In addition, both theories of personality have to do with the concept of arousal that takes center stage in the explanation of individual differences in personality in relation to evoked brain potentials. Finally, it is interesting to analyze the possibility of predicting personality dimensions based on evoked potentials and behavioral variables, and to see what role do other relevant behavioral variables have in this respect. Therefore, there are a lot of incentives for the study of this part of psychology, and, to a small extent, this research has attempted to provide the answer to some of the issues from psychophysiology of personality.

Taking into account all the presented findings and theoretical frameworks that seek to explain them, there is no doubt that the intrigue behind these findings is quite a sufficient indication of how the relationship of the P300 endogenous ERP-component and personality, and in particular the E-I dimension, is explored, yet it remains underexplored. As has been noted before, this is largely because there is still no complete and unambiguous information in general on the ERP-components, including the P300-component, which definitely has an impact in psychophysiological research of biological correlations of personalities. Another large part of the reason relates to the aforementioned methodological issues, which are not as bound to the ERP method, as much to the operationalization and setting of unique schematic frameworks for psychological paradigms that induce P300- components. The third part relates to the lack of or incomplete explanations of the existing theoretical models for the interpretation of results.

In the above-mentioned reasons, but also in a series of inconsistent findings in the study of the relationship of extraversion and the P300-wave, where: a) a number of papers has pointed to the existence of a significant positive relatedness between the P300-amplitude and the degree of introversion in previous ERP studies that generally used the auditory oddball paradigm and interpretation of results based on higher levels of arousal in introverts; b) a number of papers pointed to the absence of significant differences in the P300-amplitude between extraverts and introverts, after the adoption of attention terms in ERP studies; and c) a specific (most recent) number of papers have pointed out a significant positive correlation between the P300-amplitude and the degree of extraversion, which mainly used the visual oddball paradigm and a more demanding task of simple discrimination with the aim of equalizing the participants in terms of the habituation speed to stimuli, lies the main initiative for the implementation of this study. In an attempt to take into account most of the methodological objections to previous ERP-studies of personality, and by controlling the number of relevant factors which have been found to affect the P300-wave, it was attempted in the current environment of technical limitations to measure as accurately as possible the latency and amplitude of the P300-wave, and to put these two measures in relation with the measured level of extraversion in the sample of female students. Thereby the focus of this study was to test the type and direction of the relationship, interpreting thereby the findings within the framework of the existing relevant theories of personality, as well as all other factors (constraints) relevant to measure of not only the P300-wave, but also other ERP-waves. Given that depending on the structure and scheme of the applied paradigm for causing evoked brain potentials enriched with various additional variables, the direction of differences in the groups of introverts and extraverts will differ.

## REFERENCES

Akerstedt, T., & Fröberg, J. (1976). Interindividual differences in circadian patterns of catecholamine excretion, body temperature, performance, and subjective arousal. *Biological Psychology*, *4*(4), 277–292. doi:10.1016/0301-0511(76)90019-3 PMID:999994

Albert, M., & Rush, M. (1983). Comparison of effects in Parkinson's disease and schizophrenia. *Psychopharmacology Bulletin*, *19*, 118–120.

Anokhin, A. P., Vedeniapin, A. B., Sirevaag, E. J., Bauer, L. O., OConnor, S. J., Kuperman, S., & Rohrbaugh, J. W. et al. (2000). The P300 brain potential is reduced in smokers. *Psychophyarmacology*, *149*(4), 409–413. doi:10.1007/s002130000387 PMID:10867969

Austermann, M., Grotemeyer, K. H., Evers, S., Rodding, D., & Husstedt, I. W. (1998). The influence of acetylsalicyclic acid on cognitive processing – en event-related potentials study. *Psychophyarmacology*, *138*(3-4), 369–374. doi:10.1007/s002130050683 PMID:9725760

Austin, M., Mitchell, P., & Goodwin, G. M. (2001). Cognitive deficits in depression. *The British Journal of Psychiatry*, *178*(3), 200–206. doi:10.1192/bjp.178.3.200 PMID:11230029

Baal, G. C. M. van, Geus, E. J. C. & de, Boomsma, D. I. (1997). Longitudinal Study of Genetic Influences on ERP-P3 during Childhood. In G. C. M. van Baal (Ed.), *A Genetic Perspective on the Developing Brain* (pp. 37-61). Vrije Universiteit, Print Partners Ipskamp.

Bange, F., & Bathie, N. (1998). Visual cognitive dysfunction in depression: An event-related potential study. *Electroencephalography and Clinical Neurophysiology*, *108*(5), 472–481. doi:10.1016/S0168-5597(98)00024-0 PMID:9780017

Baribeau-Braun, J., & Leserve, N. (1983). Event-related potential assessment of psychomotor retardation in depresives. *Advances in Biological Psychiatry*, *13*, 211–224. doi:10.1159/000408534

Barratt, E. S., Stanford, M. S., Kent, T. A., & Felthous, A. (1997). Neurophyschological and cognitive psychophysiological substrates of impulsive aggression. *Biological Psychiatry*, *41*(10), 1045–1061. doi:10.1016/S0006-3223(96)00175-8 PMID:9129785

Bauer, L. O., Costa, L., & Hesselbrock, V. M. (2001). Effects of alcoholism, anxiety and depression on P300 in women: A pilot study. *Journal of Studies on Alcohol*, *62*(5), 571–579. doi:10.15288/jsa.2001.62.571 PMID:11702796

Bauer, L. O., & Hesselbrock, V. M. (1999a). P300 decrements in teenagers with conduct problems: Implications for substance abuse risk and brain development. *Biological Psychiatry*, *46*(2), 263–272. doi:10.1016/S0006-3223(98)00335-7 PMID:10418702

Bauer, L. O., & Hesselbrock, V. M. (1999b). Subtypes of family history and conduct disorder: Effects on P300 during the Stroop test. *Neuropsychophyrmacology*, *21*(1), 51–62. doi:10.1016/S0893-133X(98)00139-0 PMID:10379519

Bazylevich, T. F. (1974). The expression of strenght of the regulative brain system in the dynamics of the somatosensory evoked potential. In V. D. Nebylitsyn (Ed.), *Problems of differential psychophysiology. Electrophysiological studies on the fundamental properties of the nervous system* (Vol. 8). Moscow: Nauka.

Beauducel, A., Brocke, B., & Leue, A. (2006). Energetical bases of extraversion: Effort, arousal, EEG, and performance. *International Journal of Psychophysiology*, *62*(2), 212–223. doi:10.1016/j.ijpsycho.2005.12.001 PMID:16426692

Blackman, J. D., Towle, V. L., Lewis, G. F., Spire, J.-P., & Polonsky, K. S. (1990). Hypoglycemic thresholds for cognitive dysfunctions in humans. *Diabetes*, *39*(7), 828–835. doi:10.2337/diab.39.7.828 PMID:2191886

Blackwood, D. H. R., Erbmeier, K. P., & Muir, W. J. (1994). Correlation of regional cerebral blood flow equivalents measured by single photon emission computerized tomography with P300 latency and eye movement abnormality in schizophrenia. *Acta Psychiatrica Scandinavica*, *90*(3), 157–166. doi:10.1111/j.1600-0447.1994.tb01572.x PMID:7810338

Blackwood, D. H. R., Whalley, L. J., Christie, J. E., Blackburn, I. M., St Clair, D. M., & McInnes, A. (1987). Changes in auditory P3 event-related potential in schizophrenia and depression. *The British Journal of Psychiatry*, *150*(2), 154–160. doi:10.1192/bjp.150.2.154 PMID:2888501

Blumenthal, T. D. (2001). Extraversion, attention, and startle response reactivity. *Personality and Individual Differences*, *30*(4), 495–503. doi:10.1016/S0191-8869(00)00153-7

Brebner, J. (1983). A model of extraversion. *Australian Journal of Psychology*, *35*(3), 349–359. doi:10.1080/00049538308258748

Brebner, J. (1990). Psychological and neurophysiological factors in stimulus-response compatibility. In R. W. Proctor & R. T. Gilmour (Eds.), *Stimulus-response compatibility: An integrated perspective. Advances in psychology* (Vol. 65, pp. 246–260). doi:10.1016/S0166-4115(08)61225-X

Brebner, J., & Cooper, C. (1974). The effect of a low rate of regular signals upon the reaction times of introverts and extraverts. *Journal of Research in Personality*, *8*(3), 263–276. doi:10.1016/0092-6566(74)90037-3

Brinar, V., Brzović, Z., Vukadin, S., & Zurak, N. (1996). Neurologija – udžbenik za medicinske sestre, rentgen tehničare i fizioterapeute [Neurology – the handbook for medical nurses, roentgen technicians and physical therapists]. Prometej, Znanstvena biblioteka, Knjiga 3.

Broadhurst, A., & Glass, A. (1969). Relationship of personality measures of alpha rhythm of the electroencephalogram. *The British Journal of Psychiatry*, *115*(519), 199–204. doi:10.1192/bjp.115.519.199 PMID:5778196

Brocke, B., Tasche, K. G., & Beauducel, A. (1996). Biopsychological Foundations of Extraversion: Differential Effort Reactivity and the Differential P300 Effect. *Personality and Individual Differences*, *21*(5), 727–738. doi:10.1016/0191-8869(96)00117-1

Brocke, B., Tasche, K. G., & Beauducel, A. (1997). Biopsychological Foundations of Extraversion: Differential Effort Reactivity and the State Control. *Personality and Individual Differences*, *22*(4), 447–458. doi:10.1016/S0191-8869(96)00226-7

Browman, C. P. (1979). Diurnal variation of the human auditory evoked potential. *Physiological Psychology*, *7*(3), 287–290. doi:10.3758/BF03326642

Browman, C. P., & Sullivan, H. T. (1980). Diurnal periodicity of the human vertex potential. *Perceptual and Motor Skills*, *51*(2), 643–646. doi:10.2466/pms.1980.51.2.643 PMID:7192381

Bruder, G. E., Tenke, C., Stewart, J. E., Towey, J. P., Leite, P., Voglmaier, M., & Quitkin, F. M. (1995). Brain event-related potentials to complex tones in depressed patients: Relations to perceptual asymmetry and clinical features. *Psychophysiology*, *32*(4), 373–381. doi:10.1111/j.1469-8986.1995.tb01220.x PMID:7652114

Bruder, G. E., Towey, J. P., Stewart, J. W., Friedman, M., Tenke, C., & Quitkin, F. M. (1991). Brain event-related potentials to complex tones in depressed patients: Relations to perceptual asymmetry and clinical features. *Psychophysiology*, *32*(4), 373–381. doi:10.1111/j.1469-8986.1995.tb01220.x PMID:7652114

Bruin, K. J., Kenemans, J. L., Verbaten, M. N., & Van der Heijden, A. C. H. (2000). Habituation: An event-related potential and dipole source analysis study. *International Journal of Psychophysiology*, *36*(3), 199–209. doi:10.1016/S0167-8760(99)00114-2 PMID:10754194

Bruneau, N., Roux, S., Perse, J., & Lelord, G. (1984). Frontal evoked responses, stimulus intensity control, and the extraversion dimension. *Annals of the New York Academy of Sciences*, *425*(1), 546–550. doi:10.1111/j.1749-6632.1984.tb23575.x PMID:6588872

Buchsbaum, M. S., Haier, R. J., & Johnson, J. (1983). Augmenting and reducing: Individual differences in evoked potentials. In A. Gale & J. A. Edwards (Eds.), *Physiological correlates of human behavior: Individual differences and psychopathology* (Vol. 3). London: Academic Press. doi:10.1016/B978-0-12-273903-3.50013-4

Buchsbaum, M. S., & Stevens, S. S. (1971). Neural events and the psychophysical law. *Science*, *172*(3982), 502. doi:10.1126/science.172.3982.502 PMID:5550509

Buckingham, R. M. (2002). Extraversion, neuroticism and the four temperaments of antiquity: An investigation of Physiological reactivity. *Personality and Individual Differences*, *32*(2), 225–246. doi:10.1016/S0191-8869(01)00020-4

Bullock, W. A., & Gilliland, K. (1993). Eysencks arousal theory of introversion/ekstraversion: A converging measures investigation. *Journal of Personality and Social Psychology*, *64*(1), 113–123. doi:10.1037/0022-3514.64.1.113 PMID:8421248

Cahhil, J. M., & Polich, J. (1992). P300, Probability, and Introverted/Extroverted Personality Types. *Biological Psychology*, *33*(1), 23–35. doi:10.1016/0301-0511(92)90003-D PMID:1599997

Callaway, E., & Naghdi, S. (1981). An information processing model for schizophrenia. *Archives of General Psychiatry*, *39*(3), 339–347. doi:10.1001/archpsyc.1982.04290030069012 PMID:7065844

Campbell, J. B. (1983). Differential relationships of extraversion, impulsivity, and sociability to study habits. *Journal of Research in Personality*, *17*(3), 308–314. doi:10.1016/0092-6566(83)90022-3

Campbell, J. B. (1992). Extraversion and noise sensitivity: A replication to Dornic and Ekehammars study. *Personality and Individual Differences*, *13*(8), 953–956. doi:10.1016/0191-8869(92)90015-H

Campbell, J. B., & Hawley, C. W. (1982). Study habits and Eysencks theory of extraversion-introversion. *Journal of Research in Personality*, *16*(2), 139–146. doi:10.1016/0092-6566(82)90070-8

Canli, T., Zhao, Z., Kang, E., & Gross, J. (2001). An fMRI study of personality unfluences on brain reactivity to emotional stimuli. *Behavioral Neuroscience*, *115*(1), 33–42. doi:10.1037/0735-7044.115.1.33 PMID:11256451

Chuprikova, N. I. (1977). The analysis of psychological structure and physiological mechanisms of activity as a of a diagnosis of nervous system properties. In A. A. Smirnov (Ed.), *Psychology and psychophysiology of individual differences*. Moscow: Pedagogika.

Claridge, G. S., & Herrington, R. N. (1963). An EEG correlate of the Archimedes spiral after-effect and its relationship with personality. *Behaviour Research and Therapy*, *1*(2-4), 217–229. doi:10.1016/0005-7967(63)90030-5 PMID:14153348

Coles, M. G. H., Gale, A., & Kline, P. (1971). Personality and habituation of the orienting rection: Tonic and response measures of electrodermal activity. *Psychophysiology*, *8*(1), 59–63. doi:10.1111/j.1469-8986.1971.tb00436.x

Comerchero, M. D., & Polich, J. (1999). P3a and P3b from typical Auditory and Visual Stimuli. *Clinical Neurophysiology*, *110*(1), 24–30. doi:10.1016/S0168-5597(98)00033-1 PMID:10348317

Como, P., Simons, R., & Zuckerman, M. (1984). Psychophysiological indices of sensation seeking as a function of stimulus intensity. *Psychophysiology*, *21*, 572–573.

Coquery, J. M. (1979). Alertness and attention: Recent theorethical perspectives and new areas of exploration. *Review of Eelctroencephalography and Clinical Neurophysiology*, *9*, 307–315. doi:10.1016/S0370-4475(79)80014-3

Coren, S. (1999). Arousal predisposition as a predictor of antisocial and delinquent behavior. *Personality and Individual Differences*, *27*(5), 815–820. doi:10.1016/S0191-8869(99)00028-8

Cornblatt, B. A., & Keilp, J. G. (1994). Impaired attention, genetics, and the pathophysiology of schizophrenia. *Schizophrenia Bulletin*, *20*(1), 31–46. doi:10.1093/schbul/20.1.31 PMID:8197420

Costa, L., Bauer, L., Kuperman, S., Porjesz, B., OConnor, S., Hesselbrock, V., & Begleiter, H. et al. (2000). Frontal P300 decrements, alcohol dependence, and antisocial personality disorder. *Biological Psychiatry*, *47*(12), 1064–1071. doi:10.1016/S0006-3223(99)00317-0 PMID:10862806

Coursey, R. D., Buchsbaum, M. S., & Frankel, B. L. (1975). Personality measures and evoked responses in chronic insomniacs. *Journal of Abnormal Psychology*, *84*(3), 239–249. doi:10.1037/h0076716 PMID:1133252

Cox-Fuenzalida, L.-E., Gilliland, K., & Swickert, R. J. (2001). Congruency of the relationship between extraversion and the brainstem auditory evoked response based on the EPI versus the EPQ. *Journal of Research in Personality*, *35*(2), 117–126. doi:10.1006/jrpe.2000.2299

Criado, J. R., & Ehlers, C. L. (2007). Electrophysiological responses to affective stimuli in Mexican Americans: Relationship to alcohol dependence and personality traits. *Pharmacology, Biochemistry, and Behavior*, *88*(2), 148–157. doi:10.1016/j.pbb.2007.07.019 PMID:17764730

Dabić-Jeftić, M., & Mikula, I. (1994a). Evocirani potencijali kore mozga – Osnovne postavke i klinička primjena [Evoked brain potentials – Fundamental postulates and clinical application]. Školska knjiga.

Dabić-Jeftić, M., & Mikula, I. (1994b). Brainstem Auditory Evoked Potentials (BAER) in Drug Addicts. *Alcoholism*, *30*(1), 17–22.

Dabić-Jeftić, M., Mikula, I., & Martinjak, D. (1991). Auditory event-related potentials in heroin addicts. *Psychiatria Danubina*, *4*, 469–483.

Danilova, N. N. (1986). Dynamics of AEP and heart rate as indicators of individual arousal level and learning. In J. Strelau, F. H. Farley & A. Gale (Eds.), The biological bases of personality and behavior: Vol. 2. Psychophysiology, performance, and application, (pp. 91-96). Hemisphere Publishing Corporation.

Daruna, J. H., Karrer, R., & Rosen, A. J. (1985). Introversion, attention, and late positive component of event-related potentials. *Biological Psychology*, *20*(4), 249–259. doi:10.1016/0301-0511(85)90001-8 PMID:4041517

Davis, G. C., Buchsbaum, M. S., & Bunney, W. E. Jr. (1978). Naloxone decreases diurnal variation in pain sensitivity and somatosensory evoked potentials. *Life Sciences*, *23*(14), 1449–1460. doi:10.1016/0024-3205(78)90126-1 PMID:568705

De Feo, P., Gallai, V., Mazzotta, G., Grispino, G., Torlone, E., Perriello, G., & Bolli, G. et al. (1988). Modest decrements in plasma glucose concentration cause early impairment in cognitive function and later activation of glucose counterregulation in the absence hypoglycemic symptoms in normal man. *The Journal of Clinical Investigation*, *22*(2), 436–444. doi:10.1172/JCI113616 PMID:3403713

De Pascalis, V. (1993). Hemispheric Asymmetry, Personality and Temperament. *Personality and Individual Differences*, *14*(6), 825–834. doi:10.1016/0191-8869(93)90095-K

De Pascalis, V. (1994). Personality and temperament in the event-related potentials during stimulus recognition tasks. *Personality and Individual Differences*, *16*(6), 877–889. doi:10.1016/0191-8869(94)90232-1

De Pascalis, V. (2004). On the Psychophysiology of Extraversion. In R. M. Stelmack (Ed.), *On the Psychobiology of Personality: Essays in Honor of Marvin Zuckerman* (pp. 295–327). Elsevier Ltd. doi:10.1016/B978-008044209-9/50017-8

De Pascalis, V., & Montirosso, R. (1988). Extraversion, neuroticism and individual differences in event-related potentials. *Personality and Individual Differences*, *9*(2), 353–360. doi:10.1016/0191-8869(88)90098-0

De Pascalis, V., & Speranza, O. (2000). Personality effects on attentional shifts to emotional charged cues: ERP, behavioural and HR data. *Personality and Individual Differences*, *29*(2), 217–238. doi:10.1016/S0191-8869(99)00189-0

De Pascalis, V., Strelau, J., & Zawadzki, B. (1999). The effect of temperamental traits on event-related potentials, heart rate and reaction time. *Personality and Individual Differences*, *26*(3), 441–465. doi:10.1016/S0191-8869(98)00151-2

Defrance, J. F., Ginsber, L. D., Rosenber, B. A., & Sharma, J. C. (1996). Topographical analysis of adolescent affective disorders. *The International Journal of Neuroscience*, *86*(1-2), 119–141. doi:10.3109/00207459608986704 PMID:8828066

Deldin, P. J., Duncan, C. C., & Miller, G. A. (1994). Season, gender, and P300. *Biological Psychology*, *39*(1), 15–28. doi:10.1016/0301-0511(94)90054-X PMID:7880945

Diner, B. C., Holcomb, P. J., & Dykman, R. A. (1985). P300 in major depressive disorder. *Psychiatry Research*, *15*(3), 175–184. doi:10.1016/0165-1781(85)90074-5 PMID:3862153

Ditraglia, G. M., & Polich, J. (1991). P300 and Introverted/Extroverted Personality Types. *Psychophysiology*, *28*(2), 177–184. doi:10.1111/j.1469-8986.1991.tb00410.x PMID:1946884

Donchin, E., & Coles, M. G. H. (1988). Precomentary: Is the P300 Component a Manifestation of Context Updating? *Behavioral and Brain Sciences*, *11*(3), 355–372. doi:10.1017/S0140525X00058027

Donchin, E., Ritter, W., & McCallum, W. C. (1978). Cognitive Psychophysiology: The Endogenous components of the ERP. In E. Callaway, P. Tueting, & S. Koslow (Eds.), *Event-related Brain Potentials in man* (pp. 55–118). New York: Academic Press. doi:10.1016/B978-0-12-155150-6.50019-5

Dornic, S., & Ehehammar, B. (1990). Extraversion, neuroticism, and noise sensitivity. *Personality and Individual Differences*, *11*(9), 989–992. doi:10.1016/0191-8869(90)90283-W

Doucet, C., & Stelmack, R. M. (2000). An event-related potential analysis of extraversion and individual differences in cognitive processing speed and response execution. *Journal of Personality and Social Psychology, 78*(5), 956–964. doi:10.1037/0022-3514.78.5.956 PMID:10821201

Driesen, N., & Raz, N. (1995). The influence of sex, age and handedness of corpus callosum morphology: A meta-analysis. *Psychobiology (Austin, Tex.), 23*, 240–247.

Dustman, R. E., Schenkenberg, T., Lewis, E. G., & Beck, E. C. (1977). The cerebral evoked potential: Life.span changes and twin studies. In J. E. Desmedt (Ed.), *Visual evoked potentials in man: New developments. Methodology of patterned visual stimulation, neurophysiology of visual functions in man, clinical applications* (pp. 363–377). Oxford, UK: Oxford University Press.

Eaves, L. J., Eysenck, H. J., & Martin, N. G. (1989). *Genes, culture, and personality: An empirical approach.* New York: Academic Press.

Enoch, M. A., White, K. V., Harris, C. R., Rohrbaugh, J. W., & Goldman, D. (2001). Alcohol use disorders and anxiety disorders: Relation to the P300 event-related potential. *Alcoholism, Clinical and Experimental Research, 25*(9), 1293–1300. doi:10.1111/j.1530-0277.2001.tb02350.x PMID:11584148

Eysenck, H. J. (1967). *Biological basis of personality.* Springfield, IL: Charles C Thomas Publisher.

Eysenck, H. J. (1990). Biological Dimensions of Personality. In L. E. Pervin (Ed.), *Handbook of Personality* (pp. 244–276). John Wiley & Sons, Inc.

Eysenck, H. J. (1994). EEG evoked potentials. In R. J. Stenberg (Ed.), Encyclopedia of human intelligence (pp. 391-395). Macmillan Publishing Company.

Eysenck, H. J. (1997). Personality and Experimental Psychology: The Unification of Psychology and the Possibility of a Paradigm. *Journal of Personality and Social Psychology, 73*(6), 1224–1237. doi:10.1037/0022-3514.73.6.1224

Eysenck, H. J., & Eysenck, M. W. (1985). Chapter eight: The psychophysiology of personality. In *Personality and individual differences: A natural science approach* (pp. 217–236). New York: Plenum Press. doi:10.1007/978-1-4613-2413-3_8

Eysenck, H. J., & Eysenck, S. B. G. (1994). *Priručnik za Eysenckove skale ličnosti: EPS-odrasli. [The Manual for Eysenck's personality scales: EPS-adults].* Jastrebarsko, Croatia: Naklada Slap.

Eysenck, S. B. G., & Eysenck, H. J. (1970). A factor-analysis study of the Lie Scale of the Junior Eysenck Personality Inventory. *Personality*, *1*, 3–10.

Eysenck, S. B. G., Nias, D. K., & Eysenck, H. J. (1971). Interpretation of childrens Lie Scale scores. *The British Journal of Educational Psychology*, *41*(1), 23–31. doi:10.1111/j.2044-8279.1971.tb00654.x PMID:5547174

Fahrenberg, J. (1987). Concepts of activation and arousal in theory of emotionality (neuroticism). In J. Strelau & H. J. Eysenck (Eds.), *Personality dimensions and arousal* (pp. 99–120). New York: Plenum Press. doi:10.1007/978-1-4899-2043-0_6

Fenton, G. W., & Scotton, L. (1967). Personality and alpha rhythm. *The British Journal of Psychiatry*, *113*(504), 1283–1289. doi:10.1192/bjp.113.504.1283 PMID:6075456

Fjell, A. M., Walhovd, K. B., Meling, S., & Johansen, M. B. (2005). Basic information processing of neurotics and stables: An experimental ERP approach to personality and distractibility. *Scandinavian Journal of Psychology*, *46*(6), 493–502. doi:10.1111/j.1467-9450.2005.00481.x PMID:16277650

Ford, J. M., Mathalon, D. H., Marsh, L., Faustman, W. O., Harris, D., Hoff, A. L., & Pfefferbaum, A. et al. (1999). P300 amplitude is related to clinical state in severely and moderately I11 patients with schizophrenia. *Biological Psychiatry*, *46*(1), 94–101. doi:10.1016/S0006-3223(98)00290-X PMID:10394478

Ford, J. M., Pfefferbaum, A., & Roth, W. (1992). P3 and schizophrenia. *Annals of the New York Academy of Sciences*, *658*(1), 146–162. doi:10.1111/j.1749-6632.1992.tb22843.x PMID:1353949

Fröberg, J. (1977). Twenty-four-hour patterns in human performance, subjective and physiological variables and differences between morning and evening active subjects. *Biological Psychology*, *5*(2), 119–134. doi:10.1016/0301-0511(77)90008-4 PMID:884171

Gaeta, H., Friedman, D., Ritter, W., & Cheng, J. (1998). An event-related potential study of age-related changes in sensitivity to stimulus deviance. *Neurobiology of Aging*, *19*(5), 447–459. doi:10.1016/S0197-4580(98)00087-6 PMID:9880047

Gale, A. (1981). EEG studies of extraversion-introversion: what's the next step? In R. Lynn (Ed.), *Dimensions of personality: Papers in honour of H. J. Eysenck* (pp. 181–207). Oxford, UK: Pergamon.

Gale, A. (1983). Electroencephalographic Studies of Extraversion-Introversion: A Case Study in the Psychophysiology of Individual Differences. *Personality and Individual Differences*, *4*(4), 371–380. doi:10.1016/0191-8869(83)90002-8

Gale, A. (1987). The Electroencephalogram. In A. Gale & B. Christie (Eds.), *Psychophysiology and the Electronic Workplace* (pp. 223–237). John Wiley & Sons, Ltd.

Gale, A., Coles, M., & Blaydon, J. (1969). Extraversion-introversion and the EEG. *British Journal of Psychology*, *60*(2), 209–223. doi:10.1111/j.2044-8295.1969.tb01194.x PMID:5787680

Gale, A., Coles, M. G. H., Kline, P., & Penfold, V. (1971). Extraversion-introversion, neuroticism and the EEG: Basal and response measures during habituation of the orienting response. *British Journal of Psychology*, *62*(4), 533–543. doi:10.1111/j.2044-8295.1971.tb02069.x PMID:5121644

Gale, A., Edwards, J., Morris, P., Moore, R., & Forrester, D. (2001). Extraversion-introversion, neuroticism-stability, and EEG indicators of positive and negative empathic mood. *Personality and Individual Differences*, *30*(3), 449–461. doi:10.1016/S0191-8869(00)00036-2

Gallai, V., Mazzotta, G., Firenze, C., & Del Gatto, F. (1988). A study of the P300 component during minor hypoglycemia. *Acta Neurologica*, *10*, 178–186. PMID:3051900

Gangadhar, B. N., Ancy, J., Janakiramaiah, N., & Umapathy, C. (1993). P300 amplitude in non-bipolar, melancholic depression. *Journal of Affective Disorders*, *28*(1), 57–60. doi:10.1016/0165-0327(93)90077-W PMID:8326081

Geen, R. G., McCown, E. J., & Broyles, J. W. (1985). Efects of noise on sensitivity of introverts and extraverts to signals in a vigilance task. *Personality and Individual Differences*, *6*(2), 237–241. doi:10.1016/0191-8869(85)90114-X

Geisler, M. W., & Polich, J. (1990). P300 and time of day: Circadian rhythms, food intake, and body temperature. *Biological Psychology*, *31*(2), 117–136. doi:10.1016/0301-0511(90)90012-L PMID:2103747

Giedke, H., Thier, P., & Bolz, J. (1981). The relationship between P3-latency and reaction time in depression. *Biological Psychology*, *13*, 31–49. doi:10.1016/0301-0511(81)90026-0 PMID:7343001

Gloor, P. (1969). *Hans Berger on the electroencephalogram of man: The fourteen original reports on the electroencephalogram. Electroencephalography and Clinical Neurophysiology, Supplement No. 28*. Amsterdam: Elsevier Publishing Company.

Golding, J. F., Ashton, C. H., Marsh, V. R., & Thompson, J. W. (1986). Early and late SEPs – the later the potential the greater the relevance to personality. *Personality and Individual Differences*, *7*(6), 787–794. doi:10.1016/0191-8869(86)90077-2

Golubeva, E. A., Izyumovy, S. A., & Pechenkov, V. V. (1977). Parameters of the evoked potentials and their relation to the efficiency of involuntary and voluntary memory. In M. N. Borisova, E. A. Golubeva, N. S. Leites, A. E. Olshannikova, I. W. Ravich-Shcherbo, V. I. Rozhdestvenskaya, & V. M. Rusalov (Eds.), *Problems of differential psychophysiology* (Vol. 9). Moscow: Pedagogika.

Gordon, E., Kraiuhin, C., Harris, A., Meares, R., & Howson, A. (1986). The differential diagnosis of dementia using P300 latency. *Biological Psychiatry*, *21*(12), 1121–1132. doi:10.1016/0006-3223(86)90220-9 PMID:3756262

Gray, J. A. (1991). Neural systems, emotion and personality. In J. Madden IV, (Ed.), *Neurobiology of learning, emotion and affect* (pp. 273–306). New York: Raven Press.

Gray, N. S., Pickering, A. D., & Gray, J. A. (1994). Psychoticism and dopamine D2 binding in the basal ganglia using single photon emission tomography. *Personality and Individual Differences*, *17*(3), 431–434. doi:10.1016/0191-8869(94)90289-5

Grebb, J. A., Weinberger, D. R., & Morihis, J. M. (1986). Electroencephalogram and evoked potential studies of schizophrenia. In H. A. Nasrallah & D. R. Weinberger (Eds.), Handbook of schizophrenia: vol. 1. The neurology of schizophrenia (pp. 121-140). Elsevier.

Green, R. G. (1984). Preferred stimulation levels in introverts and extroverts: Effects on arousal and performancedoi. *Journal of Personality and Social Psychology*, *46*(6), 1303–1312. doi:10.1037/0022-3514.46.6.1303

Grossberg, S. (1982). *Studies of Mind and Brain*. Amsterdam: Kluwer. doi:10.1007/978-94-009-7758-7

Gurrera, R. J., ODonnell, B. F., Nestor, P. G., Gainski, J., & McCarley, R. W. (2001). The P3 Auditory Event-Related Brain Potential Indexes Major Personality Traits. *Biological Psychiatry*, *49*(11), 921–929. doi:10.1016/S0006-3223(00)01067-2 PMID:11377410

Hansen, J. C., & Hillyard, S. A. (1980). Endogenous brain potentials associated with selective auditory attention. *Electroencephalography and Clinical Neurophysiology*, *49*(3-4), 277–290. doi:10.1016/0013-4694(80)90222-9 PMID:6158404

Hare, R. D. (1978). Electrodermal and cardiovascular correlates of psychopathology. In R. D. Hare & D. Schalling (Eds.), *Psychopathic behavior: Approaches to research* (pp. 107–144). New York: Willey.

Hare, R. D. (1993). *Without conscience: The disturbing world of the psychopaths among us*. New York: Pocket.

Heninger, G. R., McDonald, R. K., Goff, W. R., & Sollberger, A. (1969). Diurnal variations in the cerebral evoked response and EEG: Relations to 17-hydroxycorticosteroid levels. *Archives of Neurology*, *21*(3), 330–337. doi:10.1001/archneur.1969.00480150120015 PMID:5306582

Hillyard, S. A. (1969). Supplement C: The CNV and the vertex evoked potential during signal detection: A preliminary report. In E. Donchin & D. B. Lindsey (Eds.), Average evoked potentials: Methods, results, and evaluations (pp. 349-395). National Aeronautics and space administration.

Hillyard, S. A., Hink, R. F., Schwent, V. L., & Picton, T. W. (1973). Electrical signs of selective attention in the human brain. *Science*, *182*(4108), 177–180. doi:10.1126/science.182.4108.177 PMID:4730062

Hirayasu, Y., Samura, M., Ohta, H., & Ogura, C. (2000). Sex effects on rate of change of P300 latency with age. *Clinical Neurophysiology*, *111*(2), 187–194. doi:10.1016/S1388-2457(99)00233-3 PMID:10680553

Hoffman, L. D., Friedmann, A., Saltman, P., & Polich, J. (1999). Neuroelectric assessment of nutrient intake. *International Journal of Psychophysiology*, *32*(2), 93–106. doi:10.1016/S0167-8760(99)00004-5 PMID:10380944

Hoffman, L. D., & Polich, J. (1998). EEG, ERPs, and Food Consumption. *Biological Psychology*, *48*(2), 139–151. doi:10.1016/S0301-0511(98)00010-6 PMID:9700015

Hoffman, L. D., & Polich, J. (1999). P300, Handedness, and Corpus Callosal Size: Gender, Modality, and Task. *International Journal of Psychophysiology, 31*(2), 163–174. doi:10.1016/S0167-8760(98)00050-6 PMID:9987062

Horne, J. A., Brass, C. G., & Pettit, A. N. (1980). Circadian performance differences between 'morning' and 'evening' 'types'. *Ergonomics, 23*, 129–136. doi:10.1080/00140138008924715

Horne, J. A., & Östberg, O. (1976). Morningness-eveningness questionnaire. *International Journal of Chronobiology, 4*, 97–110. PMID:1027738

Hornykiewicz, O. (1975). Parkinsonism induced by dopaminergic antagonists. In D. B. Calne & A. Barbeau (Eds.), *Advances in Neurology* (Vol. 9). New York: Raven Press.

Houlihan, M. E., Pritchard, W. S., Guy, T. D., & Robinson, J. H. (2002). Smoking/nicotine affects the magnitude and onset of lateralized readiness potentials. *Journal of Psychophysiology, 16*(1), 37–45. doi:10.1027//0269-8803.16.1.37

Houlihan, M. E., Pritchard, W. S., & Robinson, J. H. (2001). Effects of smoking/nicotine on performace and event-related potentials during a short-term memory scanning task. *Psychophyarmacology, 156*(4), 388–396. doi:10.1007/s002130100751 PMID:11498715

Houston, R. J., Bauer, L. O., & Hesselbrock, V. M. (2003). Depression and familial risk for substance dependence: A P300 study of younf women. *Psychiatry Research: Neuroimaging, 124*(1), 49–62. doi:10.1016/S0925-4927(03)00074-X PMID:14511795

Houston, R. J., Bauer, L. O., & Hesselbrock, V. M. (2004). P300 evidence of cognitive inflexibility in female adolescents at risk for reccurent depression. *Progress in Neuro-Psychopharmacology & Biological Psychiatry, 28*(3), 529–536. doi:10.1016/j.pnpbp.2004.01.004 PMID:15093961

Hugdahl, K. (1995b). Collecting and analyzing data: Electrodermal activity. In *Psychophysiology: The Mind-Body Perspective* (pp. 101–130). Harvard University Press.

Johnston, V. S., & Wang, X.-T. (1991). The relationship between menstrual phase and the P3 component of ERPs. *Psychophysiology, 28*(4), 400–507. doi:10.1111/j.1469-8986.1991.tb00723.x PMID:1745720

Johnstone, S. J., Barry, R. J., Anderson, J. W., & Coyle, S. F. (1996). Age-related changes in child and adolescent event-related potential component morphology, amplitude and latency to standard and target stimuli in an auditory oddball task. *International Journal of Psychophysiology*, *24*(3), 223–238. doi:10.1016/S0167-8760(96)00065-7 PMID:8993997

Jones, T., McCarthy, G., Tamborlane, W., Caprio, S., Roessler, E., Kraemer, D., & Serwin, R. et al. (1990). Mild hypoglycemia and impairment of brain-stem and cortical evoked potentials in normal subjects. *Diabetes*, *39*(12), 1550–1555. doi:10.2337/diab.39.12.1550 PMID:2245879

Kaplan, H. I., Sadock, B. J., & Grebb, J. A. (1994). Psychiatric emergencies. In H. I. Kaplan, B. J. Sadock, & J. A. Grebb (Eds.), *Synopsis of Psychiatry* (pp. 803–811). Baltimore, MD: Williams & Wilkins.

Kaustio, O., Partanen, J., Valkonen-Korhonen, M., Viinamäki, H., & Lehtonen, J. (2002). Affective and psychotic symptoms relate to different types of P300 alterations in depressive disorder. *Journal of Affective Disorders*, *71*(1-3), 43–50. doi:10.1016/S0165-0327(01)00410-4 PMID:12167500

Kayser, J., Tenke, C. E., & Bruder, G. E. (1998). Dissociation of brain ERP topographies for tonal and phonetic oddball tasks. *Psychophysiology*, *35*(5), 576–590. doi:10.1017/S0048577298970214 PMID:9715101

Keister, M. E., & McLaughlin, R. J. (1972). Vigilance performance related to extraversion-introversion and caffeine. *Journal of Experimental Research in Personality*, *6*(1), 5–11.

Kenemans, J. L., Verbaten, M. N., Melis, C., & Slangen, J. (1992). Visual stimuli change and the orienting reaction: Event-related potential evidence for a two-stage process. *Biological Psychology*, *33*(2-3), 97–114. doi:10.1016/0301-0511(92)90026-Q PMID:1525300

Kerkhof, G. (1980). Interindividual differences in the diurnal variations of the human auditory evoked potentials. *Physiological Psychology*, *8*(1), 141–143. doi:10.3758/BF03326463

Kerkhof, G., Koving, H. J., Willemse, V. D., Geest, M., & Rietveld, W. J. (1980). Diurnal differences between morning-type and evening-type subjects in self-rated alertness, body temperature, and the visual and auditory evoked potential. *Neuroscience Letters*, *16*(1), 11–15. doi:10.1016/0304-3940(80)90093-2 PMID:6892051

Kern, M., Wells, J. A., Stephens, J. M., Elton, C. W., Friedman, J. E., Tapscott, E. B., & Dohm, G. L. et al. (1990). Insulin responsiveness in skeletal muscle is determined by glucose transporter (Glut 4) protein level. *The Biochemical Journal*, *270*(2), 397–400. doi:10.1042/bj2700397 PMID:2205203

Klyagin, V. S. (1974). Diagnostic relevance of individual stability of the total power EEG activity. In K. M. Gurevich (Ed.), *Psychophysiological problems of higher level professional experience* (Vol. 1). Moscow: Sovetska Rossiya.

Knott, V. J. (1991). Neuropsychological aspects of smoking behaviour: A neuroelectric perspective. *British Journal of Addiction*, *86*(5), 511–515. doi:10.1111/j.1360-0443.1991.tb01799.x PMID:1650268

Knott, V. J., Harr, A., & Mahoney, C. (1999). Smoking History and Aging-Associated Cognitive Decline: An Event-related Brain Potential Study. *Neuropsychobiology*, *40*(2), 95–106. doi:10.1159/000026604 PMID:10474064

Kohn, P. M. (1987). Issues in the measurement of arousability. In J. Strelau & H. J. Eysenck (Eds.), *Personality Dimensions and Arousal* (pp. 233–250). New York: Plenum Press. doi:10.1007/978-1-4899-2043-0_14

Kok, A. (2000). Age-related changes in involuntary and voluntary attention as reflected in components of the event-related potential (ERP). *Biological Psychology*, *54*(1-3), 107–143. doi:10.1016/S0301-0511(00)00054-5 PMID:11035221

Kosmidis, M. H., Duncan, C. C., & Mirsky, A. F. (1998). Sex Differences in Seasonal Variations in P300. *Biological Psychology*, *49*(3), 249–268. doi:10.1016/S0301-0511(98)00043-X PMID:9858056

Kramer, A. F., Siveraag, E. J., & Braune, R. (1987). A psychophysiological assessment of operator workload durign simulated flight missions. *Human Factors*, *29*, 145–160. PMID:3610180

Krizmanić, M. & Kolesarić, V. (1994). *Priručnik za primjenu Skale depresiivnosti D-92* [The Manual for the application of Depression Scale- D]. Naklada Slap, Jastrebarsko.

Kutas, M., & Hillyard, S. A. (1980). Reading senseless sentences: Brain potentials reflect semnatic incongruity. *Science*, *207*(4427), 203–205. doi:10.1126/science.7350657 PMID:7350657

Lemere, F. (1936). The significance of individual differences in the Berger rhythm. *Brain*, *9*(3), 366–375. doi:10.1093/brain/59.3.366

Lew, G. S., & Polich, J. (1993). P300, habituation and response mode. *Physiology & Behavior*, *53*(1), 111–117. doi:10.1016/0031-9384(93)90018-B PMID:8434050

Lin, E., & Polich, J. (1999). P300 habituation patterns: Individual differences from ultradian rhythms. *Perceptual and Motor Skills*, *88*(3c), 1111–1125. doi:10.2466/pms.1999.88.3c.1111 PMID:10485091

Lindgren, M., Stenberg, G., & Rosen, I. (1999). Directed forgetting, event-related potentials and nicotine. *Human Psychopharmacology*, *14*(1), 19–29. doi:10.1002/(SICI)1099-1077(199901)14:1<19::AID-HUP60>3.0.CO;2-2

Lloyd, K. G. (1978). Observations concerning neurotransmitter interaction in schizophrenia. In L. L. Butcher (Ed.), *Cholinergic-Monoaminergic interactions in the Brain*. New York: Academic Press. doi:10.1016/B978-0-12-147850-6.50023-4

Lolas, F., Camposano, S., & Etcheberrrigaray, R. (1989). Augmenting/reducing and personality: A psychometric and evoked potential study in Chilean sample. *Personality and Individual Differences*, *10*(11), 1173–1176. doi:10.1016/0191-8869(89)90081-0

Lorist, M. M., Snel, J., & Kok, A. (1994a). Influence of caffeine on information processing in well-rested and fatigued subjects. *Psychopharmacology*, *113*(3-4), 4115–4421. doi:10.1007/BF02245217 PMID:7862853

Lorist, M. M., Snel, J., Kok, A., & Mulder, G. (1994b). Influence of caffeine on selective attention in well-rested and fatigued subjects. *Psychophysiology*, *31*(6), 525–534. doi:10.1111/j.1469-8986.1994.tb02345.x PMID:7846213

Lukas, J. H. (1982). Human augmenting-reducing and sensation seeking. *Psychophysiology*, *19*, 333–334.

Lukas, J. H., & Mullins, L. F. (1985). Auditory augmenters are sensation seekers and perform better under high work-loads. *Psychophysiology*, *22*, 580–581.

Maher, B. A. (1977). *Contributions to the Psychopathology of Schizophrenia*. New York: Academic Press.

Marton, M., & Urban, I. (1966). An electroencephalographic investigation of individual differences in the process of conditioning.*Proceedings of the 18th International Congress of Experimental psychology, Symposium 9,*106-109.

Maryutina, T. M. (1974). Visual evoked potentials in adults and children. In V. D. Nebylitsyn (Ed.), *Problems of differential psychophysiology. Electrophysiological studies on the fundamental properties of the nervous system* (Vol. 8). Moscow: Nauka.

Maryutina, T. M. (1978). On the genetic determinants of evoked potentials in man. In B. F. Lomov & I. V. Ravich-Schrerbo (Eds.), *The problems of genetic psychophysiology in man*. Moscow: Nauka.

Mathews, G. (1997). An introduction to the cognitive science of personality and emotion. In *Cognitive science perspectives on personality and emotion* (pp. 3–30). Amsterdam: Elsevier. doi:10.1016/S0166-4115(97)80118-5

Mathews, G. (1999). Personality and skill: A cognitive-adaptive framework. In *The future of learning and individual differences research: Processes, traits, and content* (pp. 251–270). Washington, DC: American Psychological Association.

Mathews, G. (2000). A cognitive science critigue of biological theories of personality traits. *History and Phylosophy of Psychology*, *2*, 1–17.

Matthews, G. (2004). Neuroticism from the Top Down: Psychophysiology and Negative Emotionality. In R. M. Stelmack (Ed.), *On the Psychobiology of Personality: Essays in Honor of Marvin Zuckerman* (pp. 249–266). Elsevier Ltd. doi:10.1016/B978-008044209-9/50015-4

Matthews, G., & Gilliland, K. (1999). The personality theories of H. J. Eysenck and J. A. Gray: A comparative review. *Personality and Individual Differences*, *26*(4), 583–626. doi:10.1016/S0191-8869(98)00158-5

Matthews, G., & Gilliland, K. (2001). Personality, biology and cognitive science: A reply to Corr (2001). *Personality and Individual Differences*, *30*(2), 353–362. doi:10.1016/S0191-8869(00)00029-5

Mecklinger, A., & Ullsperger, P. (1993). P3 varies with stimulus categorisation rather than probability. *Electroencephalography and Clinical Neurophysiology*, *86*(6), 395–407. doi:10.1016/0013-4694(93)90135-I PMID:7686474

Michaelis, W., & Eysenck, H. J. (1971). The determination of personality inventory factor patterns and intercorrelations by changes in real-life motivation. *The Journal of Genetic Psychology*, *118*(2), 223–234. doi:10.1080/00221325.1971.10532611

Momirović, A. (2008). Povezanost evociranih kognitivnih potencijala s rezultatima psihologijskih testova. In A. Vulić-Prtorić, V. Ćubela-Adorić, A. Proroković, I. Sorić & P. Valerjev (Eds.), Paper summaries: 16th Psychology Days in Zadar (p. 85). Zadar: University of Zadar, Department of Psychology.

Moruzzi, G., & Magoun, H. W. (1949). Brainstem reticular formation and activation of the EEG. *Electroencephalography and Clinical Neurophysiology, 1*(1-4), 455–473. doi:10.1016/0013-4694(49)90219-9 PMID:18421835

Muir, W. J., St Clair, D. M., & Blackwood, D. H. R. (1991). Long-latenca auditory event-related potentials in schizophrenia and in bipolar and unipolar affective disorder. *Psychological Medicine, 21*, 867–879. doi:10.1017/S003329170002986X PMID:1780401

Näätänen, R. (1992). *Attention and brain function*. Hillsdale, NJ: Lawrence Erlbaum.

Näätänen, R., Alho, K., & Sams, M. (1985). Selective information processing and event-related brain potentials. In F. Klix, R. Näätänen, & K. Zimmer (Eds.), *Psychophysiological approaches to human information processing* (pp. 73–92). Amsterdam: Elsevier Science Publishers. doi:10.1016/S0166-4115(08)61597-6

Nebylitsyn, V. D. (1961). Extinction with reinforcement of conditioned EEG as an index of strenght of nervous system. *Doklady Academii Pedagogischeskikh Nauk SSSR, 3*, 97–100.

Nebylitsyn, V. D. (1963). The structure of the basic properties of the human nervous system. *Voprosy Psihologii, 9*, 21–34.

Nieman, D. H., Ongerboer de Visser, B. W., Koelman, J. H. T. M., Hofman, W. F., & Linszen, D. H. (1998). A model of P300 event-related potential deficits in recent-onset schizophrenia. *International Clinical Psychopharmacology, 13*, S67–S73. doi:10.1097/00004850-199801001-00012

OConnor, K. (1980). Electrocortical positivity and personality. *Perceptual and Motor Skills, 51*(3), 924–926. doi:10.2466/pms.1980.51.3.924 PMID:7208240

OConnor, K. (1983). Individual differences in components of slow cortical potentials: Implications for models of information processing. *Personality and Individual Differences, 4*(4), 403–410. doi:10.1016/0191-8869(83)90006-5

OConnor, S., Bauer, L. O., Tasman, A., & Hesselbrock, V. M. (1994). Reduced P300 amplitudes of ERPs are associated with both a family history of alcoholism and antisocial personality disorder. *Progress in Neuro-Psychopharmacology & Biological Psychiatry*, *18*(8), 1307–1321. doi:10.1016/0278-5846(94)90095-7 PMID:7863018

OGorman, J. G. (1977). Individual differences in habituation of human physiological responses: A review of theory, method and findings in the study of personality correlates in non-clinical populations. *Biological Psychology*, *5*(4), 257–318. doi:10.1016/0301-0511(77)90017-5 PMID:338041

OGorman, J. G., & Mallis, L. R. (1984). Extraversion and the EEG: II. A test of Gales hypothesis. *Biological Psychology*, *19*(2), 113–127. doi:10.1016/0301-0511(84)90050-4 PMID:6518221

Oliver-Rodriguez, J. C., Guan, Z., & Johnston, V. S. (1999). Gender differences in late positive components evoked by human faces. *Psychophysiology*, *36*(2), 176–185. doi:10.1111/1469-8986.3620176 PMID:10194964

Orlebeke, J. F., Kok, A., & Zeillemaker, C. W. (1984). Augmenting-reducing (disinhibition) and the processing of auditory stimulus intensity. *Psychophysiology*, *21*, 591.

Ortiz, T., & Maojo, V. (1993). Comparison of the P300 wave in introverts and extraverts. *Personality and Individual Differences*, *15*(1), 109–112. doi:10.1016/0191-8869(93)90051-4

Otten, L. J., Gaillard, A. W., & Wientjes, C. J. (1995). The relation between event-related brain potential, heart rate, and blood pressure responses in an S1-S2 paradigm. *Biological Psychology*, *39*(2-3), 81–102. doi:10.1016/0301-0511(94)00969-5 PMID:7734631

Ottowitz, W. E., Dougherty, D. D., & Savage, C. R. (2002). The neural network basis for abnormalities of attention and executive function in major depressive disorder: Implications for application of the medical disease model to psychiatric disorders. *Harvard Review of Psychiatry*, *10*(2), 86–99. doi:10.1080/10673220216210 PMID:11897749

Pass, H. L., Klorman, R., Salzman, L. F., Klein, R., & Kaskey, G. B. (1980). The late positive component of the evoked response in acute schizophrenic during a test sustained attention. *Biological Psychiatry*, *15*, 9–20. PMID:7357059

Pasynkova, A. V., Guseva, E. P., & Lipovetsky, S. S. (1980). The relation of later evoked potentials' components to indicators of activation and efficiency of learning and memorizing. In V. M. Rusalov & E. A. Golubeva (Eds.), *Psychophysiological investigations on intellectual self-regulation and activity*. Moscow: Nauka.

Patterson, J. V., Michalewski, H. J., & Starr, A. (1988). Latency variability of the components of auditory event-related potentials to infrequent stimuli in aging, Alzheimer-type demention, and depression. *Electroencephalography and Clinical Neurophysiology*, *71*(6), 450–460. doi:10.1016/0168-5597(88)90049-4 PMID:2460326

Pavlov, I. P. (1928). *Lectures on conditioned reflexes*. New York: Liveright.

Petrie, A. (1967). *Individuality in pain and suffering*. Chicago, IL: Chicago University Press.

Pfefferbaum, A., Ford, J. M., White, P. M., & Roth, W. T. (1989). P3 in schizophrenia is affected by stimulus modality, response requirements, medication status, and negative symptoms. *Archives of General Psychiatry*, *46*(11), 1035–1044. doi:10.1001/archpsyc.1989.01810110077011 PMID:2573328

Pfefferbaum, A., Wenegrat, B. G., Ford, J. M., Roth, W. T., & Kopell, B. S. (1984). Clinical application of the P3 component of event-related potentials. II: Dementia, depression, and schizophrenia. *Electroencephalography and Clinical Neurophysiology*, *59*(2), 104–124. doi:10.1016/0168-5597(84)90027-3 PMID:6200305

Picton, T. W. (1980). The use of human event-related potentials in psychology. In I. Martin & P. H. Venables (Eds.), *Techniques in psychophysiology* (pp. 357–395). John Wiley & Sons, Ltd.

Pitzer, A., & Polich, J. (1997). EEG, ERPs, and Cognitive Development. *Psychophysiology*, *34*, S71.

Plooij-van Gorsel, E. (1981). EEG and cardiac correlates of neurotocism: A psychophysiological comparison of neurotics and normal controls in relation to personality. *Biological Psychology*, *13*, 141–156. doi:10.1016/0301-0511(81)90032-6 PMID:7342986

Plooij-van Gorsel, E. (1984). Evoked potential correlates of information processing and habituation in depressive illness. *Annals of the New York Academy of Sciences*, *425*(1), 609–616. doi:10.1111/j.1749-6632.1984.tb23585.x PMID:6588881

Polich, J. (1987). Task difficulty, probability and inter-stimulus interval as determinants of P300 from auditory stimuli. *Electroencephalography and Clinical Neurophysiology*, *68*(4), 311–320. doi:10.1016/0168-5597(87)90052-9 PMID:2439311

Polich, J. (1989). Habituation of P300 from Auditory Stimuli. *Psychobiology (Austin, Tex.)*, *17*(1), 19–28.

Polich, J. (1993). Cognitive Brain Potentials. *Current Directions in Psychological Science*, *2*(6), 175–179. doi:10.1111/1467-8721.ep10769728

Polich, J. (1996). Meta-analysis of P300 normative aging studies. *Psychophysiology*, *33*(4), 334–353. doi:10.1111/j.1469-8986.1996.tb01058.x PMID:8753933

Polich, J. (1997). EEG and ERP Assessment of Normal Aging. *Clinical Neurophysiology*, *104*, 244–256. PMID:9186239

Polich, J. (1998). P300 Clinical Utility and Control of Variability. *Journal of Clinical Neurophysiology*, *15*(1), 14–33. doi:10.1097/00004691-199801000-00004 PMID:9502510

Polich, J. (1999). P300 in clinical applications. In E. Niedermeyer & F. Lopes de Silva (Eds.), Electroencephalography: Basic Principles, Clinical Applications and Related Fields (4th ed.; pp. 1073-1091). Baltimore, MD: Urban & Schwarzenberg.

Polich, J. (2004). *Marijuana and ERPs*. Retrieved December 30, 2003, from http://p300.scrips.edu/mjstudy.htm

Polich, J., & Geisler, M. W. (1990). P300 seasonal variation. *Biological Psychology*, *32*(2-3), 173–179. doi:10.1016/0301-0511(91)90008-5 PMID:1790269

Polich, J., & Hoffman, L. D. (1998). P300 and Handedness: On the Possible Contribution of the Corpus Calosal Size to ERPs. *Psychophysiology*, *35*(5), 497–507. doi:10.1017/S0048577298970792 PMID:9715094

Polich, J., & Kok, A. (1995). Cognitive and Biological Determinants of P300: An Integrative Review. *Biological Psychology*, *41*(2), 103–146. doi:10.1016/0301-0511(95)05130-9 PMID:8534788

Polich, J., & Lardon, M. T. (1997). P300 and long-term physical exercise. *Electroencephalography and Clinical Neurophysiology*, *103*(4), 493–498. doi:10.1016/S0013-4694(97)96033-8 PMID:9368494

Polich, J., & Martin, S. (1992). P300, Cognitive Capability, and Personality: A Correlational Study of University Undergraduates. *Personality and Individual Differences, 13*(5), 533–543. doi:10.1016/0191-8869(92)90194-T

Polich, J., Polock, V. E., & Bloom, F. E. (1994). Meta-analysis of P300-Amplitude from Males at Risk for Alcoholism. *Psychological Bulletin, 115*(1), 55–73. doi:10.1037/0033-2909.115.1.55 PMID:8310100

Porjesz, B., & Begleiter, H. (1990). Event-related potentials in individuals at risk for alcoholism. *Alcohol (Fayetteville, N.Y.), 7*(5), 465–469. doi:10.1016/0741-8329(90)90033-9 PMID:2222850

Porjesz, B., & Begleiter, H. (1998). Human evoked brain potentials and alcohol. *Alcoholism, Clinical and Experimental Research, 5*, 394–317. PMID:7018313

Pozzessere, G., Valle, E., De Crignis, S., Cordischi, V. M., Fattapposta, F., Rizzo, P. A., & Di Mario, U. et al. (1991). Abnormalities of cognitive functions in IDDM revealed by P300 event-related potential analysis: Comparison with short-latency evoked potentials and psychometric tests. *Diabetes, 40*(8), 952–958. doi:10.2337/diab.40.8.952 PMID:1860560

Pritchard, W. S. (1989). P300 and EPQ/STPI Personality Traits. *Personality and Individual Differences, 10*(1), 15–24. doi:10.1016/0191-8869(89)90172-4

Pylyshyn, Z. W. (1999). What's in your mind? In E. Lepore & Z. W. Pylyshyn (Eds.), *What is cognitive science?* Malden, MA: Blackwell.

Raine, A., Venables, P. H., & Williams, M. (1990). Autonomic orienting responses in 15-year-old male subjects and criminal behavior at age 24. *The American Journal of Psychiatry, 147*(7), 933–937. doi:10.1176/ajp.147.7.933 PMID:2356879

Rammsayer, T., & Stahl, J. (2002). Extraversion-related differences in motor activation as revealed by lateralized readiness potentials. *International Journal of Psychophysiology, 45*, 19.

Rammsayer, T., & Stahl, J. (2004). Extraversion-related differences in response organization: Evidence from lateralized readiness potentials. *Biological Psychology, 66*(1), 35–49. doi:10.1016/j.biopsycho.2003.08.003 PMID:15019169

Regan, D. (1972). *Evoked potentials in psychology, sensory physiology and clinical medicine*. London: Chapman and Hall. doi:10.1007/978-94-011-6890-8

Revelle, W., Anderson, K. J., & Humphreys, M. S. (1987). Empirical tests and theoretical extensions of arousal-based theories of personality. In J. Strelau & H. J. Eysenck (Eds.), *Personality dimensions and arousal* (pp. 17–36). New York: Plenum. doi:10.1007/978-1-4899-2043-0_2

Revelle, W., Humphreys, M. S., Simon, L., & Gilliland, K. (1980). The interactive effect of personality, time of day, and caffeine: A test of the arousal model. *Journal of Experimental Psychology. General*, *109*(1), 1–31. doi:10.1037/0096-3445.109.1.1 PMID:6445402

Reynolds, G. P. (1983). Increased concentrations and lateral asymmetry of amygdala dopamine in schizophrenia. *Nature*, *305*(5934), 527–529. doi:10.1038/305527a0 PMID:6621699

Reynolds, G. P. (1987). Post-mortem neurochemical studies in human postmortem brain tissue. In H. Hafner, W. F. Gattaz, & W. Janzarik (Eds.), *Search for the Causes of Schizophrenia* (pp. 236–240). Heidelberg, Germany: Springer. doi:10.1007/978-3-642-71765-9_21

Robinson, D. L. (1982). Properties of the diffuse thalamocortical system and human personality: A direct test of Pavlovian/Eysenckian theory. *Personality and Individual Differences*, *3*(1), 1–16. doi:10.1016/0191-8869(82)90069-1

Robinson, D. L. (1999). The technical, neurological, and psychological significance of alpha‘, delta and theta waves confounded in EEG evoked potentials: A study of peak latencies. *Clinical Neurophysiology*, *110*(8), 1427–1434. doi:10.1016/S1388-2457(99)00078-4 PMID:10454278

Robinson, D. L. (2000). The technical, neurological, and psychological significance of alpha‘, delta and theta waves confounded in EEG evoked potentials: A study of peak amplitudes. *Personality and Individual Differences*, *28*(4), 673–693. doi:10.1016/S0191-8869(99)00130-0

Robinson, D. L. (2001). How brain arousal system determines different temperament types and the major dimensions of personality. *Personality and Individual Differences*, *31*(8), 1233–1259. doi:10.1016/S0191-8869(00)00211-7

Rohtman, H. H. (1970). Effects of high frequences and intersubject variability on the auditory evoked cortical response. *The Journal of the Acoustical Society of America*, *47*(2B), 569–573. doi:10.1121/1.1911930 PMID:5439656

Röschke, J., & Wagner, P. (2003). A confirmatory study on the mechanisms behind reduced P300 waves in depression. *Neuropsychopharmacology*, *28*(S1), S9–S12. doi:10.1038/sj.npp.1300139 PMID:12827138

Roth, W. T., Pfefferbaum, A., Kelly, A. F., Berger, P. A., & Kopell, B. S. (1981). Auditory event-related potentials in schizophrenia and depression. *Psychiatry Research*, *4*(2), 199–212. doi:10.1016/0165-1781(81)90023-8 PMID:6939010

Rugg, M. D. (1992). Event-related Potentials in Clinical Neuropsychology. In J. R. Crawford, D. M. Parker & W. W. McKinlay (Eds.), A Handbook of Neuropsychological Assessment (pp. 393-411), Lawrence Erlbaum Associates Publishers.

Rusalov, V. M. (1974). Polar-amplitude asymmetry of evoked potentials. In V. D. Nebylitsyn (Ed.), *Problems of differential psychophysiology. Electrophysiological studies on the fundamental properties of the nervous system* (Vol. 8). Moscow: Nauka.

Rust, J. (1975). Cortical evoked potential, personality, and intelligence. *Journal of Comparative and Physiological Psychology*, *89*(10), 1220–1226. doi:10.1037/h0077178 PMID:1238436

Salisbury, D. F., Shenton, M. E., Sherwood, A. R., Fischer, I. A., Yurgelun-Todd, D. A., Tohen, M., & McCarley, R. W. (1998). First episode schizophrenic psychosis differs from first episode affective psychosis and controls in P300 amplitude over left temporal lobe. *Archives of General Psychiatry*, *55*(2), 173–180. doi:10.1001/archpsyc.55.2.173 PMID:9477932

Santosh, P. J., Malhotra, S., Raghunathan, M., & Mehra, Y. N. (1994). A study of P300 in melancholic depression: Correlation with psychotic features. *Biological Psychiatry*, *35*(7), 474–479. doi:10.1016/0006-3223(94)90046-9 PMID:8018798

Sarah, G., Gordon, E., Kraiuhin, C., Coyle, S., Howson, A., & Meares, R. (1994). The P300 ERP component: An index of cognitive dysfunction in depression? *Journal of Affective Disorders*, *31*(1), 29–38. doi:10.1016/0165-0327(94)90124-4 PMID:8046158

Savage, R. D. (1964). Electrocerebral activity, extraversion and neuroticism. *The British Journal of Psychiatry*, *110*(464), 89–100. doi:10.1192/bjp.110.464.98 PMID:14103379

Snyder, E., Hillyard, S. A., & Galambos, R. (1980). Similarities and Differences among the P3 Waves to Detected Signals in Three Modalities. *Psychophysiology*, *17*(2), 112–122. doi:10.1111/j.1469-8986.1980.tb00120.x PMID:7375612

Souza, V. B. N., Muir, W. J., Walker, M. T., Glabus, M. F., Roxborough, H. M., Sharp, C. W., & Blackwood, D. H. R. et al. (1995). Auditory P300 event-related potentials and neuropsychological performance in schizophrenia. *Biological Psychiatry*, *37*(5), 300–310. doi:10.1016/0006-3223(94)00131-L PMID:7748981

Squires, N. K., & Ollo, C. (1999). Comparison of endogenous event-related potentials in attend and non-attend conditions: Latency changes with normal aging. *Clinical Neurophysiology*, *110*(3), 564–574. doi:10.1016/S1388-2457(99)00003-6 PMID:10363780

Stelmack, R. M. (1981). The psychophysiology of extraversion and neuroticism. In H. J. Eysenck (Ed.), *A model for personality* (pp. 38–63). Springer-Verlag Berlin Heidelberg. doi:10.1007/978-3-642-67783-0_2

Stelmack, R. M. (1997). The Psychophysics and Psychophysiology of Extraversion and Arousal. In H. Nyborg (Ed.), *The Scientific Study of Human Nature: Tribute to Hans J. Eysenck at Eighty* (pp. 388–403). Oxford, UK: Pergamon Press.

Stelmack, R. M., Achorn, E., & Michaud, A. (1977). Extraversion and individual differences in auditory evoked response. *Psychophysiology*, *14*(4), 368–374. doi:10.1111/j.1469-8986.1977.tb02966.x PMID:882616

Stelmack, R. M., & Campbell, K. B. (1974). Extraversion and auditory sensitivity to high and low frequency. *Perceptual and Motor Skills*, *38*(3), 875–879. doi:10.2466/pms.1974.38.3.875 PMID:4842444

Stelmack, R. M., Campbell, K. B., & Bell, I. (1993). Extraversion and brainstem auditory evoked potentials during sleep and wakefulness. *Personality and Individual Differences*, *14*(3), 447–453. doi:10.1016/0191-8869(93)90314-S

Stelmack, R. M., & Geen, R. G. (1992). The Psychophysiology of Extraversion. In A. Gale & M. W. Eysenck (Eds.), *Handbook of Individual Differences: Biological Perspectives* (pp. 227–254). New York: John Wiley & Sons, Ltd.

Stelmack, R. M., & Houlihan, M. (1995). Event-Related Potentials, Personality, and Intelligence: Concepts, Issues, and Evidence. In D. H. Saklofske & M. Zeidner (Eds.), *International Handbook of Personality and Intelligence* (pp. 349–365). New York: Plenum Press. doi:10.1007/978-1-4757-5571-8_17

Stelmack, R. M., Houlihan, M., & McGarry-Roberts, P. A. (1993). Personality, reaction time, and event-related potentials. *Journal of Personality and Social Psychology*, *65*(2), 399–409. doi:10.1037/0022-3514.65.2.399

Stelmack, R. M., & Michaud-Achorn, A. (1985). Extraversion, attention, and habituation of the auditory evoked response. *Journal of Research in Personality*, *19*(4), 416–428. doi:10.1016/0092-6566(85)90009-1

Stelmack, R. M., & Wilson, K. G. (1982). Extraversion and the effects of frequency and intensity on the auditory brainstem evoked response. *Personality and Individual Differences*, *3*(4), 373–380. doi:10.1016/0191-8869(82)90003-4

Stenberg, G. (1992). Personality and the EEG: Arousal and emotional arousability. *Personality and Individual Differences*, *13*(10), 1097–1113. doi:10.1016/0191-8869(92)90025-K

Stenberg, G. (1994). Extraversion and the P300 in a Visual Classification Task. *Personality and Individual Differences*, *16*(4), 543–560. doi:10.1016/0191-8869(94)90182-1

Stenberg, G., Rosén, I., & Risberg, J. (1988). Personality and augmenting/reducing in visual and auditory evoked potentials. *Personality and Individual Differences*, *9*(3), 571–579. doi:10.1016/0191-8869(88)90155-9

Stenberg, G., Rosen, I., & Risberg, J. (1990). Attention, and Personality in Augmenting/Reducing of Visual Evoked Potentials. *Personality and Individual Differences*, *11*(12), 1243–1254. doi:10.1016/0191-8869(90)90151-G

Stevens, J. (1993). An anatomy of schizophrenia? *Archives of General Psychiatry*, *29*(2), 177–189. doi:10.1001/archpsyc.1973.04200020023003 PMID:4147475

Strelau, J. (1982). Biologically determined dimensions of personality or temperament. *Personality and Individual Differences*, *3*(4), 355–360. doi:10.1016/0191-8869(82)90001-0

Strelau, J. (1983a). *Temperament, Personality, Activity*. London: Academic Press.

Strelau, J. (1987). Personality Dimensions Based on Arousal Theories. In J. Strelau & H. J. Eysenck (Eds.), Personality Dimensions and Arousal (pp. 269-286). New York: Plenum Press. doi:10.1007/978-1-4899-2043-0_16

Strelau, J. (1991). Are psychophysiological/psychophysical scores good candidates for diagnosing temperament/personality traits and for a demonstration of the construct validity of psychometrically measured traits? *European Journal of Personality*, *5*(5), 323–342. doi:10.1002/per.2410050502

Strelau, J., & Zawadzki, B. (1993). The Formal-Characteristics of Behavior-Temperament Inventory (FCB-TI): Theoretical assumption and scale construction. *European Journal of Personality*, *7*(5), 313–336. doi:10.1002/per.2410070504

Strelau, J., & Zawadzki, B. (1995). The Formal-Characteristics of Behavior-Temperament Inventory (FCB-TI): Validity studies. *European Journal of Personality*, *9*(3), 207–229. doi:10.1002/per.2410090304

Suls, J. (2001). Affect, stress, and personality. In J. P. Forgas (Ed.), *Handbook of affect and social cognition* (pp. 392–409). Mahwah, NJ: Erlbaum.

Sutton, S., Braren, M., Zubin, J., & John, E. R. (1965). Evoked potential correlates of stimulus uncertainty. *Science*, *150*(3700), 1187–1188. doi:10.1126/science.150.3700.1187 PMID:5852977

Swickert, R. J., & Gilliland, K. (1998). Relationship between the brainstem auditory evoked response and extraversion, impulsivity, and sociability. *Journal of Research in Personality*, *32*(3), 314–330. doi:10.1006/jrpe.1998.2216

Szelenberger, W. (1983). Brain stem auditory evoked potentials and personality. *Biological Psychiatry*, *18*(2), 157–174. PMID:6830929

Tatalović Vorkapić, S. (2009). Biological correlates of P300 and its relationship with extraversion. *Collegium Antropologicum*, *33*(4), 1215–1222. PMID:20102071

Tatalović Vorkapić, S. (2011). Electrocortical differences in sanguine, choleric, phlegmatic and melancholic. *Romanian Journal of Psychology. Psychotherapy and Neuroscience*, *1*(2), 67–96.

Teder, W. (1994). *Selective attention and auditory event-related potentials* (Doctoral Dissertation). University of Helsinki, Helsinki, Finland.

Thier, P., Axmann, D., & Giedke, H. (1986). Slow brain potentials and psychomotor retardation in depression. *Electroencephalography and Clinical Neurophysiology*, *63*(6), 570–581. doi:10.1016/0013-4694(86)90144-6 PMID:2422006

Tran, Y., Craig, A., & McIsaac, P. (2001). Extraversion-introversion and 813 Hz waves in frontal cortical regions. *Personality and Individual Differences*, *30*(2), 205–215. doi:10.1016/S0191-8869(00)00027-1

Tsuji, Y., & Kobayashi, T. (1988). Short and long ultradian EEG components in daytime arousal. *Electroencephalography and Clinical Neurophysiology*, *70*(2), 110–117. doi:10.1016/0013-4694(88)90111-3 PMID:2456189

Turetsky, B., Colbath, E. A., & Gur, R. E. (1998). P3 subcomponent abnormalities in schizophrenia: II. Longitudinal stability and relationship to symptom change. *Biological Psychiatry*, *43*(1), 31–39. doi:10.1016/S0006-3223(97)00261-8 PMID:9442342

Urretavizcaya, M., Moreno, I., Benlloch, L., Cardoner, N., Serrallonga, J., Menchón, J. M., & Valleyo, J. (2003). Auditory event-related potentials in 50 melancholic patients: Increased N100, N200 and P300 latencies and diminished P300 amplitude. *Journal of Affective Disorders*, *74*(3), 293–297. doi:10.1016/S0165-0327(02)00016-2 PMID:12738049

van Beijsterveldt, C. E. M., Molenaar, P. C. M., Geus, E. J. C., & de Boomsma, D. I. (1996). Heritability of human brain functioning as assessed by electroencephalography. In C. E. M. van Beijsterveldt (Ed.), *The Genetics of Electrophysiological Indices of Brain Activity* (pp. 29–49). Dissertatierecks, Faculteit Psychologie, Universiteit van Amsterdam.

Vanderwolf, C. H., & Robinson, T. E. (1981). Reticulo-cortical activity and behavior: A critique of the arousal theory and a new synthesis. *Behavioral and Brain Sciences*, *4*(03), 459–514. doi:10.1017/S0140525X00009869

Vandoolaeghe, E., van Hunsel, F., Nuyten, D., & Maes, M. (1998). Auditory event-related potentials in major depression: Prolonged P300 latency and increased P200 amplitude. *Journal of Affective Disorders*, *48*(2-3), 105–113. doi:10.1016/S0165-0327(97)00165-1 PMID:9543199

Vaughn, H. G., & Ritter, W. (1970). The sources of auditory evoked responses recorded from the human scalp. *Electroencephalography and Clinical Neurophysiology*, *28*(4), 360–367. doi:10.1016/0013-4694(70)90228-2 PMID:4191187

Venturini, R., De Pascalis, V., Imperiali, M. G., & San Martini, P. (1981). EEG alpha reactivity and extraversion-introversion. *Personality and Individual Differences*, *2*(3), 215–220. doi:10.1016/0191-8869(81)90026-X

Von Knorring, L. (1981). Visual evoked responses and platelet monoamine oxidase in patients suffering from alcoholism. In H. Begleiter (Ed.), *The biological effects of alcohol*. New York: Plenum press.

Wesnes, K., & Warburton, D. M. (1983). Effects of smoking on rapid information processing performance. *Neuropsychobiology*, *9*(4), 223–229. doi:10.1159/000117969 PMID:6646394

Wilson, M. A., & Languis, M. L. (1990). A topographic study of differences in the P300 between introverts and extraverts. *Brain Topography*, *2*(4), 269–274. doi:10.1007/BF01129655 PMID:2223383

Winter, K., Broadhurst, A., & Glass, A. (1972). Neuroticism, extraversion and EEG amplitude. *Journal of Experimental Research in Personality*, *6*, 44–51.

Yagi, Y., Coburn, K. L., Estes, K. M., & Arruda, J. E. (1999). Effects of Aerobic Exercise and Gender on Visual and Auditory P300, Reaction Time, and Accuracy. *European Journal of Applied Physiology*, *80*(5), 402–408. doi:10.1007/s004210050611 PMID:10502073

Yagi, Y., Estes, K. M., & Coburn, K. L. (1997). Changes in Information Processing during Aeribuc Exercise. *Bulletin of Seinan Jogakuin Junior College*, *44*, 27–34.

Yanai, I., Fujikawa, T., Osada, M., Yamawaki, S., & Touhouda, Y. (1997). Changes in auditory P300 in patients with major depression and silent cerebral infarction. *Journal of Affective Disorders*, *46*(3), 263–271. doi:10.1016/S0165-0327(97)00100-6 PMID:9547123

Yerkes, R. M., & Dodson, J. D. (1908). The relation of strenght of stimulus to rapidity of habit-formation. *The Journal of Comparative Neurology and Psychology*, *18*(5), 459–482. doi:10.1002/cne.920180503

Young, J. P. R., Lader, M. H., & Fenton, G. W. (1971). The relationship of extraversion and neuroticism to the EEG. *The British Journal of Psychiatry*, *119*(553), 667–670. doi:10.1192/bjp.119.553.667 PMID:5169077

Zuckerman, M. (1969). Theoretical formulations. In J. P. Zubek (Ed.), *Sensory deprivation: Fifteen years of research* (pp. 407–432). New York: Appleton-Century-Crofts.

Zuckerman, M. (1987). Is sensation seeking a predisposing trait for alcoholism? In E. Gottheil, K. A. Druley, S. Pashko, & S. P. Weinstein (Eds.), *Stress and addiction* (pp. 283–301). New York: Brunner/Mazel.

Zuckerman, M. (1991). Psychobiology of personality. Cambridge University Press.

Zuckerman, M., Kuhlman, D. M., Joireman, J., Teta, P., & Kraft, M. (1993). A comparison of three structural models for personality: The big three, the big five, and the alternative five. *Journal of Personality and Social Psychology*, *65*(4), 757–768. doi:10.1037/0022-3514.65.4.757

Zuckerman, M., Murtaugh, T. M., & Siegel, J. (1974). Sensation seeking and cortical augmenting-reducing. *Psychophysiology*, *11*(5), 535–542. doi:10.1111/j.1469-8986.1974.tb01109.x PMID:4415722

# Chapter 4
# Empirical Research on the Relationship Between Personality and Evoked Brain Potentials


## ABSTRACT

*In this section, research aim, problems and hypothesis with the methods and determined research results will be presented. This correlational design research that has been run on a sample of N=54 students in Croatia will be described. The main findings regarding the relationship between personality traits extraversion and evoked brain potentials will be presented. Personality traits that were explored are: extraversion, neuroticism, psychoticism, social desirability, addiction, criminality, empathy, impulsivity, adventurousness, strength of excitation, strength of inhibition, mobility, and depression. Latencies and amplitudes in two trials were investigated for the following evoked brain potentials: N1, P2, N2, P3, and Slow wave activity. Visual oddball paradigm was used for evoking brain activity measured on two occipital and two parietal electrodes. Results on controlled variables, such as: age, sight characteristics, coffee drinking, smoking, taking medications, alcohol and drug consumption, and body exercise, are introduced as well. The correlation analyses revealed a significant relationship between personality traits and evoked brain potentials, especially trait adventurousness and social desirability, due to a too simple and monotonous visual task that was use. The determined findings from the PCA factor analysis with Varimax rotation determined 15 factors that explained 79,611% of the total variance. Series of Hierarchical regression analyses for each personality trait individually revealed, as it was expected, certain visual evoked potentials as significant predictors.*


DOI: 10.4018/978-1-5225-2283-6.ch004

# RESEARCH AIM, PROBLEMS AND HYPOTHESES

## Research Aim

The main objective of this study (Tatalović Vorkapić, 2010) was to examine whether there is a possibility of predicting different personality traits operationalized within Eysenck's dimensional personality typology and Pavlov's central nervous system properties theory by means of latency and amplitude of evoked brain potentials (N1, P1, N2, P3 and SW).

## Research Problems

The following research problems were derived from the aforementioned aim:

1. To present descriptive parameters and correlation relationships of all explored personality traits and recorded evoked potentials (N1, P1, N2, P3, and SW), as well as related behavioral variables (age, vision, drinking coffee, smoking, taking medicine, drinking alcohol, taking illegal drugs, and sports activities) and recorded evoked potentials (N1, P1, N2, P3, and SW)
2. To analyze the validity of personality measurements and evoked brain potentials, as well as the general characteristics of the application of the exploratory factor analysis with the aim of determining the main components in explaining the variance of human personality, evoked potentials, and behavioral variables (age, vision, drinking coffee, smoking, taking medicine, drinking alcohol, taking illegal drugs, and sports activities)
3. To examine the possibility of prediction of Eysenck's personality dimensions (extraversion, neuroticism, psychoticism, social desirability), Pavlov's CNS properties (strength of excitation, strength of inhibition, mobility), and other personality traits (addiction, criminality, empathy, impulsivity, adventurousness, depression) by latencies of the recorded evoked potentials (N1, P1, N2, P3, and SW) and their amplitude in the first and second recording trials.

## Research Hypotheses

Regarding the stated research problems, the following research hypotheses could be defined:

1. Previously determined descriptive parameters and significant correlations between the examined personality traits and evoked brain potentials that has already been shown in previous papers will be presented. Also, a significant correlation between behavioral variables and evoked potentials is expected, given the considerable sensitivity, variability, and determination of evoked potentials of the respondents' different characteristics.
2. It is expected to determine a high possibility of the explained variance, grouping of variables with respect to the measurement type, as well as inter-correlations, e.g. mutual interconnectedness of personality traits, individual evoked potentials, and certain behavioral variables by checking the validity of personality measuring and evoked brain potentials, as well as the general characteristics of the respondents and identifying the main components in the electrophysiology of human personality.
3. Considering the significant relation between Eysenck's fundamental personality dimensions and the latency amplitude of evoked brain potentials from previous research, it is expected that evoked brain potentials will be significant predictors of the examined personality traits. However, considering that the hierarchical regression analysis will be carried out for each personality characteristic separately, different results in relation to the joint correlation analysis are expected because of the high inter-correlations between certain personality traits, which should be kept in mind in future research.

# METHODS

## Participants

A total of $N = 91$ psychology students participated in this research ($N = 15$ males and $N = 76$ females) from all study years (1$^{st}$, 2$^{nd}$, 3$^{rd}$ and 4$^{th}$) of the Department of Psychology at the Faculty of Humanities and Social Studies in Rijeka. Their average age of $M = 20.66$ years old ($SD = 1.73$) in the range of 18-25 years.

In the first part of the study, which was related to filling out a questionnaire on general information and relevant self-assessment questionnaires, all those psychology students participated who were on the day of testing present at the lecture at the Department of Psychology: first year of study $N = 28$ students (4 male), with an average age $M = 19.25$ years ($SD = 1.25$) in the range of 18 to 23 years; second year of study $N = 27$ students (4 males) with an average age $M$ = 20.44 years ($SD$ = 1.42) in the range of 19 to 25 years; third year of study $N$ = 22 students (3 males) with an average age $M$ = 21.45 years ($SD$ = 1.01) in the range of 20 to 23 years; and the fourth year of study $N$ = 14 students (4 males) with an average age $M$ = 22.64 years ($SD$ = 1.39) in the range of 21-25 years.

With regards to other data on participants whose relevance was based on their association with evoked brain potentials, which related to hand dominance (participants were further instructed to make this assessment on the basis of the hand they use to write), existing sight problems (having lenses or glasses), existence of any psychiatric/neurological diseases, drinking coffee, smoking, taking medications, alcohol consumption, drug consumption, and engaging in sports activities, the following data on the characteristics of the participants were collected based on the general information of the questionnaire: 83 (91.2%) participants evaluated the right-hand dominance, and 8 (8.8%) left-hand; 42 (46.2%) participants have vision problems or regularly use a certain correction tool (glasses or contact lenses), and 49 (53.8%) have no vision problems; 76 (83.5%) participants have no psychiatric/neurological diseases and with present no history of certain psychiatric/neurological disorders in family; 60 (65.9%) of participants stated that they consume coffee and 31 (34.1%) do not; 35 (38.5%) participants smoke and 56 (61.5%) do not; 28 (30.8%) participants take certain medications and 63 (69.2%) participants do not; 24 (26.4%) participants do not consume alcohol at all and 67 (73.6%) of participants consume alcohol; 11 (12.1%) of participants had consumed some illegal drugs in the last 15 days and 80 (87.9%) did not; and 36 (39.6%) of participants is actively engaged in a sporting activity and 55 (60.4%) of them are not.

For the second part of the research, which is related to the recording of evoked brain potentials due to the impact of the relevant variables of gender, age, and hand dominance on the amplitude and latency of evoked brain potentials (Polich & Kok, 1995; Polich, 1998, 1999, 2002), those participants were selected in relation to these variables. So that from the initial sample of participants, all male participants were excluded, all those who were not within the age range from 19 to 23 years, and those that are left-handed. After this selection, it was defined that in the context of the evoked brain potentials recording there are $N$ = 62 female participants, 8 participants gave up or did not agree to participate in the second part of the study during the recording. Finally, a final sample of $N$ = 54 participants was involved in the second part of the study, average age $M$ = 20.50 years ($SD$ = 1.28) in the age range of 19-23 years, and with the assessed right hand as the dominant hand without presence of any kind of psychiatric/neurological diseases.

Considering the year of study, participants' characteristics were as follows: $N = 16$ participants were in the first year of study, average age $M = 19.50$ years ($SD = 1.03$) in the range of 19 to 23 years; $N = 18$ participants were in the second year of study, average age $M = 20.28$ years ($SD = 1.07$) in the range of 19 to 23 years; $N = 13$ participants were in the third year of study, average age $M = 21.38$ years ($SD = 1.04$) in the range of 20 to 23 years; $N = 7$ participants were in the fourth year of study, average age $M = 21.71$ years ($SD = 0.49$) in the range of 21-22 years.

Due to the before mentioned relevant data from the general information questionnaire, the selected group of participants had the following characteristics: 22 (40.7%) participants have vision problems or regularly use a certain visual correction tool (glasses or contact lenses) and 32 (59, 3%) do not; history of some psychiatric/neurological disease is present in 11 families (20.4%) of participants and 43 (79.6%) participants are without such a history; 32 (59.3%) of participants stated that they consume coffee and 22 (40.7%) do not; 16 (29.6%) participants smoke and 38 (70.4%) do not; 15 (27.8%) participants take certain medications and 39 (72.2%) do not; 16 (29.6%) participants do not consume alcohol at all and 38 (70.4%) participants do; 4 (7.4%) participating consumed some illegal drug in the last 15 days and 50 (92.6%) did not; and 20 (37%) participants are actively engaged in a sports activity and 34 (63%) of them are not. Fifteen participants take the following medicines: Claritin, antibiotics for teeth, Ibuprofen for menstrual pain, antihistamines for allergies, birth control pills (CILEST, Triquilar), iron pills, caffetin and Nalgesin for menstrual problems, Andol for muscle relaxation, painkiller Voltaren (menstrual and toothache) and pills for gastritis, 4 of them are taking two medicines, and the other 9 take one.

## Measures

Measurements in this study were conducted on two levels: by applying questionnaire measures for a self-evaluation of personality characteristics and general characteristics, and by applying the visual oddball paradigm for measurements of evoked brain potentials. Therefore, the survey covered five groups of variables, measured with appropriate instruments:

1. Eysenck's fundamental personality dimensions: Extraversion (E), Neuroticism (N), and Psychoticism (P) Eysenck's Personality Questionnaire (EPQ-R);
2. Other personality characteristics: degree of socially desirable responding (SD), Addiction and Criminality (EPQ-R); degree of depression

(questionnaire D-92); Impulsiveness, Adventurousness and Empathy (EPQ-IVE);

3. Pavlov's CNS properties: Strength of excitation (SE), strength of inhibition (SI), and Mobility (MO) with Pavlov's Temperament Survey (PTS);
4. General characteristics of the respondents with the General Information Questionnaire (control variables): consumption of coffee; smoking; taking medication; consumption of alcohol; consumption of illegal psychoactive substances; and engaging in sports activities;
5. Amplitudes and latencies of evoked potentials: N1, P2, N2, P3, and Sw - recorded with the Device for measuring electromyography data and evoked potentials (EMG/EP) MEDELEC/TECA Sapphire[II], 4E, Vickers Medical; electrodes; other expendable material; visual oddball paradigm.

## Measurement of Eysenck's Fundamental Personality Dimensions, Social Desirability, Addiction, and Criminality

The fundamental dimensions of personality: extraversion, neuroticism, and psychoticism were measured with the method of self-evaluation using Eysenck's personality questionnaire - revised version, (EPQ-R/A), of authors Hans J. Eysenck and Sybil B. G. Eysenck (1994). Based on the theoretical framework of Eysenck's personality dimension typology, empirical validation was carried out that resulted in several versions of the applied personality questionnaires. But all previous versions of the questionnaire, as well as the last one, which was applied in this study, were intended to measure the fundamental independent personality dimensions: the extraversion - introversion dimension (E) and the neuroticism dimension - emotional stability (N), and later psychoticism dimensions (P). The latest version of Eysenck's personality questionnaire, which was applied in this study, was created on recent attempts of psychometric specialization of psychoticism subscales, which has experienced and is still experiencing a series of heated debates, as well as adding additional subscales that measure addiction and tendency to engage in crime.

Apart from that, EPQ-R also measures the Tendency to socially desirable responding, i.e. to dissimulation (L), and was originally assigned to measure personality traits of all people older than 16 years. It consists of a total of 106 items to which the participant responds by circling the answer YES or NO. The extraversion subscale contains 23 items of which one is: "Do you have many friends?", psychoticism has 32 items and one example is: "Do you enjoy to insult the people you love?", neuroticism has 24 items, of which one is: "Are you often troubled by the feeling of guilt?", giving socially desirable answers is present in 21 items, an example of which is: "Have you ever damaged or lost someone else's item?". Addiction subscale has 32 items and Criminality subscale has 34 items, and both these subscales are consist of items from extraversion, psychoticism, neuroticism and social desirability subscales, which specifically reflect the addiction or criminality. The result in each subscale is obtained by summarizing the responses according to the key from the scoring and application manual, *Manual of Eysenck Personality Scales*: *EPS-adults* (Eysenck & Eysenck, 1994). Finally, the calculated reliability level of the structural sample ($N = 902$, male = 408) was satisfying, which is partly confirmed with this study (Table 1). Reliability levels of the internal consistency type in characteristics of psychoticism and lying are somewhat lower, and extraversion and neuroticism a bit higher than those gained before, but in any case, they are within the required psychometric criteria for test reliability.

With the Subscale of lying or giving social desirable answers from Eysenck's questionnaire EPQ-R (Eysenck & Eysenck, 1994), control variable preferences to socially desirable responding wase measured, i.e. the tendency of participants to "present themselves as better than they are." As noted above, the scale showed, both in the original research and in this one, a satisfactory level of reliability. In addition to the dissimulation tendency, the scale also measures the stable personality factor that indicates social naivety/conformity. Studies have shown that, when there is a high and significant correlation between the degree of lying and neuroticism, we can speak of the measured level of dissimulation, which represents additional criteria for the exclusion of

*Table 1. Reliability coefficients for the construction sample (N = 902), internal consistency and test-retest type with 1-month interspace (adapted from Eysenck & Eysenck, 1994, p. 26), and on this study sample (N = 54)*

| EPQ | Eysenck & Eysenck (1994) | | | | This Research |
|---|---|---|---|---|---|
| | Cronbach Alpha | | Test-Retest | | Cronbach Alpha |
| | M | F | M | F | F |
| Psyc | 0.78 | 0.76 | 0.77 | 0.81 | 0.61 |
| Extr | 0.90 | 0.85 | 0.83 | 0.89 | 0.89 |
| Neur | 0.88 | 0.85 | 0.76 | 0.81 | 0.89 |
| SD | 0.82 | 0.79 | 0.76 | 0.80 | 0.68 |
| Addi | 0.78 | 0.84 | 0.75 | 0.80 | 0.72 |
| Crim | 0.75 | 0.75 | 0.77 | 0.76 | 0.76 |

those 5% of participants who achieved the highest results. Apart from that, the author's general recommendations are to conduct the correlation analysis of all relevant variables twice: first, without the exclusion of participants, followed by the exclusion of those 5% of participants who achieved the highest results. Participants are excluded only if their exclusion is significantly affecting correlation of the studied variables. Therefore, by ticking YES or NO, the participant achieves a result that indicates his tendency to give socially acceptable answers. This reduces the possibility of giving the right information about himself, more specifically, on his/her personality structure in this very study, and this is obtained by summarizing the responses based on the key from the application and scoring manual, *Manual of Eysenck Personality Scales: EPS-adults* (Eysenck & Eysenck, 1994).

## Measuring the Degree of Impulsivity, Adventurousness, and Empathy

Levels of impulsivity, adventurousness, and empathy were measured with the method of self-evaluation using Eysenck's impulsivity questionnaire, EPQ-IVE (Eysenck & Eysenck, 1994). It measures three mutually independent personality traits: Impulsivity (Imp) - a complete lack of forward planning and forecasting consequences of their actions - it highly correlates with psychoticism and less with extraversion; Adventurousness (Adv) - tendency to risky behavior with simultaneous presence of complete awareness of risks which a person exhibits – this is highly correlated with extraversion and less with psychosis; and Empathy (Emp) - tendency to compassion and caring for other people, but here there is a significant positive correlation with neuroticism and negatively with psychoticism. Although authors have so far tried to reduce the existing positive correlation between the factors of impulsivity and adventurousness, a certain level of positive correlation still exists ($r = 0.24$), and in this study ($r = 0.14, p > .31$), which explains the actual relation between them considering them only as two aspects of the same impulsivity factor. The self-evaluation questionnaire EPQ-IVE consists of 54 items to which participant also responds by ticking YES or NO. The impulsivity subscale contains 19 items (e.g. "Do you usually work fast, without checking the effect?"), adventurousness has 16 items (e.g. "Would you enjoy water skiing?"), and empathy has 19 items (e.g. "Do you get very upset when you see someone crying?"). The result in each subscale is obtained by summarizing the responses based on the key from the application and scoring manual, *Manual of Eysenck Personality Scales: EPS-adults* (Eysenck &d Eysenck, 1994). Reliability coefficients in the validation and this research can be seen in Table 2.

*Table 2. Coefficients of reliability in the two studies (the first: year 1978. and the second: year 1985.) (Adapted from Eysenck & Eysenck, 1994), and on the sample in this study (N = 54)*

| EPQ | Eysenck & Eysenck (1994) | | | | This Research |
|---|---|---|---|---|---|
| | 1978 | | 1985 | | Cronbach Alpha |
| | M | F | M | F | F |
| IMP | 0.85 | 0.82 | 0.84 | 0.83 | 0.74 |
| ADV | 0.79 | 0.78 | 0.85 | 0.84 | 0.79 |
| EMP | 0.65 | 0.64 | 0.69 | 0.69 | 0.70 |

## Measuring Depression

Given that a substantial number of papers have pointed the existence of a significant negative correlation between the degree of depression and the P300-component amplitude, in which the participants with higher levels of depression were identified with a significantly reduced amplitude of the P300-wave (Diner et al., 1985; Gangadhar et al., 1993; Muir et al., 1991; Bruder et al., 1995), and the extension of EP-latency of more depressive participants (Bruder et al., 1995; Hansenne, Pitchot, Pinto, Reggers, & Papart Ansseau, 2000), depression is the important variable for this research. For this reason, it was important to measure the depression level in the sample of this study in order to examine the relation between the evoked potentials and personality, without the moderating effect of depression. The depression variable was measured using the Depression Scale-92 (Krizmanić & Kolesarić, 1994). The authors of this scale operationalized the depression construct as a: temporary, permanent or more permanent condition, which triggers a series of changes in the perception and expression of emotions, cognitive processes, satisfying the basic needs (sleep, diet, activity, sexuality) and behavior, adding thereby questions which include Beck's cognitive triad.

It is intended for determining a global depression degree in people of both genders, aged over 16 years, and it contains 22 items. With each item in the form of questions, four answers are offered pointing to a different degree of depression (1 to 4 points), where a higher score indicates a higher degree of depression. All participants are given guidance to evaluate themselves on the offered scale by circling answers A, B, C, or D, to mark one answer that best describes their experiences and behavior in the past month. An example of such question is: "Loss of interest may also be related to other people, so it can happen that we don't want to see or hear them. Has this happened to you lately?". Answer could be one of suggested: A - other people no longer interest me; B – other people mostly interest me less than before; C – other people interest me just as they did before; D - other people are always very interesting to me. The depression questionnaire obtained a satisfactory level of reliability: first, based on the result correlation in two parts of the scales (odd and even items) corrected by Spearman-Brown's formula: for depressed participants it was $r$ =.91 and for students $r$ =.82; and second, on the basis of the internal consistency coefficient calculation (Cronbach's alpha), for depressed participants $\alpha$ =.84, as well as for students. Univariate indicators for individual samples were identified: soldiers (*M* = 43.96, *SD* = 9:50), students (*M* = 44.16, *SD* = 7.31), wounded (*M* = 46.51, *SD* = 8.10), and depressed persons (*M* = 62.62, *SD* = 9.69). This research also obtained a satisfactory level of internal consistency reliability, which was $r$ =.88.

## Measuring Pavlov's CNS Properties

Because of difficulties in determining the fundamental characteristics of the nervous system in laboratory measures (Ippolitov, 1972; Strelau, 1972, 1983a; Tadinac, 1988) and the unsatisfactory metric characteristics of the first questionnaire measure of temperament in Pavlovian terms - STI (Strelau, Angleitner, Bantelmann & Ruch, 1990; Tadinac Babić, Kulenović & Ledinski, 1989), there is a need for constructing a new questionnaire. Consequently, Pavlov's temperament questionnaire was designed (Strelau, Angleitner & Newberry, 1999) with the primary objective to evaluate Pavlov's fundamental temperament qualities and a cross-cultural comparison of these traits. The authors believe that the constructs, which should be measured by this questionnaire, are universal because they are features of neural characteristics.

Fundamental CNS properties: strength of excitation (SE), strength of inhibition (SI), and mobility (MO) are operationalized with regards to the individual's ability to adapt to environmental conditions, and they can be recognized in all types of behaviors including motor response, verbal actions, and emotional reactions (Strelau, 1983a; Strelau et al., 1999). SE refers to the ability to withstand very intense and/or prolonged stimulations without reducing the intensity of the response or appearance of behavioral disorders. SI manifests itself as the ability to terminate a behavior if needed, and to restrain from any behavior and reaction when circumstances demand so. MO refers to the ability to quickly and adequately respond to environmental changes. Until today, nineteen different language versions of the questionnaire have been constructed.

For the purpose of this research, the Croatian version was used (*Pavlovijanski upitnik temperamenta*; Lučev, Tadinac Babić, & Tatalović, 2002), which was the result of the translation from English into Croatian of the initial form of the questionnaire, *Pavlovian Temperament Survey* (PTS; Strelau et al., 1999), which originally contained 252 items. After applying the translated questionnaire on a sample of $N = 414$ participants who varied in age, gender, and education, as recommended by the original authors (Strelau et al, 1999), the final version was formed from those particles which showed the best psychometric features on the construction sample. So the applied PTS contains a total of 69 items (23 items for each subscale) and includes the defining components of three scales.

Typical items for individual subscales are: a) for the subscale of Strength of excitation: "I like very demanding tasks," b) for the subscale of Strength of inhibition: "I can conceal my anger when necessary," c) for the subscale of Mobility: "When my job changes, I quickly adapt to the situation." Items are answered by circling one of the offered answers, where participants evaluate to which extent individual claims relate to them on a Likert's type scale: 1 (does not refer to me) to 4 (fully refers to me). The result in each subscale is obtained by summarizing the responses depending on which scale a particular response belongs, as shown in the validation study (Lučev et al., 2002). Satisfactory reliability coefficients of internal consistency type were obtained on the constructional and validation sample (Lučev, Tadinac, & Tatalović Vorkapić, 2006) also in this study, as can be seen in Table 3.

*Table 3. Reliability coefficients of internal consistency for the constructional (N = 414) and validation (N = 463) samples (adapted from Lučev et al, 2006, p. 38), and on the sample in this study (N = 54)*

| PTS | Sample Type in Research | | |
|---|---|---|---|
| | **With the Purpose of Construction** | **With the Purpose of Validation** | **This Research** |
| SE | 0.87 | 0.80 | 0.86 |
| SI | 0.81 | 0.79 | 0.78 |
| MO | 0.88 | 0.83 | 0.89 |

## Measuring Behavioral Variables: General Characteristics of Respondents

Sight problems, coffee consumption, smoking, taking medication, consumption of alcohol, consumption of illegal drugs and engaging in sports activities are the variables based on whose controlling it is possible to systematically control, firstly, evoked brain potentials and, secondly, the relation between evoked potentials and temperament and basic dimensions of personality in this study. The criteria of relevance of certain variables is created on the basis of a large number of previous studies that dealt with the biological determinants of brain evoked potentials (Polich & Kok, 1995).

In the Questionnaire about general information, in addition to questions about the basic data required for a pre-selection of participants (code, gender, age, study year, and hand dominance), 7 additional questions were included to which the participants could respond by circling one of the answers, YES or NO. The remaining 7 questions were related to the existing sight problems, frequency of coffee consumption, frequency of smoking, use of any medications, frequency of alcohol consumption, consumption of illegal drugs, and engagement in sports activities. Considering the importance of the effect, which illegal drugs and medications have on the body, questions were formulated in relation to the last 30 days in questions about medication, and the last 15 days considering the consumption of illegal drugs. Data which were collected with the *Questionnaire of general data* are shown in the respondents' characteristics.

## Recording of Evoked Brain Potentials: N1, P2, N2, P3, and Sw

Evoked brain potentials (N1, P2, N2, P3, and Sw) were recorded by applying the task of simple discrimination stimuli in the visual modality, i.e. before applying the described visual oddball paradigm (Picton, Bentin, Berg, Donchin, Hillyard, Johnson, Miller, Ritter, Ruchkin, Rugg & Taylor, 2000). Tasks in which the participants needed to discriminate stimuli based on their physical characteristics are most commonly used while measuring brain evoked potentials, therefore it was also applied in this study. A task was chosen in the visual modality with regards to the basic characteristics of the measuring instrument, and better ability to capture cleaner EP-waves with reduced interference (with auditory tasks of simple discrimination, noise is more frequent during recording with respect to the visual task). The two stimuli in a random series are presented during the task with one or two, which are relatively infrequent.

The participants had to distinguish between two images by reacting to a target stimulus (e.g. mental counting of the signals in series or out loud, pressing a pushbutton, etc.) and by not responding to a standard stimulus (those images that were common and those that the participant was instructed to ignore). As the participant is actively focused on the visual oddball task, changes are recorded in the action potential of activated cortical neurons. These changes are recorded with electroencephalographic standardized equipment, which differs from the classical electroencephalograph (EEG) in terms of detecting those electrical changes or brain waves, which are time related to a given task; in this case the visual modality task, as it is previously explained. In this study MEDELEC/TECA *Sapphire$^{II}$* 4E, Vickers Medical was used for measuring electromyography data and evoked brain potentials (EMG/EP) with appropriate electrodes and needed supplies.

## *Device for Evoked Potential Measuring*

The device used to measure electromyography data and evoked brain potentials (EMG/EP), MEDELEC/TECA *Sapphire$^{II}$* 4E, Vickers Medical, consists of the following components: major components *Sapphire$^{II}$* - computer (dBASE IV) monitor with keyboard and internal printer (HP Laserjet III); four-channel preamplifier and amplifier; primary and secondary power lines; video stimulator consisting of a television monitor for displaying visual stimuli; and electrodes. The main component *Sapphire$^{II}$* represents the computer equipment with a monitor, keyboard, and internal printer (HP Laserjet III), as presented at Figure 1.

The overall Sapphire system is designed in accordance with IEC601-1, the international standard for medical electrical equipment from the well-known company MEDELEC Ltd. That mentioned standard guarantees that every person, who is being recorded for evoked potentials, as well as the one that is recording, is protected against electric shocks, and includes protection against any possible contacts with water or flammable anesthetic mixtures with air/oxygen. It contains a unit for averaging ISO9002 with additional equipment that includes a 12-bit AD converter that makes 1000 conversions on each channel. Its program parameters are stored in NV RAM and software in a PROM pack. The built-in *Sapphire$^{II}$* system software consists of convertible programs EXP2DBF and READMFF, and is compatible with MS-DOS.

The keyboard is used to access the initial framework for the application of a specific test, where one of the offered is selected: in this study, with regards to the before mentioned criteria, the visual P300 test was used, i.e. the visible oddball paradigm that includes the production of EP-waves that occur

*Figure 1. MEDELEC/TECA Sapphire$^{II}$ 4E: portable part with a keyboard and screen with visible EP-waves (older version of the Device for recording EMG/EP adapted from the website: https://www.admarneuro.com/used-emg-ncs-ep-systems)*

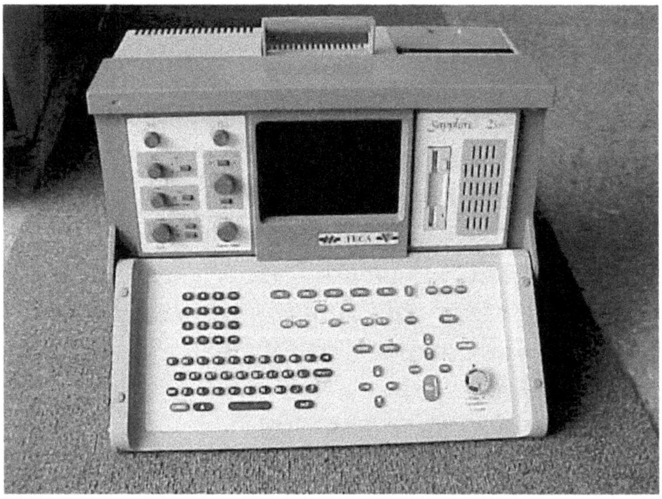

before P300, including that wave. During the task, recorded brain waves that occur in response to target stimuli on 4 channels can be seen on the screen of the displayed transmission part: $Ch^1$ = electrode O1, $Ch^2$ = electrode O2, $Ch^3$ = electrode P3, and $Ch^4$ = electrode P4, which indicate certain places of positioned electrodes.

These responses take the form of a continuous brain activity that is separate from the background EEG noise (rejection of artifacts is included), and it is time related to a given external stimulus. The display is visible in the form of the before mentioned time-window, which represents the standard form for recording evoked potentials in the studies that are researching them. The printed form of individual EP-waves represents the average values of their amplitude and latency in the first series of recordings, and in the second series of recordings, which ultimately comes down to 8 maximum target stimuli (a total of 16 target stimuli through two series of recordings), while the maximum number of non-target stimuli varies. An example of such a non-labeled image result on visual oddball paradigm can be seen in Figure 2.

4-channel preamplificr has the purpose of reinforcing the EP, i.e. brain responses to set stimuli, and a simultaneous reduction of EEG background activity. Its lines are on the back of the device. Electrode lines attached to the participant's head are connected to these four lines of the pre-amplifier, which is connected with the main Sapphire component, more specifically,

*Figure 2. Image example of unmarked average EP-waves (N1, P2, N2, P3, and Sw) in response to target stimuli on one of the research participant during the visual oddball paradigm on 4 channels: Ch[1] = electrode O1, Ch[2] = electrode O2, Ch[3] = electrode P3, and Ch[4] = electrode P4*

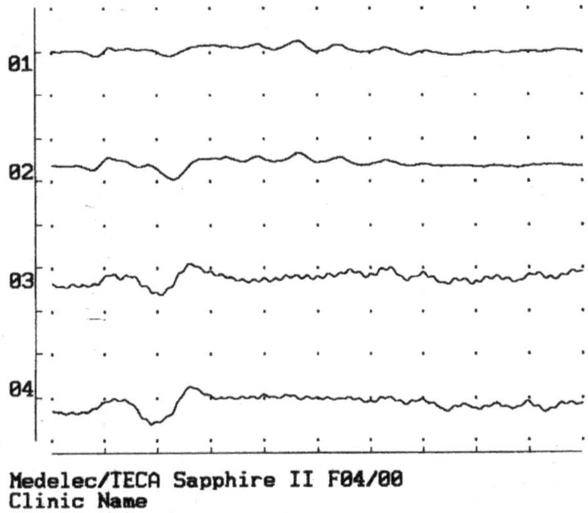


with the amplifier and filters. Recorded waves are digitally filtered (DC to 10 kHz), while maintaining resistance of less than 6kΩ. An extremely critical electrophysiological parameter is a recording time limit or time constant. Since the aim of this recording was to include both the exogenous and endogenous compounds in the visual modality, and the first have a relatively low frequency (~ 3 Hz) in contrast to the second, it was necessary to make the low filter as low as possible (Polich, 1998, 1999) in order not to distort their slow-wave activity. The criteria for recording exogenous components are not as high, given that it has already been mentioned that exogenous components are more visible, easier to capture, and harder to disrupt by some factors other than those related to stimuli features, which is not the case with endogenous components. Basic parameters set to record visible EP-waves (N1, P2, N2, P3, PV) are as follows: 4 active channels; sensitivity of 50-100μV; low filter = 0.1Hz, and high filter = 50Hz.

Major and minor electrical lines include all the power lines needed to carry out tests and EP-recordings intended for this device. The main electrical line that connects the main Sapphire component and voltage supply is also at the back of the device, next to the main switch. On the side and on the back of the device are all secondary lines: electrical lines to connect with the stimulators and electrical lines for the video monitor, headphones, external keyboard, external printer, preamplifier, output for display on a monitor on the video, and so on. The printer that is most commonly used is the internal type from Hewlett Packard LaserJet III series, and is also located on the back of the device. Information is recorded in two basic forms: pictorial, as can be seen in Figure 2, and digital, only after the procedure of manual labeling of the measured wave that can be viewed later on the monitor.

Video-stimulator (625 lines, 50 Hz): television monitor for presenting visual stimuli is connected with the main Sapphire component with one of the side cables. Monitor dimensions are 25.8 x 19.5 cm. According to a predefined ratio, it shows common/rare visual stimuli in the form of a chessboard. A red circle in the diameter of 1cm is glued in the center of the screen. Other data are visible on the display of measurement parameters of the visual oddball paradigm.

### Electrodes and Consumables

In order for each electrode to register the activity of certain brain areas, and to thereby avoid a different distance between the electrodes, the International EEG Federation has recommended the application of the nowadays very famous 10-20 system of electrodes arrangement (Šantić, 1995; Nuwer, Comi, Emerson, Fuglsang-Frederiksen, Güerito, Hinrichs, Ikeda, Luccas & Rappelsburger, 1998; Picton et al., 2000), in which the distance between the electrodes is set to 10%, 20%. The electrodes are identified by the initial letters of Latin names of those brain parts over which they are located, capital letters for main regions (F-frontal, T-temporal, P-parietal, and O-occipital lobe, C-central crease), and lowercase letters for a precise localization of electrodes. Odd numbers refer to the location on the left side of the skull, even numbers on the right side of the skull, and the central level is marked with the letter z (zero).

The entire 10-20 construction includes 19 electrodes, which are typically added to another two, to record eye movements with the aim of controlling EOG-artifacts (Faber, 1980). In order to record EP-waves (N1, P2, N2, P3, Sw) of visual modality, according to the used device characteristics, a narrowed set of five electrodes is standardly used according to a predefined arrangement of electrodes shown in Figure 3. Active electrodes are placed on O1 and O2, referent to P3 and P4, and grounding on Fz. Types of electrodes that were used in this study are surface-silver chloride electrodes (Ag-AgCl), which at its end have a double coating and fine silver composition for the minimum artifact. This type of electrode is most frequently used in practical and research studies of collecting electroencephalographic data, because it ensures the highest possible reliability, quality, and consistency. Other

*Figure 3. Arrangement of used electrodes to record the visual P300-wave according to the International 10-20 EEG system*
*Source: (adapted from Novalić, 1991)*

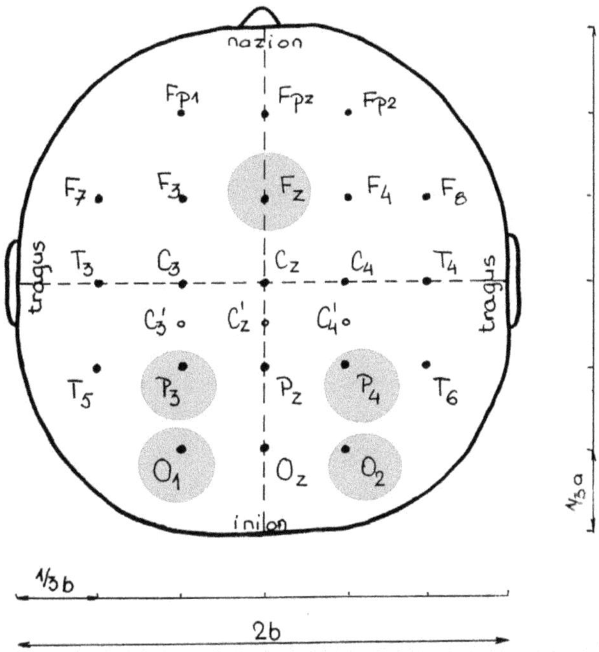


consumable material types that are used in research are related to the EEG contact paste - EC2 Grass electrode paste, cotton wool, disinfectant liquid, and medical white adhesive tape.

## Measuring Parameters of the Visual Oddball Paradigm

There is a large number of paradigms that cause evoked brain potential. Most often, excitation is caused by the application of a simple discrimination task, the so-called oddball task. In this task, two stimuli are presented in a random series with one or two which are relatively infrequent. The audio version of this task uses two different tones, the inter-stimulus interval of few seconds with a target stimulus, which is given less frequently than the non-target (standard) stimulus. Participants are asked to distinguish between the two tones by reacting to the target stimulus (e.g. mental counting of the signals in a series, pressing a push button) and by not reacting to standard stimuli. This measurement procedure is used to study a series of basic constructs in the information processing field as it was mentioned before (Polich, 1998, 1999, Picton et al, 2000), and it represents the most commonly used paradigm to obtain clinical and regulatory age information, while the oddball paradigm is an internationally accepted term for the task of simple stimuli discrimination regardless of its modality. Considering the relevant methodological variations on the theme, also, only in the auditory modality, evoked potentials can be induced by detection of target stimuli of the most different kind, for example, the rare changes in the stimuli intensity, tone level, tones in the word context, the before mentioned "clicks" in the context of sonic bangs, etc. Although the oddball paradigm is a relatively simple task, its research applications requires specific considerations that are related to: stimuli characteristics; task factors; participant's variables; electrophysiological recording methods; and measurement procedures, but not only research ones.

In the oddball task, which has been applied in this work, two stimuli are presented in a random series with one or two, which are relatively infrequent. The audio version of this task uses two different tone, while the visual version uses two different images, inter-stimulus interval of a few seconds, with a target stimulus which is presented less frequently than the non-target (standard) stimulus. Participants are asked to distinguish between the two tones by reacting to the target stimulus (e.g. mental counting of the signal in a series, pressing a push button) and not responding to the standard stimulus.

The most common default visual stimulations are inducing ERP components by: a) changing the brightness (luminance) using the strobe or flash patterns (only VEP); b) by chessboard stimuli or grids (with constant brightness, there are two possible ways of stimulation: changing the contrast between dark and bright parts of the sample or, inverse changes of dark and bright parts of the sample (only VEP); chessboard sample inversions are used to cause P300-components which vary according to the size and slope of the chessboard, and the grid pattern, which varies in size, shape, and slope of the grid), the participant has the task of counting those checkerboard patterns that are infrequent in stimulation series; c) the appearance of a checkerboard

*Figure 4. Reduced image of two visual stimuli types given in the visual oddball paradigm: the left is non-target and the right is the target stimulus on the chessboard*

with a gray background/disappearance of the chessboard in a gray background; d) counting stimuli based on: color, form, semantic category, or a combination (e.g. "In a stimuli series, drawn dogs and cats will be presented. Silently count (or press a push button) only when you see cats" (Beijsterveldt et al., 1996a; Baal, Geus & Boomsma 1997).

EP-waves (N1, P2, N2, P3, and Sw) are induced with a visual task of simple discrimination by applying a reversible chessboard, which is shown in Figure 4 (above non-target stimuli, below target stimuli). Induction of the P300 component with an alternating chessboard includes binocular stimulation of the entire participants' view field. Stimuli were presented on a black and white television monitor, in its full size. Participant's distance from the monitor is 70 cm and it is considered that an appropriate size of one chessboard is approximately 35' of the view field, because mostly size of 159 (3 mm to 70 cm) to 1° of the view angle is applied, making the size of the whole chessboard 5.2 degrees of the participant's view field (Dabić-Jeftić & Mikula, 1994a).

## Registering Evoked Potentials

Evoked potentials are the record of the size and change of differences in the electrical potential between two points on the surface of the head or body in a certain time interval. This electric potential difference is known as voltage, and the same is measured by a voltmeter between two points. As described above, the standard EEG method is used with the International EEG 10-20 system. Brain voltage observed in only one of its parts has no significant meaning. Only a simultaneous registration of the brain voltage with its various areas has diagnostic significance, as it has already been described before. The difference between the EEG and EP method is that the EP method allows a reduced number of applied electrodes on the surface of the head that are sufficient to record certain evoked potentials, as it was the case in this study.

There are three basic evoked potentials measures: amplitude, latency, and duration. The amplitude can be measured in three ways: a) from the tip of the wave orthogonal to the baseline (baseline - is determined by the potential difference recorded at the time of setting the stimulus); b) from the top of one peak to another peak; c) as surface determined by the wave and baseline. The first two are used most commonly. On the other hand, the latency measure refers to the time interval between the stimuli and certain points on the wave (usually this point it at the top of the wave spike), and it is also called absolute latency or implicit time. Inter-wave or inter-peak latency is determined by the time interval between two peaks. Finally, the wave duration is the time interval that determines the beginning and end of a wave at baseline.

*Table 4. Review of the test's measuring parameters and their values stored in the Sapphire[II] device for measuring evoked potentials*

| Measuring Parameters | Values |
|---|---|
| Active channels | Channel 1 Channel 2 Channel 3 Channel 4 |
| Sensitivity | 50 μV 50 μV |
| Low filter | 0,1 Hz 0,1 Hz |
| High filter | 50 Hz 50 Hz |
| Speed of stimulus appearance | 1s 1s |
| Stimulus form | Visual stimulation |
| Stimulus repetition level | 0,5 |
| Stimulus retention | 1s |
| Data storage form | Averaging |
| Averaging form | Exponential algorithm with automatic compensation |
| Number of target stimuli | 8 |
| Data display | Averaging |
| Artefacts rejection | Automatic/included |
| Rejection level | 5 x sensitivity |
| Stimulus type | Visual |
| Stimulation type | Binocular |
| Total number of target stimuli (2 series) | 16 |
| Contrast | 100% |
| Probability of EP appearance | 15% |
| Total number of non-target stimuli (2 series) | 64 |
| Video stimulator | 625 lines, 50Hz |
| EP labelling method | Manual |
| Principle of calculation and labelling of EP-amplitudes | From tip to tip of a wave |
| Principle of calculation and labelling of EP-latencies | Absolute latency to wave tip |
| Principle of calculation and labelling of EP-domain | 1-3 |

Source: (Sapphire[II] User Manual, 1996)

For example, the amplitude of the tip-to-tip P300-component can exceed 10 microvolts. It is believed that its latency varies between 210 milliseconds to 550 milliseconds after the provided stimulus. However, although the amplitude and latency of the P300-component vary, as long as its distribution on the surface of the head is constant, it is the same component (Donchin, 1979). Although questionable (Roth, 1978; according to Pritchard, 1981), this setting is generally accepted in the P300-wave research.

The problem of the before mentioned common signal changes in amplitude and latency during recording is solved in the way that evoked potentials are initially filtered, and then summarized by the computer software, to get an unbiased measure of the amplitude size that all recorded waves strive to achieve, and the standard deviation gives a direct measure of amplitude dispersion. In this way it was observed that the greater the range of spike-waves latencies that are summarized and the amplitude is the same, the lower amplitude and greater the duration of the summarized wave. The review of the test's measuring parameters and their values stored in the Sapphire$^{II}$ device for measuring evoked potentials are presented in the Table 4 (Sapphire$^{II}$ User Manual, 1996).

## *Averaging Technique*

As described before, it is known that the brain is permanently active and that its basic activity (EEG) has a significantly predominant size when compared with the size of evoked brain potentials. The possibility of their reading is reflected in the fact that the averaging technique involves "pulling out" of the recorded ERA from the EEG background noise (Gaussian random with arithmetic mean zero), while recording a series of event evoked impulse responses with the same waveform that occurs at the same time after the induced stimuli (Šantić, 1995; Nishida, Nakamura & Shibasaki, 1999). Therefore, repeating the excitatory situation and EEG epochs, the voltage of this response will exceed the background EEG noise and will appear as a "clean" signal, i.e. ERP. If the sinusoidal waves (as EEG waves) outside the phase add to their opposite values relative to their positive and negative amplitudes (a and b), this result is the zero amplitude. Furthermore, if the EEG signal is recorded after the repeating the assigned stimuli, the EEG signal will accidentally occur outside of this phase, and will consequently result as zero. ERP is not random with respect to each stimuli assignment, and by repeating it, each repeated EEG response will be "added" (averaged) to the previous positive and negative ERP wave spikes.

With this process, therefore, the ERP signal stands out from the total electrical activity, and is based on the fact that the brain electrical response always follows after the expiration of equal time after the stimulus. Simple computers are used for averaging that calculate the average value of the new data obtained after the assigned stimuli and data obtained from previous stimuli, which are stored in the memory of the averaging device. This process continues until the form of the ERP wave is clear. It is important to keep in mind that a certain amount of information is lost with the averaging method. Another problem associated with the tip wave analysis refers to the fact that, very often, the ERP components are not arranged in a precisely determined sequential manner, but overlap in varying degrees to form a broad complex. This problem is usually solved by calculating the arithmetic mean of ERP amplitudes within that time period that is of interest in such research. An alternative statistical method is called the window analysis, which uses a time sample in addition to all recorded untransformed ERP data, as an additional factor in ANOVA, within which the calculated difference significance of ERP components is tested by using interaction with the time variable and the factor of recording conditions.

The application of this method has showed a significant sensitivity degree for identification of different curves, even in very small ERP components (Hoormann et al., 1998). Furthermore, although it has been found that application of auditory oddball paradigm is the most practical because the measured evoked potential is more easily visible and takes less averaging procedures to obtain a crystalized wave, equally well applicable is the visual oddball paradigm as it is possible to control the ocular artifacts and to apply the existing parameters for recording evoked potentials caused by the alternating chessboard. The visual oddball paradigm is used in this work since the existence of the effect of habituation has been found in the auditory modality of the oddball paradigm that interferes with possible differences in evoked potentials, especially with the cognitive components in extroverts and introverts, which is maintained equal in the visual modality.

A formula for exponential averaging is used in the averaging process, where the new average value is gained from the ratio of the registered average values in the numerator multiplied by the ratio of the maximum target stimuli number reduced by one and the maximum target stimuli number, and data from the new target stimuli multiplied by the maximum target stimuli number in the denominator. This formula is schematically shown in Figure 5.

*Figure 5. Formula scheme for averaging*
*Source: (Sapphire[II] User Manual, 1996)*

$$NAV = \frac{RAV \times \{n-1/n\}}{NTP/n}$$

Legend:
RAV - registered averaged value
NAV - new averaged value
NTP - data from the new target stimuli
n - the maximum number of target stimuli

This averaging is characterized by calculating the average value of EP-waves amplitude and latency (N1, P2, N2, P3, and Sw) after reaching the maximum number of target stimuli, which in this study was 8. This algorithm is applied to the so-called automatic compensation option, whereby upon the occurrence of artifacts they become automatically rejected, whereupon they are prevented from entering in further process of calculating average evoked potentials values. This results in two basic values: average EP-wave amplitude and latency value (N1, P2, N2, P3, and Sw) of the first recording series and an average EP-wave amplitude and latency value (N1, P2, N2, P3, and Sw) of the second series of recordings.

## Procedures

At the Department of Psychology, Faculty of Humanities and Social Studies in Rijeka, psychology students of all study years ($1^{st}$, $2^{nd}$, $3^{rd}$, and $4^{th}$), were told in the introductory instruction that they will participate in research related to brain waves and mental activity that will be recorded using the EEG, under the technicians' and researchers' expert supervision, and that the students would be awarded getting a certain number of experimental hours as compensation for their participation in the research.

The general instructions read:

*My name is Sanja Tatalović Vorkapić and in the context of my doctoral thesis, I am conducting a research in all study years of psychology, including yours. The aim of this research is to determine the biological temperament basis and basic personality dimensions by measuring the evoked brain potential. One part of the test, with your cooperation, for which you will be rewarded with experimental hours, will be carried out now by filling out the self-evaluation questionnaire. The second part of the test will be carried out in one month, by recording evoked potentials at the Department of Neurology of the Clinical Hospital Center CHC Rijeka, according to a pre-arranged schedule. Considering that the testing is anonymous, please write to your password on the wrapper (I suggest date of birth so that the code would not be forgotten for the sake of a valid continuation of research), as well as on the envelope and on all questionnaires in the wrapper, except for the one that refers to the* Informed consent to participate in the research. *Hold that paper and store it inside the envelope. Take it home, read it and fill it out by using capital letters (on both sides). Please, bring this envelope with your password to the University in a month, when I will come again, provide you with feedback and guidance for the further course of the research. Due to the time interval between the first and second part of the research, I would kindly ask you to write a code that will be able to remember and save the envelope in a safe place to avoid losing it. Thank you. Now you can read each individual instruction and fill out the questionnaires.*

## First Part of the Testing: Application of the Self-Assessment Questionnaire and Classification of Participants

### *Questionnaire Application*

After reading the general instructions, envelopes with the General Information Questionnaire, EPQ-R/A, EPQ-IVE, PTS, D-92, the Informed consent to participate in research, and an Envelope were distributed to the students of each academic year. Statement of consent to participate in the psychological scientific research was created according to the instructions for dealing with ethical problems in conducting psychological research (Shaughnessy & Zechmeister, 1997). After carefully heard general instructions, the participants separated the statement of Informed consent to participate in the psychological scientific research, which they stored in their envelopes with a written code, and completed the self-evaluation questionnaires as described above. This part of the test lasted an average of 45-60 minutes.

### *Classification of Participants*

Before the second meeting with the research participants, all data collected in the first part of the research was statistically analyzed with the aim of creating the final sample for the study. As noted above, the criterion variables to create the final sample were based on the results of previous researches on their relation with evoked brain potentials, which are: a) gender; b) age; c) hand dominance; d) existing vision problems without correction; and e) the existence of any psychiatric/neurological diseases. Information about these participants' features were obtained by using a Questionnaire on general information, and based on its analysis all male participants were rejected from the initial sample of participants ($N = 91$), as well as all those who were not within the age range 19-23 years, and all left-handed participants. After this classification, it was found that $N = 62$ female participants would be involved in the second part of the test, which refers to the recordings of evoked brain potentials (8 participants gave up or refused to participate in the second part of the study during the recordings). Therefore, at the end of the second part of the research, $N = 54$ participants were involved, with the estimated right hand as the dominant hand, without the existence of any kind of psychiatric/neurological disease and with adequate visual correcting device in those participants who required it.

## Second Part of the Testing: EP Recording (N1, P2, N2, P3, and Sw)

EP recording (N1, P2, N2, P3, and Sw) followed at the Department of Neurology after the interval of one month had passed, once the self-evaluation questionnaires were completed. At the first meeting with the participants, they were told the following:

*Due to technical constraints and specific requirements of this research, which will be explained once the feedback on the research results are provided, those students whose codes I will now read will participate in the second part of the research. I would kindly ask you that, as I read your code, each of you individually tells me your phone number (home or cell phone), so that I can contact you about the arrival to the Department of Neurology according to a specified schedule over the next three months. Also, you will receive a paper with instructions on how to prepare for the recording of evoked brain potentials at the Department of Neurology. Every effort will be made so that you not need to be absent from your classes, and if overlaps should occur, it will be organized in agreement with your professors who will know the reason of your absence. Remember that upon arrival to the Department of Neurology you should bring your envelopes with the statement of Informed consent to participate in the psychological scientific research with printed codes that were used in this study. Thank you.*

After this, codes of all those participants who entered the final sample were read; their phone numbers collected and instructions for preparation before recording evoked potentials at the Department of Neurology were provided. Finally, it was mentioned that they would be contacted by phone from an indicated cell phone number of the researcher, most likely at the weekend, in order for them to have time to prepare for the recording over the coming week. Instructions for the preparation of EP recordings were: a) those participants who have reduced/damaged visual acuity (long-sightedness/myopia) should bring their glasses or contact lenses; b) participants should not consume food, coffee, and cigarettes 2 to 4 hours before the recording; c) participants should not have consumed alcohol 24 hours before the recording; d) participants should have clean, washed hair before the recording; e) participants should be preferably without any jewelry; f) participants should have a normal body temperature, and must be healthy, which excludes viruses, the flu or colds; g) participants should receive enough sleep before the recording; h) participants should not be affected by any medication/drugs.

The EP recordings at Department of Neurology in Rijeka were scheduled on Wednesdays from 11 am to 1 pm, and the schedule of the student's arrivals was random and did not interfere with their study commitments. As they were instructed, the students were informed during the weekends about their arrival schedule at the EP recording during the following week, and were reminded of the Instructions for the preparation and the Envelope with the declaration of Informed consent to participate in the research. If a particular student was prevented from coming to the recording for any reason, another student was randomly contacted. Therefore, recording the visual evoked potentials were conducted at the same time of the day: between 11 am and 1 pm; they were measured between 4-6 students a day, depending on the laboratory availability time that day, and the possibilities of the medical technician who conducted the recording.

### *Brain Evoked Potentials Measurements (N1, P2, N2, P3, and Sw).*

Every time after arriving at the Department of Neurology, and before entering the lab, all participants submitted their envelopes with the declarations of Informed consent to participate in the psychological scientific research. Then they were told that each individual recording would last approximately 20 to 30 minutes, in two consecutive series with a pause in the duration of approximately 1 to 2 minutes. It was up to the participants to decide in what order they would go into the laboratory for the recording, in which the medical technician and the researcher were waiting. The first participant entered at 11 am. Upon entering the laboratory, each participant said their code to the researcher, and was then told to put her personal belongings on the side of an extra bed. After that, it was checked that all jewelry/wristwatch was taken off, in case she brought some form of visual correction, if the cell phone was turned off, and if chewing gum was removed before recording.

After that, the medical technician gave all other information and instructions for recording to the participant. The participant was asked to sit on a movable chair in front of the monitor that was placed 70 cm away from her, and to sit comfortably on it. While sitting, she was given a pen to hold in her dominant hand and she was told to press the pen each time she noticed the target visual stimuli on the screen instead of pressing a push button. The medical technician then informed the participants to relax and sit still while the electrodes were put on the surface of the head, according to the previously defined parameters. The medical technician, who is specially trained to record evoked brain potentials, set 5 Ag-AgCl electrodes of surface type at equal intervals along the center line (set apart for 10% of the nasion-inion distance measured in the participants), which extend from inion to Fz, including Oz, Pz, and Cz. Before placing them, the technician used a cotton wool that had been soaked in alcohol to remove any dead skin and sweat from the surface of the head below the electrodes. Contact paste was used for contact between the electrode and the skin electrode.

The grounding electrodes– FZ was first to set, and then the reference electrodes on the locations P3 and P4, and active electrodes on the locations O1 and O2 at the end. Once the electrodes are set and fixed, electrode lines were connected, behind the participant sitting on the chair, to the four-channel preamplifier, through which the signal enters the filter prior to the defined characteristics to eliminate the noise. After filtration, the sample was converted to a digital form and was averaged with other samples. After that, the connection of the four-channel preamplifier was checked with the main component of the Sapphire$^{II}$ device, which was already included, as well as the connection of the monitor with the same main component. This was followed by the selection of the desired test to be carried out. Considering that the aim of this study was to record the waves N1, P2, N2, P3, and Sw in the visual modality, "Visual P300" was selected from the main menu.

The basic operating principle of this device, if the recording wants to capture any of the cognitive or later endogenous waves, is to choose precisely such a test because it would include all earlier exogenous components that occur. If the Visual N1 is selected, only N1 component would be recorded, which was not appropriate for this study. After the selected test, the "baseline" of participants was tested (review of the current electrical activity of the brain on the set electrode locations with no focus on the task, in the steady state, whereby impedance of the electrodes is tested, and it had to be less than 5 k). The main component of the Sapphire$^{II}$ device with a keyboard and the medical technician was placed behind the participant but to her left and the researcher was sitting next to the medical technicians, with minimal potential disruptions during the recordings. The room was quiet and the lights were dimmed.

After checking the participant's comfortability and readiness to participate in the task, the medical technician gave the following instruction:

*On the screen in front of you, a two types of chess fields will be turned on and off: chess field with larger and a chess field with smaller squares. The chess box with larger squares will be more likely to occur and does not require any task from you. But every time the chess field with smaller cubes appears, your job is to press the button once (i.e. to press the pen that you hold in your hand once). Please sit comfortably and quietly in your chair during the measurements, and look at the red dot in the middle of the screen in front of you. If you experience undue difficulty or something bothers you, please let us know before or at the end of the recording. Now we can start: first, we will show you what the two kinds of chess fields look like: with the larger and the smaller squares that you need to react to by pressing the pen, and then we will start with the recording, which will occur be in two consecutive series.*

After checking if the participant had understood the instructions, by displaying the target/non-target stimuli, the first series of recordings started, and after a few seconds the second series of visual stimuli started as well. After recording, the recorded data were stored in a separate document on the device's hardware, and on disks, so that they could be marked later.

### *Artifact Control*

Sapphire$^{II}$ device has a built in component that has already been indicated on the automatic rejection of all artifacts exceeding 5 x sensitivity. Given that it was necessary to monitor eye movements, because they may be time-related to stimuli (especially the target stimuli), a distribution field of eye movements can cover those places with active electrodes, as it was done. Also, other possible sources of extra-cranial artifacts (cranial muscles, tongue) were monitored. Therefore, throughout the examination, 8 artifacts were discarded in only three participants, and are shown in Table 5.

### *Behavioral Data*

Participants' answers to assigned visual stimuli during a defined period of time were recorded with an adequate computer program. Files were created within the same operating system for each measurement isolating the target and non-target stimuli. Processing was performed only on the target stimuli for each participant in both tests.

### *Statistical Data Processing*

Averaging the recorded data is a method that makes it easier to observe and calculate the average EP value and the latency and amplitude, but which loses a certain amount of information. Since this procedure is carried out automatically, due to laboratory equipment, the result after completing the recording and storage of recorded amplitude and latency of evoked potentials is the average EP-wave. After recording and storing images of the recorded amplitude and latency of the P300-wave for each participant, automatic averaging of recorded data was carried out (method of calculating the average value of the P300 latency and amplitude, but which also loses some information) separately for each series of recordings with a previously described artifact rejection. Three basic measures of recorded evoked potentials, amplitude, latency, and wave area (length), were manually marked and according to the suggestions that are explained in the manual compatible to the laboratory equipment (Sapphire$^{II}$ User Manual, 1996).

### EP-Wave Amplitude

The analysis of the measure amplitude peak includes two procedures: the first is determined by the EP segment for each recorded peak in that time window in which the participant was exposed to stimuli; 2) the peak of that/those of EP-components that are of research interest are determined, according to the criteria that were set before the study. As for this study, the following EP-waves were measured: N1, P2, N2, P3, and Sw, so in manual labeling it is started from the wave N1-negative polarity and latency between 80 and 100 milliseconds; over the P2-wave of positive polarity and latency between 170 and 200 milliseconds; over the N2-wave of negative polarity and latency stationary point after 200 milliseconds; to the P3-wave positive polarity and latency stationary point after 300 milliseconds (possible range of 250-600 milliseconds), and a slow-wave expected latency after 1 second and the duration of about 3-4 seconds. This analysis was carried out under the assumption that the baseline is the same for all EP components, which is questionable, and as such it is neutral, which is very difficult to achieve in the reality of measurements (Hoormann, Falkenstein, Schwarzenau & Hohnsbein, 1998). In this study, the measuring of the EP amplitude was performed from the peak of one wave to the peak of another, for which a number of previous studies have consider it the most appropriate means in terms of the real EP-amplitude display and the smallest loss (Sapphire$^{II}$ User Manual, 1996).

*Table 5. Number of discarded artifacts in this study in three participants*

| Participants Code | Discarded Artifacts Number |
|---|---|
| M.LO | 3 |
| TOPAZ | 1 |
| 1405 | 4 |
| **TOTAL** | **8** |

### EP-Wave Latency

The latency measure denotes the time interval between the stimuli and certain points on the wave, i.e. that point that marks the peak of the wave spike, also called absolute latency or implicit time. This method of EP latency measuring is applied in this study, because the other two methods (other types of absolute latency between the stimuli and the point at the beginning of the wave and not on the peak, and inter-wave/interspecific latency or delta latency - determined by time interval of two peaks whose computation depends on the used algorithm) are considered less representative of the true P300-latency representation (Sapphire[II] User Manual, 1996).

### EP-Wave Area (Duration)

Wave area/duration refers to the time interval determined by the beginning and end of the wave to the baseline, and monitor display. During the recording, it has two meanings: first, wave negativity located above the baseline, second wave positivity located below the baseline. In addition, the amplitude of the peak-to-peak of a particular EP-wave, for example, a P3-wave, can exceed 10 microvolts. It is believed that its latency varies between 210 milliseconds to 550 milliseconds after assigning a stimulus. However, although the amplitude and latency of P300 components vary, as long as its distribution at the head surface is constant, it is the same component (Donchin, 1979), which is generally accepted in EP research.

### Manual P300-Wave Labeling

EP labeling, as the very EP recording, is generally conditioned by the technical (im)possibilities of the applied device for recording evoked potentials. It may be: 1) computer digitized, i.e. automatically-electronically, where the recorded and averaged images automatically digitize with a pre-defined computer program, which is part of the recording device, while the numerical values and the corresponding amplitude and latency of EP-waves are calculated; or 2) manually (carried out by trained medical technician(s). With manually marking, which was carried in this study, after the recording of one or several series of oddball paradigms of any modality, whereby averaging the EP waves was automatic, an image file that looks unmarked is stored in a computer database for subsequent labeling. After that, the medical technician marked all recorded evoked potentials, separately for each series of recordings, for each participant according to predetermined definition of latency and amplitude of the recorded evoked potentials: N1, P2, N2, P3, and Sw. An example of such labeling is presented in Figure 6, which shows

*Figure 6. Example of labeling brain waves during the visual oddball paradigm with one participant (right: unmarked wave, left: marked wave)*

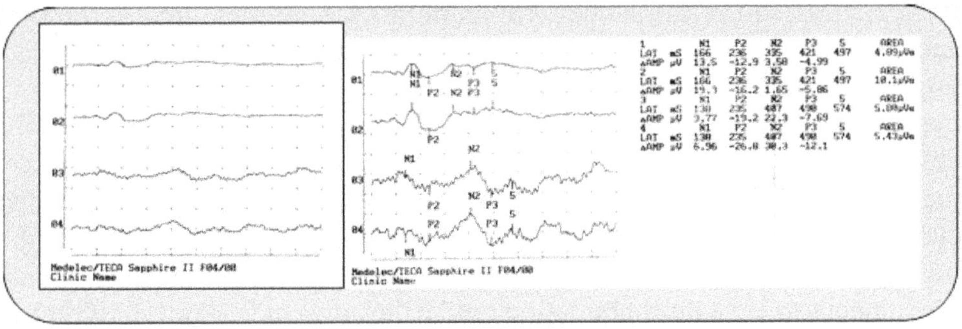


the above-unmarked averaged wave and below the same but marked, more sharpened, averaged wave of the same participant.

Thus, the medical technician who conducted the recording of evoked potentials, marked the first evoked potential N1 of one of the participants on a stored image file from the first series of recording with the cursor on the keyboard, based on the amplitude tip, which would automatically show the latency of the same components. After that, she repeated the procedure with the next EP component, in this case P2, then N2, and P3, and finally the slow wave. In conclusion, in the first series of recordings the amplitude peak was the basic principle of marking the recorded evoked potentials and their latencies. Applying the principle of EP-labeling has a drawback that is reflected in the so-called significant latency jitter of the recorded EP components (Coles, Gratton, Kramer & Miller, 1986; Hoormann et al., 1998), which is caused by factors such as fluctuations in the level of arousal and focused effort on the participant's task between different series of recordings, and is much higher in the later components, such as the P300 and slow wave. What can occur in such a situation is a quite difficult identification of the EP-amplitude peak and it is therefore often replaced with the peaks of the background EEG or noise. To avoid such errors that have resulted from the application of the amplitude peaks principle in labeling EP-latencies, it is recommended to apply the Woody's filter method (Woody, 1967), which transforms the EP-components recorded in the unique periods into a constant form by applying a complex cross-correlation. Precisely with the aim of maintaining a constant form of the recorded evoked potentials, a method of keeping the EP latency constant was applied in this study to indicate EP-waves in the second series of recordings. Latencies for each recorded evoked potential were the same in both recording series, as they were measured only in the first series of recordings and in the second, they served as a constant in labeling EP-waves.

In contrast to the EP-latency, EP-amplitudes were measured in the first and second series of recordings. In addition to the primary reason for setting the EP-latency constant while labeling evoked potential recording in the second series, which relates to the technical limitation of the used EP device and education of other medical technicians, it is important to mention the second, not less important reason. A visual inspection of the recorded evoked potentials in the first and second series of recording found that the peaks in EP-amplitudes had very similar or almost identical latencies, which are subject to a very low habituation unlike the amplitude (Polich, 1989; Lin & Polich, 1999; Bruin et al., 2000). Although this method loses significant information about specific numerical values of EP latencies in the second series of recordings, in relation to all these reasons, it was the only possible way to obtain an objective measure of evoked potentials: N1, P2, N2, P3 and Sw in both recording series, for which it is recommended that they be implemented for easy identification of recorded evoked potentials (Polich, 1998).

In other studies, in which the same EP-maker was used, the same manual way of marking evoked potentials was applied (Soysal, Atacama, Atay, Altintas, Baybas & Arpaci, 1999; Soysal, Atay, Aysal, Ozturk, Altunkaynak, & Baybas Arpaci 2001; Saxena, Bhatia, Joshi, Garg & Tandon, 2001), although the trend and recommendations in EP-research in the world today are to use advanced technology that allows smaller measurement errors, and thereby, as a smaller influence of the human factor. Consequently, few authors have tried to reduce this possibility of measurement errors caused by human factor by using several technicians (3) for manual marking of the P300-wave (Dalebout & Robey, 1997), and used those markings, which had the highest agreement between the three technicians. In this research a larger number of labeling was not used for one reason - lack of medical staff that is trained to work with the used EP-device.

## RESULTS AND DISCUSSION

### Description and Correlation Analyses of Personality Traits and Evoked Brain Potentials

Since, previous research work has been included in the presentation and interpretation of the descriptive and correlation results of personality traits and visual evoked brain potentials, only summarized results will be presented here. The main discussion will be emphasized in the part about statistical procedures that have not been run until now, such as the factor analysis and hierarchical regression analysis.

Therefore, regarding the determined results on the personality traits: extraversion, neuroticism, psychoticism, social desirability, addiction, criminality, strength of excitation, strength of inhibition, mobility, impulsivity, adventurousness, empathy, and depression, it could be seen (Figure 7) that these mean values are similar to those determined in prior studies (Eysenck & Eysenck, 1994; Strelau, Angleitner & Newberry, 1999). These descriptives are presented in detail in previous papers regarding this particular study (Tatalović Vorkapić, Tadinac & Rudež, 2010; Tatalović Vorkapić & Tadinac, 2011a; Tatalović Vorkapić, Tadinac & Lučev, 2013; Tatalović Vorkapić, 2014a; Tatalović Vorkapić, 2015; Tatalović Vorkapić & Tadinac, 2016).

Similarly, summarized descriptives of evoked brain potentials' latencies (Figure 8), amplitudes from the first trial (Figure 9), and amplitudes from the second trial (Figure 10) are presented here. Regarding the determined means, basic evoked brain potentials' parameters are within the expected range. A

*Figure 7. Means of personality traits (extraversion, neuroticism, psychoticism, social desirability, addiction, criminality, strength of excitation, strength of inhibition, mobility, impulsivity, adventurousness, empathy, and depression)*

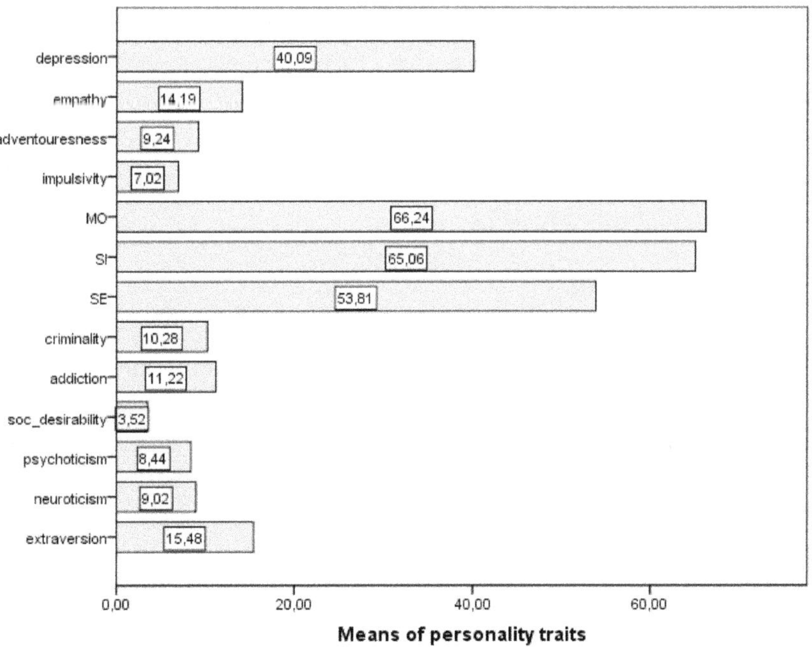

*Figure 8. Means of evoked brain potentials' latencies (evoked brain potentials: N1, P2, N2, P3 and Slow wave)*

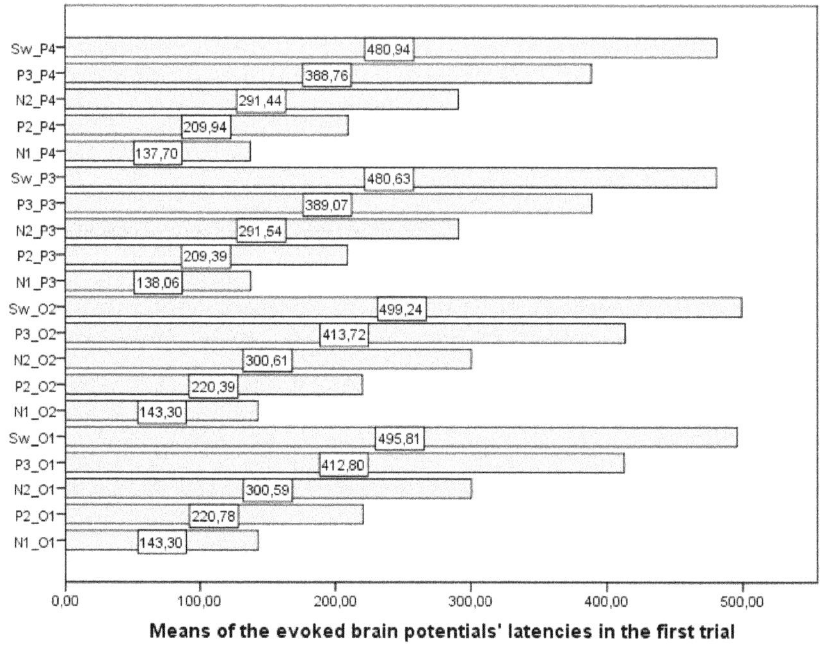


detailed description can be found in previous research (Tatalović Vorkapić, 2009; Tatalović Vorkapić, Tadinac & Rudež, 2010; Tatalović Vorkapić & Tadinac, 2011a,b; Tatalović Vorkapić, Tadinac & Lučev, 2013; Tatalović Vorkapić, 2014a; Tatalović Vorkapić, 2015; Tatalović Vorkapić & Tadinac, 2016). In addition, as it could be observed in previous work, a habituation effect has been determined, which se necessary to emphasize due to the later discussion of determined results.

## Correlation Analyses

Analysis of calculated Pearson's correlation coefficients and their levels of significance in relation to the fundamental dimensions of Eysenck's personality dimensions, Strelau's CNS dimensions, impulsivity, adventure, empathy, social desirability, and depression with the measured latencies and amplitudes of evoked potentials on all electrodes (O1, O2, P3, and P4) in the first, and for EP-amplitudes in the second series of recording, has found a number of significant connections. Table 6 shows the results of the correlation analysis of personality traits with latencies of evoked brain potentials, and Tables 7

*Figure 9. Means of evoked brain potentials' amplitude from the first trial (evoked brain potentials: N1, P2, N2, P3 and Slow wave)*

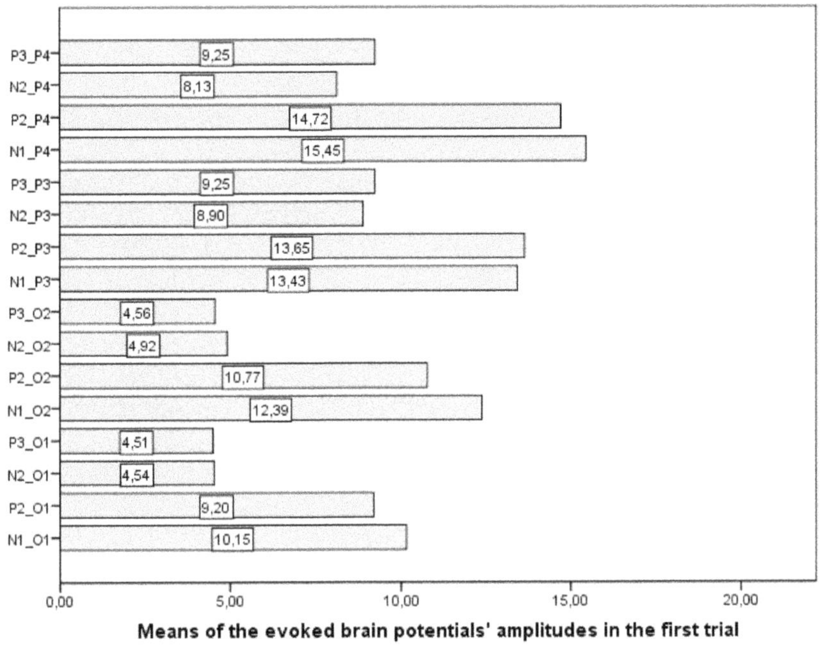


and 8 with amplitude of evoked brain potentials, while Table 7 shows the results of the first and Table 8 of the second measurement. Elevated levels of extraversion were found with a significantly shorter latency of slow-wave activity on all four electrodes, and a shorter latency P300 wave on parietal electrodes. Also, a little less consistent, but still significant, correlation on one parietal electrode was found in the elevated levels of psychoticism and shorter P3-latencies. No significant relations were found for the relationship between neuroticism and EP-latency.

Furthermore, it was found that higher levels of socially desirable responses are associated with significantly prolonged latencies and the N2-wave on all electrodes, and the P3- wave and slow-wave activity on parietal electrodes. A somewhat less consistent finding, but nevertheless significant, was determined in the relationship between depression and EP-latency, where a significant association has been determined between elevated depression and prolonged slow-wave latencies measured on parietal electrodes. Furthermore, with an increased level of addiction, significantly prolonged SW-latencies were observed on the parietal electrodes. As for adventurousness, as it was previously discussed in relation to the P3-latency (Tatalović Vorkapić, Tadinac

*Figure 10. Means of evoked brain potentials' amplitude from the second trial (evoked brain potentials: N1, P2, N2, P3 and Slow wave)*

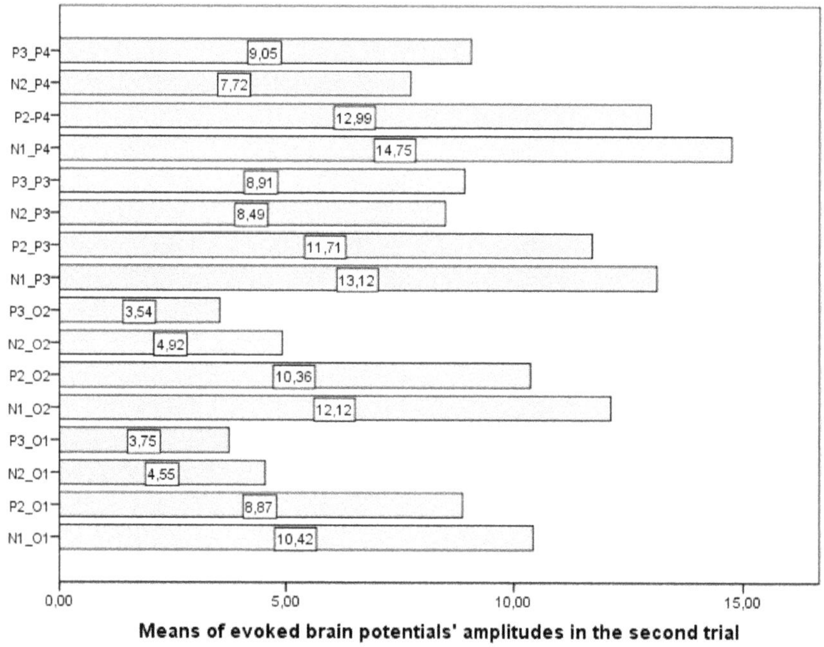


& Rudež, 2010), significantly shorter latencies of the P3-wave and the P2, N2, and slow wave latencies with a higher level of adventurousness. In other words, adventurousness has proved to be the most consistent and highest significant correlation with visual evoked potentials, which includes key components for early and late processing of information. Since this feature, operationalized within Eysenck's theory of personality as a sub-dimension of extraversion, could be most directly linked with the concept of Sensation Seeking Theory (Zuckerman, 1969), one of the basic guidelines for future research is to study the relationship of brain evoked potentials and personality operationalized within Zuckerman's theory (1969).

Given that, in addition to the significant association of adventurousness and latencies of evoked brain potentials, the correlation between social desirability and EP-latency has proved to be extremely significant, it is important to point out this finding. As it was pointed out in the previous article (Tatalović Vorkapić, 2015), significant positive correlations between N2-P3-Sw-latency on occipital and parietal electrodes and social desirability have been confirmed by previous findings on extended EP-latencies in providing socially desirable responses when self-assessment questionnaires are applied. This finding clearly points to the implications related to a possible improvement of those measurements that use self-assessment questionnaires, particularly in the context of measurements in personality psychology. In fact, given that lying requires more cognitive resources, which requires certain time span, it is possible to reduce the level of socially desirable responding with a limited time span during the completion of self-assessment questionnaires. But this is only a hypothesis that should be tested in future research (Tatalović Vorkapić, 2015). It is also important to bear in mind the mutually significant correlations of personality traits, which lead to a changed attitude with evoked brain potentials. In fact, starting from a holistic approach, these correlations analyses were carried out together with all personality traits and evoked potentials, considering that such an analysis has not been carried out so far in this study. However, these correlations are different when individual or group relationship of personality traits and evoked brain potentials is observed, which will later be noticed with regards to being able to predict each characteristic individually based on EPs.

When it comes to the analyzed relations between the EP amplitude and personality traits in the first series (Table 7) and second series recordings (Table 8), it is observable that the determined correlations are significantly smaller than what was expected in relation to the theoretical background. So, as has been pointed out in previous works (Tatalović Vorkapić, Tadinac & Rudež, 2010; Tatalović Vorkapić, Tadinac & Lučev, 2013), extraversion and tendency to socially desirable responses have not proved to have a significant connection with the measured EP-amplitudes, neither in the first nor in the second series of recordings.

On the other hand, impulsivity has showed a significant positive correlation with the N2-amplitude on the first occipital electrode and empathy a negative significant correlation also with the N2-component, but on the other parietal electrode. It is to be expected that impulsive individuals will exhibit a significantly higher extraction of stimuli characteristics and a selection of target stimuli during the selection task, which the N2-wave reflects, as well as that the fronto-central distribution of the N2-wave is commonly found in persons who experience empathy (Tatalović Vorkapić, 2011). However, an inconsistency of established correlations, i.e. a correlation recorded only on one electrode becomes questionable, and, as it has already been mentioned in previous works, the cause can be found in the characteristics of a monotonous task which is applied (Sternberg, 1994), given the determined effect of habituation (Tatalović Vorkapić, Tadinac & Rudež, 2010). Therefore, it is extremely important to conduct research that will vary in the task difficulty. Psychoticism, neuroticism, and depression showed a signifi-

*Table 6. Correlation coefficients and significant levels of personality traits and evoked brain potentials' latencies in the first trial (N1, P2, N2, P3 and Sw) on two occipital (O1 & O2) and two parietal (P3 & P4) electrodes*

| | Evoked Brain Potentials' Latencies From the First Trial | | | | | | | | | | | | | | | | | | | |
|---|---|---|---|---|---|---|---|---|---|---|---|---|---|---|---|---|---|---|---|---|
| | O1 Electrode | | | | | O2 Electrode | | | | | P3 Electrode | | | | | P4 Electrode | | | | |
| | N1 | P2 | N2 | P3 | SW | N1 | P2 | N2 | P3 | SW | N1 | P2 | N2 | P3 | SW | N1 | P2 | N2 | P3 | SW |
| EXT | -.091 | -.018 | -.052 | -.190 | **-.284*** | -.091 | -.015 | -.049 | -.202 | **-.290*** | -.087 | -.250 | -.197 | **-.306*** | **-.360**** | -.063 | -.258 | -.199 | **-.308*** | **-.353**** |
| | .515 | .897 | .711 | .168 | **.038** | .515 | .912 | .726 | .144 | **.033** | .533 | .069 | .153 | **.024** | **.008** | .649 | .060 | .148 | **.023** | **.009** |
| NEU | -.023 | -.151 | -.013 | -.034 | .092 | -.023 | -.148 | -.014 | -.056 | .082 | .028 | .101 | -.069 | .088 | .179 | .018 | .105 | -.070 | .090 | .179 |
| | .871 | .275 | .923 | .808 | .508 | .871 | .284 | .922 | .688 | .556 | .839 | .468 | .621 | .527 | .194 | .899 | .451 | .616 | .520 | .194 |
| PSY | -.145 | -.006 | .046 | -.071 | -.128 | -.145 | .018 | .053 | -.078 | -.146 | -.046 | -.123 | -.159 | -.257 | -.200 | -.060 | -.115 | -.158 | **-.265** | -.211 |
| | .297 | .966 | .743 | .612 | .357 | .297 | .896 | .704 | .575 | .293 | .739 | .374 | .251 | .061 | .148 | .664 | .407 | .254 | **.053** | .125 |
| SD | .097 | .161 | **.268** | .086 | .126 | .097 | .160 | **.268** | .113 | .126 | .078 | .157 | **.276*** | **.336*** | **.378**** | .065 | .133 | **.277*** | **.338*** | **.370**** |
| | .484 | .244 | **.050** | .537 | .364 | .484 | .247 | **.050** | .415 | .364 | .575 | .256 | **.043** | **.013** | **.005** | .640 | .337 | **.043** | **.012** | **.006** |
| ADD | -.056 | -.135 | .025 | .096 | .158 | -.056 | -.130 | .030 | .097 | .167 | -.061 | .040 | -.001 | .195 | **.293*** | -.081 | .049 | -.002 | .197 | **.300*** |
| | .689 | .332 | .855 | .488 | .254 | .689 | .351 | .830 | .487 | .228 | .661 | .774 | .993 | .158 | **.032** | .561 | .726 | .986 | .154 | **.027** |
| CRI | -.132 | -.199 | .048 | -.004 | .086 | -.132 | -.185 | .051 | -.023 | .073 | -.021 | .015 | -.091 | .089 | .196 | -.032 | .013 | -.092 | .088 | .198 |
| | .342 | .148 | .730 | .975 | .536 | .342 | .181 | .716 | .870 | .599 | .880 | .912 | .515 | .523 | .156 | .816 | .926 | .509 | .528 | .151 |
| SE | -.016 | .113 | .029 | -.015 | .007 | -.016 | .130 | .034 | .002 | .029 | -.096 | -.083 | -.102 | -.222 | -.190 | -.084 | -.103 | -.101 | -.222 | -.185 |
| | .909 | .415 | .833 | .917 | .960 | .909 | .351 | .807 | .989 | .835 | .492 | .548 | .462 | .106 | .169 | .545 | .456 | .466 | .106 | .181 |
| SI | .229 | .212 | .097 | .083 | -.060 | .229 | .219 | .096 | .103 | -.045 | .030 | .110 | .096 | -.004 | -.133 | .033 | .098 | .097 | -.002 | -.129 |
| | .096 | .125 | .487 | .553 | .667 | .096 | .112 | .489 | .458 | .745 | .829 | .429 | .488 | .976 | .337 | .813 | .483 | .487 | .989 | .352 |
| MO | .009 | .163 | .071 | -.023 | -.038 | .009 | .181 | .079 | -.025 | -.055 | -.056 | -.175 | -.092 | -.210 | -.238 | -.049 | -.194 | -.092 | -.215 | -.244 |
| | .946 | .238 | .610 | .870 | .784 | .946 | .191 | .568 | .855 | .694 | .690 | .207 | .507 | .128 | .082 | .724 | .161 | .508 | .118 | .075 |
| IMP | .005 | -.155 | -.132 | -.164 | -.102 | .005 | -.142 | -.127 | -.160 | -.122 | -.014 | -.152 | -.174 | -.230 | -.223 | -.011 | -.150 | -.175 | -.228 | -.220 |
| | .971 | .262 | .340 | .235 | .463 | .971 | .304 | .359 | .248 | .380 | .920 | .271 | .207 | .094 | .105 | .934 | .280 | .205 | .097 | .111 |

*continued on following page*

*Table 6. Continued*

| | Evoked Brain Potentials' Latencies From the First Trial | | | | | | | | | | | | | | | | | | | |
|---|---|---|---|---|---|---|---|---|---|---|---|---|---|---|---|---|---|---|---|---|
| | O1 Electrode | | | | | O2 Electrode | | | | | P3 Electrode | | | | | P4 Electrode | | | | |
| | N1 | P2 | N2 | P3 | SW | N1 | P2 | N2 | P3 | SW | N1 | P2 | N2 | P3 | SW | N1 | P2 | N2 | P3 | SW |
| ADV | -.075 | -.054 | -.065 | -.110 | -.091 | -.075 | -.048 | -.064 | -.094 | -.106 | -.123 | **-.276*** | **-.376**** | **-.484**** | **-.396**** | -.101 | **-.281*** | **-.375**** | **-.483**** | **-.385**** |
| | .591 | .699 | .643 | .430 | .515 | .591 | .729 | .645 | .498 | .445 | .374 | **.043** | **.005** | **.000** | **.003** | .470 | **.039** | **.005** | **.000** | **.004** |
| EMP | .054 | -.157 | -.124 | -.085 | -.075 | .054 | -.159 | -.136 | -.064 | -.063 | -.010 | .110 | -.062 | .005 | .026 | -.011 | .093 | -.061 | .015 | .040 |
| | .697 | .258 | .370 | .543 | .591 | .697 | .251 | .327 | .646 | .653 | .940 | .428 | .656 | .970 | .851 | .939 | .504 | .663 | .914 | .775 |
| DEP | -.114 | -.179 | .058 | .128 | .258 | -.114 | -.162 | .055 | .113 | .240 | -.035 | .158 | .189 | .244 | **.334*** | -.045 | .168 | .189 | .250 | **.335*** |
| | .411 | .195 | .678 | .355 | .060 | .411 | .243 | .693 | .416 | .081 | .804 | .254 | .170 | .076 | **.014** | .744 | .225 | .170 | .069 | **.013** |

* p<.05; ** p<.01

**Personality Traits:** EXT=extraversion, NEU=neuroticism, PSY=psychoticism, SD=social desirability, ADD=addiction, CRI=criminality, SE=strength of excitation, SI=strength of inhibition, MO=mobility, IMP=impulsivity, ADV=adventurousness, EMO=empathy and DEP=depression

cant correlation with EP-amplitudes only in the second series of recordings (Tatalović Vorkapić & Tadinac, 2016).

These are personality traits that are sensitive to the flow of a specific task and engagement of respondents in the task. As it was expected in the context of the over-arousal hypothesis, higher levels of psychoticism showed a significant association with higher amplitudes on the P3-wave on both parietal electrodes in the second round of recordings and with the amplitude of the N2-wave from the second series of recordings only on the P4-electrode. A higher level of neuroticism is significantly associated with a lower N2-amplitude on one parietal electrode, again only in the second series of recordings. As for depression, a relationship was determined between its elevated and reduced N2-amplitudes from the second series of recordings on both parietal electrodes.

However, it is crucial to point out that the issue of the importance of the difficulty of task variance is raised even in these correlations, even though they are not consistent and were recorded only in the second series of recordings; therefore, this should be researched in future studies. In addition to these personality characteristics, Strelau's CNS dimensions have demonstrated a significant correlation with EP-amplitudes. Analysis of the established relationship between the strength of excitation and amplitude of N1, P2, and P3 components in the first and second series of recordings has found that there is no significant positive correlation between these variables.

In other words, an increase of the aforementioned waves, which mark, on the one hand, selective attention and early treatment, and, on the other hand, automatic and controlled extraction of stimuli properties in directing attention and changes in immediate memory, is associated with the increased excitation power of the sample. A significant positive correlation with EP amplitude was also determined in relation to mobility. In contrast, the strength of inhibition showed completely opposite directions of the most significant connections of EP-amplitudes in the first and second series of recordings.

Although these findings were explained in detail in previous work (Tatalović Vorkapić, Tadinac & Lučev, 2013), it is important to point out that the fundamental conclusion is also linked to the need to control the task difficulty variable, and the application of a greater number of recordings in future research of electrophysiology of human personality. In addition, it is important to emphasize that in addition to group relations, it is important to study individual relationships of individual personality traits with specific parameters of evoked brain potentials.

Although the results related to correlations between behavioral variables and the P3-wave were shown in previous work (Tatalović Vorkapić, 2009), due to the importance of the effect of these variables on evoked brain potentials, here are also shown the relations between the mentioned variables with all measured EP-components. Pearson's correlation coefficients (Table 9) were calculated between the already mentioned variables: age, vision problems, drinking coffee, smoking, taking medicine, alcohol, drug use, and recreational activities and the EP-latencies recorded on four electrodes (O1, O2, P3, and P4).

Significant associations were determined between wearing glasses with long P3-latencies on occipital electrodes. T-test analyses showed that the prolonged P3-latencies were significantly more common in participants who reported that they do not to use any vision correction, as opposed to shorter P300-latencies that were significantly more prevalent among those who reported that they use glasses or contact lenses (on the O1 electrode, $t_{(52)}$=2.37, $p$=.02; on the O2 electrode $t_{(52)}$=2.44, $p$=.02).

Also, there was significant association between drinking coffee and shortened slow-wave latencies on O1 ($r$ =.31, $p$ <0.05) and on O2 ($r$ =.29, $p$ <0.05), which indicates that participants who drank coffee had a significantly shorter Sw-latency on both occipital electrodes (on O1 $t_{(52)}$=2.37, $p$=.02; and on O2 $t_{(52)}$=2.21, $p$=.03). Moreover, significant relations were revealed between smoking and the shortened slow-wave latency on parietal electrodes, and smoking and the shortened P3-latency on the P4-lectrode. Thus, participants who declared as smokers had significantly shortened slow-wave latencies (on P3 $t_{(52)}$=2, $p$=.05; on P4 $t_{(52)}$=2.11, $p$=.04) and P3-latencies on the P4 electrode ($t_{(52)}$=2.36, $p$=.02).

Regarding the analysis of relations between EP-amplitudes recorded on four electrodes (O1, O2, P3, and P4), in the first and second series of measurements and behavioral variables, it is observable from Table 10 that almost all behavioral variables showed some sort of significant association with the recorded EP-amplitudes. There is a noticeable drop in the N1-amplitude on the O2 electrode in the second series of recordings that is significantly associated with smoking, and significantly reduced N1-amplitudes on O2 ($t_{(52)}$=1.98, $p$=.05) were found in participants who smoke. Further analysis of the variables of smoking shows that it is also associated with a decrease in the N2-amplitude on the P3-electrode and the P3-amplitude on the O1 electrode in the first series of measurements. In other words, participants who smoke also showed significantly reduced N2-amplitudes and P3-components in the first series recording. An interesting finding relates to a significant association between smoking and an increase in the P3-amplitude on the P4-electrode in the second series of recordings.

*Table 7. Correlation coefficients and significant levels of personality traits and evoked brain potentials' amplitudes in the first trial (N1, P2, N2, P3 and Sw) on two occipital (O1 & O2) and two parietal (P3 & P4) electrodes*

| | Evoked Brain Potentials' Amplitudes From the First Trial | | | | | | | | | | | | | | | |
|---|---|---|---|---|---|---|---|---|---|---|---|---|---|---|---|---|
| | O1 Electrode | | | | O2 Electrode | | | | P3 Electrode | | | | P4 Electrode | | | |
| | N1 | P2 | N2 | P3 | N1 | P2 | N2 | P3 | N1 | P2 | N2 | P3 | N1 | P2 | N2 | P3 |
| EXT | -.091 | -.088 | .070 | -.082 | -.193 | -.004 | .052 | -.043 | .147 | .160 | .189 | -.006 | .048 | .071 | .199 | .010 |
| | .511 | .526 | .617 | .555 | .161 | .979 | .709 | .758 | .289 | .247 | .171 | .966 | .729 | .608 | .149 | .944 |
| NEU | .011 | -.095 | -.055 | -.092 | .040 | -.076 | -.016 | -.107 | -.056 | -.111 | -.074 | .014 | .022 | -.089 | -.229 | .045 |
| | .935 | .493 | .695 | .509 | .776 | .585 | .906 | .439 | .686 | .424 | .594 | .922 | .875 | .523 | .096 | .746 |
| PSY | -.095 | .014 | .096 | -.057 | -.071 | .095 | .191 | -.115 | .058 | .113 | .060 | .071 | .016 | .069 | .207 | .207 |
| | .492 | .920 | .491 | .683 | .609 | .495 | .166 | .407 | .675 | .416 | .668 | .609 | .910 | .618 | .133 | .132 |
| SD | -.009 | -.092 | -.231 | -.139 | -.110 | -.132 | -.222 | -.085 | -.101 | -.240 | .083 | -.068 | -.243 | -.284* | .116 | -.161 |
| | .950 | .510 | .093 | .315 | .429 | .342 | .107 | .543 | .466 | .080 | .553 | .625 | .076 | .038 | .402 | .245 |
| ADD | .081 | -.006 | -.074 | -.146 | .095 | .039 | .027 | -.189 | -.156 | -.146 | -.136 | -.005 | -.076 | -.128 | -.141 | .022 |
| | .562 | .966 | .595 | .291 | .495 | .778 | .846 | .171 | .260 | .291 | .325 | .973 | .584 | .356 | .308 | .876 |
| CRI | .029 | -.073 | -.051 | -.189 | .005 | -.007 | .040 | -.212 | -.064 | -.099 | -.011 | -.001 | -.071 | -.156 | -.056 | .041 |
| | .838 | .600 | .715 | .172 | .970 | .962 | .775 | .125 | .643 | .478 | .939 | .995 | .610 | .261 | .689 | .766 |
| SE | .065 | .087 | -.016 | .107 | .052 | .118 | .002 | .118 | **.308*** | .203 | .112 | .051 | -.024 | .114 | .202 | .108 |
| | .642 | .530 | .907 | .443 | .708 | .397 | .991 | .395 | **.024** | .140 | .420 | .713 | .860 | .411 | .143 | .439 |
| SI | .220 | .230 | .057 | .095 | -.064 | .179 | .091 | .052 | .132 | .113 | .014 | .046 | -.139 | .022 | **.352**** | .013 |
| | .109 | .094 | .685 | .494 | .647 | .196 | .512 | .711 | .343 | .418 | .918 | .742 | .315 | .873 | **.009** | .923 |
| MO | -.006 | .143 | .053 | .141 | -.009 | .250 | .061 | .111 | .156 | **.278*** | .159 | .033 | .008 | .192 | .262 | .031 |
| | .967 | .302 | .701 | .311 | .948 | .068 | .661 | .423 | .258 | **.042** | .252 | .815 | .953 | .165 | .055 | .821 |

*continued on following page*

*Table 7. Continued*

| | Evoked Brain Potentials' Amplitudes From the First Trial | | | | | | | | | | | | | | | |
|---|---|---|---|---|---|---|---|---|---|---|---|---|---|---|---|---|
| | O1 Electrode | | | | O2 Electrode | | | | P3 Electrode | | | | P4 Electrode | | | |
| | N1 | P2 | N2 | P3 | N1 | P2 | N2 | P3 | N1 | P2 | N2 | P3 | N1 | P2 | N2 | P3 |
| IMP | -.262 | -.084 | **.323*** | -.031 | -.063 | .093 | **.290*** | -.013 | -.248 | .056 | -.060 | .041 | -.175 | -.036 | -.092 | .116 |
| | .055 | .548 | **.017** | .822 | .653 | .503 | **.033** | .926 | .071 | .685 | .665 | .767 | .205 | .796 | .509 | .405 |
| ADV | .029 | -.059 | -.089 | -.061 | .147 | -.003 | -.076 | -.006 | .097 | .129 | .021 | -.223 | .187 | .180 | -.153 | -.068 |
| | .834 | .673 | .523 | .662 | .287 | .984 | .587 | .965 | .483 | .352 | .878 | .105 | .176 | .192 | .270 | .627 |
| EMP | .076 | .213 | .264 | .134 | .123 | .177 | .140 | .052 | -.012 | .188 | -.185 | .125 | .028 | .122 | **-.357**** | .157 |
| | .587 | .123 | .055 | .333 | .374 | .201 | .312 | .711 | .931 | .173 | .182 | .369 | .843 | .379 | **.008** | .256 |
| DEP | .097 | -.078 | -.005 | -.097 | .139 | -.070 | .037 | -.142 | -.187 | -.240 | -.154 | .003 | -.033 | -.186 | -.116 | -.002 |
| | .484 | .577 | .970 | .486 | .316 | .615 | .793 | .307 | .175 | .081 | .265 | .982 | .813 | .179 | .403 | .989 |

* $p<.05$; ** $p<.01$

**Personality Traits:** EXT=extraversion, NEU=neuroticism, PSY=psychoticism, SD=social desirability, ADD=addiction, CRI=criminality, SE=strength of excitation, SI=strength of inhibition, MO=mobility, IMP=impulsivity, ADV=adventurousness, EMO=empathy and DEP=depression

*Table 8. Correlation coefficients and significant levels of personality traits and evoked brain potentials' amplitudes in the second trial (N1, P2, N2, P3 and Sw) on two occipital (O1 & O2) and two parietal (P3 & P4) electrodes*

| | Evoked Brain Potentials' Amplitudes From the Second Trial | | | | | | | | | | | | | | | |
|---|---|---|---|---|---|---|---|---|---|---|---|---|---|---|---|---|
| | O1 Electrode | | | | O2 Electrode | | | | P3 Electrode | | | | P4 Electrode | | | |
| | N1 | P2 | N2 | P3 | N1 | P2 | N2 | P3 | N1 | P2 | N2 | P3 | N1 | P2 | N2 | P3 |
| EXT | -.173 | -.105 | .013 | -.081 | -.237 | .004 | .000 | -.120 | .161 | .117 | .157 | .054 | .109 | .074 | .230 | .036 |
| | .210 | .451 | .923 | .562 | .084 | .976 | 1.000 | .388 | .244 | .399 | .256 | .700 | .431 | .593 | .094 | .796 |
| NEU | -.025 | -.103 | -.044 | .055 | .016 | -.109 | .028 | .169 | -.019 | -.115 | -.241 | .005 | .045 | -.136 | **-.314*** | -.076 |
| | .856 | .460 | .753 | .691 | .908 | .432 | .840 | .222 | .893 | .408 | .079 | .970 | .748 | .325 | **.021** | .587 |
| PSY | -.101 | -.022 | .079 | .145 | -.011 | .096 | .173 | .059 | .017 | .137 | .093 | **.359**** | -.060 | .124 | **.341*** | **.339*** |
| | .468 | .874 | .568 | .294 | .936 | .489 | .210 | .672 | .901 | .322 | .505 | **.008** | .668 | .373 | **.012** | **.012** |
| SD | -.017 | -.062 | -.145 | -.159 | -.154 | -.121 | -.243 | -.204 | .007 | -.055 | -.054 | -.168 | -.078 | -.086 | -.036 | -.222 |
| | .903 | .656 | .296 | .251 | .267 | .382 | .077 | .138 | .958 | .690 | .699 | .226 | .576 | .534 | .798 | .107 |
| ADD | .082 | -.047 | -.104 | .006 | .078 | -.007 | .018 | .162 | -.137 | -.148 | -.240 | .070 | -.045 | -.139 | -.196 | .049 |
| | .557 | .737 | .455 | .967 | .576 | .961 | .899 | .243 | .323 | .287 | .081 | .614 | .746 | .315 | .156 | .723 |
| CRI | -.048 | -.118 | -.072 | .003 | -.051 | -.055 | .026 | .114 | .002 | -.095 | -.200 | .108 | .032 | -.160 | -.173 | .027 |
| | .732 | .396 | .603 | .980 | .713 | .695 | .852 | .410 | .986 | .493 | .148 | .439 | .817 | .247 | .212 | .848 |
| SE | .107 | .142 | -.034 | .087 | .037 | .134 | -.030 | .006 | **.273*** | .180 | .307* | .242 | .008 | .149 | .262 | **.304*** |
| | .441 | .307 | .806 | .529 | .790 | .333 | .830 | .968 | **.046** | .192 | .024 | .078 | .954 | .281 | .056 | **.026** |
| SI | .144 | .248 | -.018 | -.147 | -.209 | .184 | .023 | -.227 | .207 | .213 | -.078 | **-.269*** | -.008 | .156 | .152 | -.063 |
| | .299 | .071 | .899 | .289 | .129 | .182 | .868 | .098 | .133 | .122 | .574 | **.049** | .952 | .259 | .273 | .649 |
| MO | -.066 | .160 | .074 | .100 | -.076 | .216 | .018 | -.024 | .262 | **.319*** | **.376**** | .201 | .144 | .247 | **.270*** | .182 |
| | .635 | .249 | .597 | .474 | .586 | .117 | .897 | .864 | .056 | **.019** | **.005** | .145 | .301 | .072 | **.048** | .188 |

*continued on following page*

*Table 8. Continued*

| | Evoked Brain Potentials' Amplitudes From the Second Trial | | | | | | | | | | | | | | | |
|---|---|---|---|---|---|---|---|---|---|---|---|---|---|---|---|---|
| | O1 Electrode | | | | O2 Electrode | | | | P3 Electrode | | | | P4 Electrode | | | |
| | N1 | P2 | N2 | P3 | N1 | P2 | N2 | P3 | N1 | P2 | N2 | P3 | N1 | P2 | N2 | P3 |
| IMP | **-.302*** | -.061 | .232 | .039 | -.126 | .115 | .214 | .055 | .007 | -.037 | .094 | .173 | -.054 | -.095 | .077 | .108 |
| | **.026** | .659 | .092 | .777 | .365 | .409 | .121 | .693 | .961 | .792 | .498 | .212 | .698 | .494 | .579 | .435 |
| ADV | .025 | -.029 | -.138 | .036 | .148 | .044 | -.076 | .097 | -.044 | .062 | .192 | .049 | .204 | .136 | .153 | .091 |
| | .859 | .836 | .318 | .799 | .287 | .752 | .585 | .485 | .752 | .658 | .163 | .725 | .139 | .325 | .268 | .511 |
| EMP | .151 | .227 | .129 | -.070 | .086 | .129 | .179 | .003 | -.034 | .088 | .022 | -.082 | .008 | .048 | -.155 | -.010 |
| | .274 | .099 | .354 | .614 | .538 | .352 | .196 | .981 | .808 | .526 | .875 | .557 | .953 | .731 | .262 | .941 |
| DEP | .086 | -.090 | -.099 | .031 | .117 | -.097 | .056 | .123 | -.066 | -.213 | **-.380**** | -.112 | .014 | -.183 | **-.274*** | -.133 |
| | .536 | .517 | .478 | .825 | .400 | .485 | .685 | .374 | .637 | .121 | **.005** | .421 | .919 | .186 | **.045** | .337 |

* p<.05; ** p<.01

**Personality Traits:** EXT=extraversion, NEU=neuroticism, PSY=psychoticism, SD=social desirability, ADD=addiction, CRI=criminality, SE=strength of excitation, SI=strength of inhibition, MO=mobility, IMP=impulsivity, ADV=adventurousness, EMO=empathy and DEP=depression

*Table 9. Correlation coefficients between EP-latencies on four electrodes ($O_1$, $O_2$, $P_3$ & $P_4$) and behavioral variables: age, sight, drinking coffee, smoking, taking medications, alcohol consumption, taking drugs and sports*

| EP-Latencies | | Age | Sight | Drinking Coffee | Smoking | Taking Medications | Alcohol Consumption | Taking Drugs | Sports |
|---|---|---|---|---|---|---|---|---|---|
| O1 | N1 | -.09 | .21 | .14 | .20 | .01 | .02 | .11 | -.09 |
| | P2 | -.01 | .22 | .05 | .26 | -.15 | .19 | -.05 | -.06 |
| | N2 | -.18 | .09 | .02 | .08 | -.02 | .13 | -.01 | .03 |
| | P3 | .12 | **.31*** | .14 | .14 | -.03 | .14 | .02 | -.02 |
| | Sw | -.03 | .12 | **.31*** | .19 | -.18 | .10 | .03 | -.10 |
| O2 | N1 | -.09 | .21 | .14 | .20 | .01 | .02 | .11 | -.09 |
| | P2 | -.03 | .21 | .07 | .25 | -.17 | .21 | -.06 | -.07 |
| | N2 | -.18 | .10 | .02 | .08 | -.02 | .13 | -.01 | .02 |
| | P3 | .13 | **.31*** | .14 | .17 | -.02 | .13 | .06 | -.07 |
| | Sw | .02 | .14 | **.29*** | .24 | -.15 | .12 | .07 | -.14 |
| P3 | N1 | -.06 | .12 | .09 | .08 | -.03 | -.04 | .10 | -.10 |
| | P2 | -.11 | .18 | .18 | .16 | .07 | .14 | .16 | .11 |
| | N2 | -.08 | -.01 | .10 | .21 | .25 | .20 | .19 | .21 |
| | P3 | .02 | .11 | .22 | .26 | .16 | .15 | .13 | .05 |
| | Sw | -.03 | .05 | .26 | **.27*** | .16 | .21 | .20 | .16 |
| P4 | N1 | -.05 | .11 | .10 | .08 | -.06 | -.05 | .10 | -.10 |
| | P2 | -.07 | .20 | .17 | .17 | .07 | .12 | .17 | .11 |
| | N2 | -.09 | -.01 | .10 | .21 | .25 | .20 | .19 | .21 |
| | P3 | .01 | .10 | .23 | **.26*** | .16 | .15 | .15 | .05 |
| | Sw | -.03 | .04 | .26 | **.28*** | .15 | .20 | .22 | .13 |

* p<0.05,** p<0.01

In other words, in contrast to previous findings, it appears that in the second series of recordings there is an abrupt change in participants who smoke as far as this cognitive EP-wave is concerned, i.e. instead of the current reduction in the P3-amplitude, there is now a significant increase. By testing the significance of differences between individual groups of participants in their EP-amplitudes, participants who smoke had significantly lower N2-amplitudes in the first series of recordings on the P3-electrode ($t_{(52)}=1.98$, $p=.05$), and P3-amplitudes in first series of recordings on the O1 electrode ($t_{(52)}=1.98$, $p=.05$). This finding is logical, given the established strong influence of caffeine and nicotine on the state of cortical arousal (Polich & Kok, 1995).

*Table 10. Matrix correlation between EP-amplitudes on four electrodes (O1, O2, P3, and P4) in the first (Amp1) and second (Amp2) series of measurements and behavioral variables: age (Age), sight problems (Sight), drinking coffee (Coffee), smoking (Smoking), taking medication (medication), alcoholic beverages (Alcohol), taking drugs (Drugs), and sports activities (Sports)*

| EP-Amplitudes | | | Age | Sight | Drinking Coffee | Smoking | Taking Medications | Alcohol Consumption | Taking Drugs | Sports |
|---|---|---|---|---|---|---|---|---|---|---|
| O1 | N1 | Amp1 | .05 | .16 | -.06 | .22 | -.04 | .15 | .02 | -.02 |
| | | Amp2 | .10 | .12 | -.16 | .17 | -.04 | .24 | .22 | .07 |
| | P2 | Amp1 | -.21 | -.07 | .16 | .05 | **-.30*** | .02 | .20 | -.10 |
| | | Amp2 | -.18 | -.09 | .19 | .03 | **-.27*** | .19 | **.34**** | -.12 |
| | N2 | Amp1 | .14 | -.01 | .02 | .13 | .15 | -.15 | .17 | .21 |
| | | Amp2 | .04 | -.12 | .13 | .11 | .09 | .07 | .02 | .21 |
| | P3 | Amp1 | -.03 | .02 | .16 | **.26*** | -.08 | .11 | .04 | -.08 |
| | | Amp2 | -.24 | **-.28*** | .25 | .02 | .02 | .00 | -.17 | -.17 |
| O2 | N1 | Amp1 | -.03 | -.09 | .25 | .25 | -.23 | .10 | .08 | .05 |
| | | Amp2 | .01 | -.07 | .20 | **.26*** | -.23 | .07 | .16 | .06 |
| | P2 | Amp1 | **-.38**** | -.13 | **.36**** | .22 | -.21 | -.01 | .22 | **-.27*** |
| | | Amp2 | **-.35**** | -.19 | **.41**** | .26 | -.18 | .10 | **.26*** | -.23 |
| | N2 | Amp1 | .14 | .07 | .20 | .21 | -.05 | -.18 | .15 | .10 |
| | | Amp2 | .05 | -.06 | .23 | .24 | -.02 | -.06 | .04 | .07 |
| | P3 | Amp1 | -.02 | .08 | .10 | .20 | -.01 | .13 | .06 | -.03 |
| | | Amp2 | **-.42**** | **-.40**** | **.32*** | .04 | -.18 | .04 | .07 | -.22 |
| P3 | N1 | Amp1 | **.27*** | **.27*** | -.05 | .02 | .11 | .06 | -.01 | .01 |
| | | Amp2 | -.10 | -.16 | .22 | -.01 | -.13 | -.03 | .12 | -.12 |
| | P2 | Amp1 | -.02 | .01 | .12 | .07 | .08 | .10 | .07 | -.18 |
| | | Amp2 | -.14 | -.02 | **.30*** | .11 | .05 | -.10 | -.03 | -.20 |
| | N2 | Amp1 | .04 | .22 | .06 | **.26*** | .07 | -.11 | .19 | -.19 |
| | | Amp2 | .09 | -.11 | -.12 | -.04 | -.22 | .02 | -.18 | -.03 |
| | P3 | Amp1 | -.04 | .02 | .13 | .20 | .11 | .06 | .19 | .16 |
| | | Amp2 | -.08 | -.23 | -.02 | -.34 | -.11 | .10 | -.10 | .13 |
| P4 | N1 | Amp1 | **.28*** | -.01 | -.13 | .21 | -.04 | -.13 | .07 | .12 |
| | | Amp2 | .04 | **-.30*** | .18 | .16 | -.25 | -.05 | .02 | .00 |
| | P2 | Amp1 | .00 | -.09 | .05 | .14 | -.09 | .12 | .24 | -.14 |
| | | Amp2 | -.25 | -.10 | **.37**** | .22 | -.09 | -.01 | .14 | -.22 |
| | N2 | Amp1 | .02 | .10 | .06 | .17 | .13 | .08 | -.22 | -.07 |
| | | Amp2 | -.05 | -.11 | -.05 | -.11 | -.18 | -.01 | -.14 | -.17 |
| | **P3** | Amp1 | -.01 | -.01 | .12 | .10 | -.05 | -.01 | .09 | .22 |
| | | Amp2 | -.13 | -.26 | .07 | **-.27*** | **-.31*** | .03 | .14 | .04 |

* p<0.05 ** p<0.01

By analyzing the relation between age and EP-amplitudes, significant associations were found between age and the N1-amplitude in the first series of recording on parietal electrodes, between age and the P2-amplitude in the first series of recordings on the O2 electrode, and the second series of recordings on the O2-electrode, and between age and the P3-amplitude in the second series of recordings on the O2 electrode. In other words, if the N1-wave is observed, it can be seen that significant associations between younger age and lower amplitudes, whereas quite the opposite direction is observed in amplitudes of the P2 and P3 wave in the first and second series of recordings, i.e. the younger the age the higher the amplitudes of these later waves. Testing the significance of the differences has pointed to the existence of significant differences between younger and older participants with regards to the EP-components, so that younger participants had significantly lower N1-amplitudes on the P3-electrode ($t_{(52)}$=2.18, $p$=.03) and on the P4-electrode ($t_{(52)}$=2.18, $p$=.04).

In contrast, with subsequent EP-components, as noted above, younger participants showed significantly higher P2-amplitudes on the O2-electrode both in the first ($t_{(52)}$=3.16, $p$=.01) and the second series of recordings ($t_{(52)}$=2.77, $p$=.01), and a significantly higher P3-amplitude also on the O2 electrode in the second series of recordings ($t_{(52)}$=2.48, $p$=.02). Developmental changes in the brain, including brain potentials, have been thoroughly researched (Dabić-Jeftić & Mikula, 1994a), and the results indicate a different direction of connectedness between age and evoked potentials, depending on age. It is obvious that in this study the tested sample is not age-homogeneous in terms of the differences in the measured evoked potentials, which should be kept in mind in future research.

Furthermore, a significant relationship was detected between drinking coffee and EP-amplitudes, so that the drinking of coffee is significantly associated with a lower P3-amplitude in the second series of measurements on the O2 electrode. The same trend of connectedness is visible with other relations of drinking coffee with EP-amplitudes, i.e. with a significant association between drinking coffee and a lower P2-amplitude of the O2 electrode in the first and second series of measurements, and only in the second series of measurements but also on parietal electrodes. Notably, it was a fairly consistent finding in relation to others with respect to the significant association found between the P2-amplitude in the second series of measurements and drinking coffee on 3 out of 4 used electrodes during EP-recording.

In addition, significant differences were found between those participants who drink and do not drink coffee in the amplitudes of P2 and P3 waves. As with the P3-amplitude in the second series of measurements on the O2 electrode, which was significantly lower in participants who drink coffee ($t_{(52)}$=2.20, $p$=.04), it was found that the P2-amplitudes on the O2 electrode both in the first ($t_{(52)}$=2.61, $p$=.01) and second series of measurements ($t_{(52)}$=3.01, $p$=.01), and only in the second series of measurement on the P3 electrode ($t_{(52)}$=2.12, $p$=.04) and the P4 electrode ($t_{(52)}$=2.63, $p$=.01) were significantly lower in participants who drink coffee. These results are consistent with the findings by Revelle and colleagues (1980), where moderate doses of caffeine affected the deterioration of performance on cognitive tasks in introverts and improved the performance in extraverts.

In addition, a significant connection was found between participants who wear glasses or some form of visual correction and significantly lower N1-amplitudes in the first series of recordings on the P3 electrodes. But, in contrast to this finding, there is a significant association between participants who wear glasses and a significantly higher N1-amplitude in the second series of recordings on the P4-electrode, and the P3-amplitudes in the second series of recordings on the O1 electrode ($r = -.28$, $p<0.05$) and the O2 electrode. It is clear that the factor of vision, i.e. using some form of visual correction is very important in measuring the EP-latency, especially the P3-latency in this study. It was also found that those participants who do not wear glasses or contact lenses have a tendency for a longer time of evaluation and categorization of target stimuli as opposed to those that use visual aids.

Finally, there is significant association between the EP amplitude and taking medication, and drug use. In particular, taking medications, such as prednisone, antibiotics for teeth, ibuprofen for menstrual cramps, antihistamines for allergies, birth control pills (CILEST, Triquilar), iron pills, caffetin, and Nalgesin for menstrual problems, Andol for muscle relaxation, painkiller Voltaren (menstrual cramps and toothache), and tablets against gastritis, is significantly associated with higher amplitudes in the second series of recording of the P2-wave on the O1-electrode, and the P3-wave on the P4-electrode. Given that all these are very different medicines, and evoked potentials are sensitive to different physiological changes that can take place, it is difficult to explain the nature of this association, which is one of the guidelines for future research.

By contrast, the relation of drug use takes another direction, i.e. there is a significant connection between participants who take drugs and lower P2-amplitudes in the second series of recordings on occipital electrodes. By analyzing the differences between individual groups of participants, it was found that those participants who used drugs had a significantly higher P2-amplitude in the second series of recordings on the O1-electrode ($t_{(52)}$=1.99, $p$=.05), and the P3-amplitude on the P4-electrode ($t_{(52)}$=2.34, $p$=.02). In addition, participants who consumed some of the illegal drugs in the last 15 days showed significantly reduced P2-amplitudes in the second series of measurements on the O1 electrode ($t_{(52)}$=2.63, $p$=.01) and the O2 electrode ($t_{(52)}$=1.98, $p$=.05).

## Factor Analysis Results

With the aim of exploring the validity of applied measurement and the variance percentage that could be explained by the measurement of:

1. Eysenck's Personality traits (Extraversion, neuroticism and psychoticism), Strelau' temperament dimensions of CNS (strength of excitation, strength of inhibition and mobility) and others (social desirability, addiction, criminality, impulsivity, adventurousness, empathy and depression);
2. latencies and amplitudes (from the first and second trial) of evoked brain potentials (N1, P2, N2, P3 and Sw) on two occipital (O1 & O2) and two parietal (P3 & P4) electrodes; and
3. behavioral variables (age, sight, drinking coffee, smoking, taking medications, alcohol consumption, taking drugs and sports), an Exploratory Factor analysis on Principal Components with Varimax Rotation has been run.

In the first step, nineteen components have been determined, which explained 86.629% of the total variance of human personality, evoked potentials and behavioral variables, as it could be observed at the Figure 11. Since, after fifteen components, there is an alignment, as it could be observed at the Scree plot, so in the second step Factor analysis on the principal components with Varimax rotation and 15 factors has been run. Initial Eigenvalues and percentage of cumulative and total variance could be seen in the Table 11. It could be discussed that together, all fifteen factors explained a significant percentage of the total variance, i.e. 79.611% of personality, brain electrophysiology and some behavioral variables. Overall, based on the previously described reliability levels and this percentage of the total variance explained, it could be concluded that applied measurement in this study has the high level of validity. In addition, determined results are in accordance with previous results of research done by DePascalis (1993, 1994).

After nineteen rotations, a factorial structure has been determined for the variables that have been entered in this factor analysis and it could be observed in the Table 12. Also, component plot in the rotated space could be observed at Figure 12.

*Figure 11. Scree plot of eigenvalues and component number determined in the Factor analysis of personality traits, visual evoked potentials and behavioral variables*

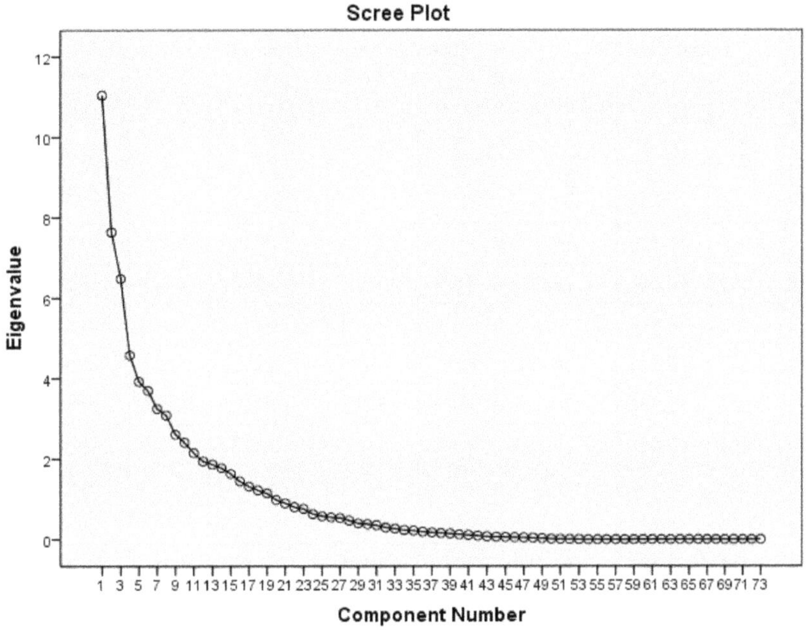


The first factor is structured of N2-P2-Sw-latencies on parietal electrodes with adventurousness, what confirmed prior findings about the strongest and the most consistent relationship between EP-latencies on parietal electrodes and adventurousness. Taking medications has similar loadings on the first and the fourteenth factor, and since it has greater theoretical argumentation to be the part of the fourteenth factor, it is structured as its element. In addition, due to taking medications variable's similar loadings on several factors, this variable could be removed from the analysis.

The second factor is structured of several personality traits: neuroticism, addiction, criminality, depression, strength of excitation, mobility and extraversion. Their negative and positive loadings perfectly reflect the presumed theoretical background within their personality theories.

The third factor consists of N1-P2-latencies on both occipital and both parietal electrodes. It is logical that particularly these EP-components are closely connected because of their psychological function within an early information processing.

Furthermore, the forth factor consist of P3-Sw-latencies only on occipital electrodes, and the fifth factor of N2-component with its latencies and ampli-

*Table 11. Total variance explained determined in the Factor analysis on the Principal components with Varimax rotation and fixed number of factors for extraction (15)*

| Total Variance Explained | | | | | | | | | | |
|---|---|---|---|---|---|---|---|---|---|---|
| Component | | Initial Eigenvalues | | | Extraction Sums of Squared Loadings | | | Rotation Sums of Squared Loadings | | |
| | | Total | % of Variance | Cumulative % | Total | % of Variance | Cumulative % | Total | % of Variance | Cumulative % |
| Dimension | 1 | 11.045 | 15.130 | 15.130 | 11.045 | 15.130 | 15.130 | 6.579 | 9.013 | 9.013 |
| | 2 | 7.641 | 10.467 | 25.597 | 7.641 | 10.467 | 25.597 | 5.791 | 7.933 | 16.946 |
| | 3 | 6.486 | 8.885 | 34.482 | 6.486 | 8.885 | 34.482 | 5.486 | 7.515 | 24.461 |
| | 4 | 4.577 | 6.270 | 40.752 | 4.577 | 6.270 | 40.752 | 5.013 | 6.867 | 31.329 |
| | 5 | 3.921 | 5.371 | 46.123 | 3.921 | 5.371 | 46.123 | 4.850 | 6.643 | 37.972 |
| | 6 | 3.698 | 5.066 | 51.189 | 3.698 | 5.066 | 51.189 | 4.030 | 5.521 | 43.493 |
| | 7 | 3.254 | 4.457 | 55.646 | 3.254 | 4.457 | 55.646 | 3.409 | 4.670 | 48.163 |
| | 8 | 3.087 | 4.229 | 59.875 | 3.087 | 4.229 | 59.875 | 3.377 | 4.626 | 52.789 |
| | 9 | 2.614 | 3.581 | 63.455 | 2.614 | 3.581 | 63.455 | 3.260 | 4.466 | 57.255 |
| | 10 | 2.414 | 3.307 | 66.763 | 2.414 | 3.307 | 66.763 | 3.066 | 4.200 | 61.455 |
| | 11 | 2.154 | 2.951 | 69.714 | 2.154 | 2.951 | 69.714 | 3.056 | 4.186 | 65.640 |
| | 12 | 1.947 | 2.668 | 72.382 | 1.947 | 2.668 | 72.382 | 2.851 | 3.905 | 69.546 |
| | 13 | 1.870 | 2.562 | 74.943 | 1.870 | 2.562 | 74.943 | 2.675 | 3.665 | 73.211 |
| | 14 | 1.778 | 2.435 | 77.379 | 1.778 | 2.435 | 77.379 | 2.349 | 3.217 | 76.428 |
| | 15 | 1.630 | 2.233 | 79.611 | 1.630 | 2.233 | 79.611 | 2.324 | 3.184 | 79.611 |

tude in both trials only on occipital electrodes. It is interesting to determine that taking drugs has positioned with P2-amplitude on occipital electrodes mostly in both trials.

The seventh factor is structured of N1-amplitudes in both trials on parietal and occipital electrodes, and the eight factors consists of N1-N2-P3 amplitudes from both trials on parietal electrodes.

Psychoticism has joined with N2-P3-amplitudes on parietal electrodes only in the second trial and together they reflect the ninth factor. The tenth factor consists of N1-P2-amplitudes only in the second trial on parietal electrodes and of behavioral variable engagement in sport activities. The eleventh factor is structured of the sight (having glasses) and P3-amplitudes in both trials but only on occipital electrodes, and the twelfth factor consists of N2-P2-amplitudes in the first trial on parietal electrodes and empathy. Strength

*Table 12. Rotated component matrix*

| | Component | | | | | | | | | | | | | | |
|---|---|---|---|---|---|---|---|---|---|---|---|---|---|---|---|
| | 1 | 2 | 3 | 4 | 5 | 6 | 7 | 8 | 9 | 10 | 11 | 12 | 13 | 14 | 15 |
| N2-latency_P3 | .910 | | | | | | | | | | | | | | |
| N2-latency_P4 | .910 | | | | | | | | | | | | | | |
| P3-latency_P3 | .831 | | | | | | | | | | | | | | |
| P3-latency_P4 | .831 | | | | | | | | | | | | | | |
| Sw-latency_P3 | .801 | | | .350 | | | | | | | | | | | |
| Sw-latency_P4 | .789 | | | .347 | | | | | | | | | | | |
| Adventurousness | -.502 | .309 | | | | | | | | | -.303 | | | | |
| Taking medications | .366 | | | | | | -.303 | | | | | | | .363 | |
| Neuroticism | | -.904 | | | | | | | | | | | | | |
| Addiction | | -.896 | | | | | | | | | | | | | |
| Criminality | | -.862 | | | | | | | | | | | | | |
| Depression | | -.855 | | | | | | | | | | | | | |
| SE | | .704 | | | | | | | .314 | | | | | | |
| MO | | .680 | | | | | | | | | | | | .338 | |
| Extraversion | | .561 | | | | | | | | | | | | .545 | |
| N1-latency_P3 | | | .905 | | | | | | | | | | | | |
| N1-latency_P4 | | | .897 | | | | | | | | | | | | |
| N1-latency_O2 | | | .789 | | | | | | | | | | | | |
| N1-latency_O1 | | | .789 | | | | | | | | | | | | |
| P2-latency_P3 | .462 | | .707 | | | | | | | | | | | | |

*continued on following page*

*Table 12. Continued*

| | Component | | | | | | | | | | | | | | |
|---|---|---|---|---|---|---|---|---|---|---|---|---|---|---|---|
| | 1 | 2 | 3 | 4 | 5 | 6 | 7 | 8 | 9 | 10 | 11 | 12 | 13 | 14 | 15 |
| P2-latency_P4 | .470 | | .698 | | | | | | | | | | | | |
| P2-latency_O1 | | | .531 | .443 | | | | | | -.405 | | | | | |
| P2-latency_O2 | | | .526 | .455 | | | | | | -.385 | | | | | |
| Sw-latency_O2 | | | | .861 | | | | | | | | | | | |
| Sw-latency_O1 | | | | .855 | | | | | | | | | | | |
| P3-latency_O2 | .304 | | | .843 | | | | | | | | | | | |
| P3-latency_O1 | .306 | | | .836 | | | | | | | | | | | |
| N2-amplitude2_O2 | | | | | .892 | | | | | | | | | | |
| N2-amplitude1_O2 | | | | | .871 | | | | | | | | | | |
| N2-amplitude1_O1 | | | | | .864 | | | | | | | | | | |
| N2-amplitude2_O1 | | | | | .782 | | | | | | | | | | |
| N2-latency_O2 | | | | .406 | -.524 | | | | | -.316 | | | | | |
| N2-latency_O1 | | | .308 | .408 | -.517 | | | | | -.316 | | | | | |
| P2_amplitude1_O2 | | | | | | .861 | | | | | | | | | |
| P2_amplitude1_O1 | | | | | | .829 | | | | | | | | | |
| P2_amplitude2_O1 | | | | | | .755 | | | | | | | .328 | | |
| P2_amplitude2_O2 | | | | | | .747 | .306 | | | | | | | | |
| Taking drugs | | | | | | .388 | | | | | | -.333 | | -.344 | |
| P2_amplitude1_P4 | | .303 | | | | .327 | .316 | | | | | | | -.320 | -.307 |
| N1-amplitude2_P4 | | | | | | | .806 | | | | | | | | |

*continued on following page*

*Table 12. Continued*

| | Component | | | | | | | | | | | | | | |
|---|---|---|---|---|---|---|---|---|---|---|---|---|---|---|---|
| | **1** | **2** | **3** | **4** | **5** | **6** | **7** | **8** | **9** | **10** | **11** | **12** | **13** | **14** | **15** |
| N1-amplitude1_P4 | | | | | | | .760 | .393 | | | | | | | |
| N1-amplitude2_O2 | | | | | .440 | | .751 | | | | | | | | |
| N1-amplitude1_O2 | | | | | .434 | | .633 | | | | | | .328 | | |
| P3-amplitude1_P3 | | | | | | | | .800 | | | | | | | |
| N1-amplitude1_P3 | | | | | | | | .694 | | .348 | | | | | |
| P3-amplitude1_P4 | | | | | | | | .693 | | | | | | | |
| N2-amplitude2_P4 | | | | | | | | -.500 | .373 | | | | | | |
| P3-amplitude2_P4 | | | | | | | | | .819 | | | | | | |
| P3-amplitude2_P3 | | | | | | | | | .803 | | | | | | |
| Psychoticism | | | | | | | | | .492 | | | .329 | | .413 | -.320 |
| N2-amplitude2_P3 | -.320 | .304 | | | | | | | .400 | | | | | | |
| P2_amplitude2_P3 | | | | | | | | | | .774 | | | | | |
| N1_amplitude2_P3 | | | | | | | | .327 | | .629 | | | | | |
| P2_amplitude2_P4 | | .323 | | | | .311 | .426 | | | .551 | | | | | |
| Sports | | | | | | | | | | -.388 | | | | | |
| P3-amplitude2_O2 | | | | | | | | | | | .736 | | | | |
| P3-amplitude2_O1 | | | | | | | | | | | .718 | | | | |
| P3-amplitude1_O2 | | | | | | | | .419 | | | .654 | | | | |
| P3-amplitude1_O1 | | | | | | | | .403 | | | .634 | | | | |
| Sight (Glasses) | | | | .307 | | | | | | | -.370 | | | | |

*continued on following page*

*Table 12. Continued*

| | Component | | | | | | | | | | | | | | |
|---|---|---|---|---|---|---|---|---|---|---|---|---|---|---|---|
| | **1** | **2** | **3** | **4** | **5** | **6** | **7** | **8** | **9** | **10** | **11** | **12** | **13** | **14** | **15** |
| N2-amplitude1_P3 | | | | | | | | | | | | .842 | | | |
| N2-amplitude1_P4 | | | | | | | | | | | | .810 | | | |
| P2-amplitude1_P3 | | | | | | | | | | .447 | | .458 | | | |
| Empathy | | | | | | | | | | | | -.350 | | | |
| N1-amplitude1_O1 | | | | | | | | | | | | | .821 | | |
| N1-amplitude2_O1 | | | | | | | | | | | | | .773 | | |
| SI | | .385 | | | | | | | | | | | .489 | | |
| Impulsivity | | | | | | | | | | | | | | .754 | |
| Alcohol consumption | | | | | | | | | | | | | | -.414 | |
| Drinking coffee | | | | | | | | | | .331 | | | | | .675 |
| Soc_desirability | .377 | | | | | | | | | | | | | | .546 |
| Smoking | | | | | | | | | -.380 | | | | | | .464 |
| Age | | | | | | -.429 | | | | | | | | | -.455 |

of inhibition has the highest loadings with N1-amplitudes in both trials on occipital electrodes on the thirteenth factor, and impulsivity, alcohol consumption and taking medications on the fourteenth factor. Finally, behavioral variables such as drinking coffee, smoking and age together with social desirability or conformism placed in the fifteenth factor.

Within this discussion, it is very important to emphasize that certain personality traits are placed within the same factor, same as certain evoked potentials' latencies or amplitudes, what has confirmed prior hypothesis and prior research results. However, it is interesting that some of them, such as psychoticism, empathy, strength of inhibition has the highest loadings in the factors where certain evoked potentials' latencies or amplitudes are placed too. Therefore, determined results are pointing in the fact that some personality traits are more closely connected with evoked brain potentials rather than with other personality traits or behavioral variables. This does not immediately mean that they also have the greater biological background than other personality traits, but rather the fact that each variable in this factor analysis has been measured in a specific way, so the measurement variance could play an important role in these loadings. Anyway, the determined fac-

*Figure 12. Component plot in rotated space*

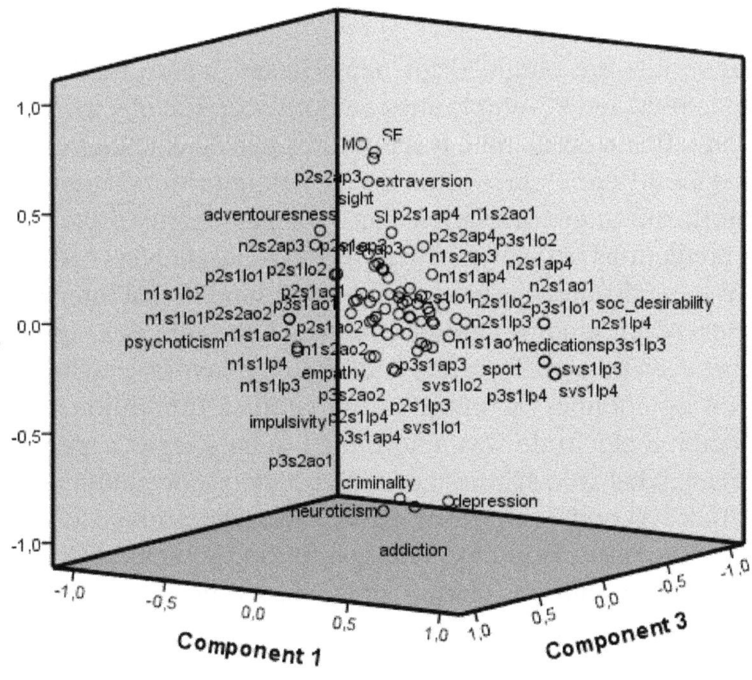

tor structure regarding the personality traits and evoked potentials confirmed prior research results and theoretical background, same as regarding the measured behavioral variables.

## Hierarchical Regression Analyses

Thirteen Hierarchical regression analyses are run with the aim of exploring the significant predictors for each personality traits. In the first step N1, P2, N2, P3 and Sw latencies are tested, in the second step N1, P2, N2 and P3 amplitudes in the first trial are tested and in the third step N1, P2, N2 and P3 amplitudes in the second trial are tested.

As it could be observed in Table 13, the results of hierarchical regression analysis of N1, P2, N2, P3 and Sw latencies (the first step), N1, P2, N2 and P3 amplitudes in the first trial (the second step) and N1, P2, N2 and P3 amplitudes in the second trial (the third step) as predictors of extraversion, neuroticism, psychoticism and social desirability are presented.

Regarding Eysenck's personality dimensions, it could be seen that latencies and amplitudes in both trails are not significant predictors for these four traits at general level. However, even though general contributions of evoked potentials are not significant, some latencies and amplitudes of evoked potentials are significant predictors. Therefore, for extraversion N1-latencies on parietal electrodes and P3-amplitude on one occipital electrode are significant predictors

Similar results are obtained for neuroticism, where N1-latency on one parietal electrode and P3-amplitudes on both occipital electrode and in both trials are significant predictors. It is interesting to detect that these predictors showed rather different correlation levels within prior correlation analyses, due to significant inter-correlations between personality traits.

These predictions are analyzed within individual analyses of each personality trait, so these differences have their background in that inter-correlations. Nevertheless, each kind of analyses showed that there is a significant relationship between personality traits and evoked potentials, so later on will be given specific guidelines for future research studies. In addition, P2-amplitude on one occipital electrode was determined to be a significant predictor for psychoticism, what is in accordance with previous correlation analyses, and N2-amplitudes on both occipital electrodes were determined to be significant predictors for social desirability. This last finding is rather different from the results obtained within correlation analyses, so further research should be the one to clear these relationships.

*Table 13. Four Regression analyses of N1, P2, N2, P3 and Sw latencies (the first step), N1, P2, N2 and P3 amplitudes in the first trial (the second step) and N1, P2, N2 and P3 amplitudes in the second trial (the third step) as predictors of extraversion, neuroticism, psychoticism and social desirability*

| Model Summary: Extraversion | | | | | | | | | |
|---|---|---|---|---|---|---|---|---|---|
| Model | R | $R^2$ | Adjusted $R^2$ | Std. Error of the Estimate | Change Statistics | | | | |
| | | | | | $R^2$ Change | F Change | df1 | df2 | Sig. F Change |
| 1_Latencies | .586 | .344 | .006 | 5.42156 | .344 | 1.018 | 18 | 35 | .465 |
| 2_Amplitudes1 | .760 | .578 | -.178 | 5.90276 | .234 | .658 | 16 | 19 | .799 |
| 3_Amplitudes2 | .908 | .824 | .068 | 5.25082 | .246 | 1.557 | 9 | 10 | .250 |
| Significant predictors | | | B | Beta | | | | | |
| N1-latency_P4 | | | -.907* | -5.059* | | | | | |
| N1-latency_P3 | | | -.862* | -4.766* | | | | | |
| P3-amplitude2_O1 | | | -1.944** | -1.140** | | | | | |
| Model Summary: Neuroticism | | | | | | | | | |
| Model | R | $R^2$ | Adjusted $R^2$ | Std. Error of the Estimate | Change Statistics | | | | |
| | | | | | $R^2$ Change | F Change | df1 | df2 | Sig. F Change |
| 1_Latencies | .612 | .375 | .053 | 5.47026 | .375 | 1.165 | 18 | 35 | .339 |
| 2_Amplitudes1 | .871 | .759 | .328 | 4.60936 | .384 | 1.893 | 16 | 19 | .092 |
| 3_Amplitudes2 | .952 | .906 | .504 | 3.95768 | .147 | 1.752 | 9 | 10 | .197 |
| Significant predictors | | | B | Beta | | | | | |
| N1-latency_P4 | | | -.078** | -.717** | | | | | |
| P3-amplitude1_O1 | | | -1.549* | -.802* | | | | | |
| P3-amplitude1_O2 | | | -1.330** | -.759** | | | | | |
| P3-amplitude2_O2 | | | -2.296* | -1.093 | | | | | |
| Model Summary: Psychoticism | | | | | | | | | |
| Model | R | $R^2$ | Adjusted $R^2$ | Std. Error of the Estimate | Change Statistics | | | | |
| | | | | | $R^2$ Change | F Change | df1 | df2 | Sig. F Change |
| 1_Latencies | .533 | .285 | -.083 | 3.22039 | .285 | .773 | 18 | 35 | .715 |
| 2_Amplitudes1 | .798 | .637 | -.013 | 3.11456 | .352 | 1.151 | 16 | 19 | .381 |
| 3_Amplitudes2 | .903 | .815 | .018 | 3.06637 | .178 | 1.067 | 9 | 10 | .457 |
| Significant predictors | | | B | Beta | | | | | |
| P2-amplitude1_O1 | | | -.441* | -.723* | | | | | |

*continued on following page*

*Table 13. Continued*

| Model Summary: Social Desirability | | | | | | | | | |
|---|---|---|---|---|---|---|---|---|---|
| Model | R | $R^2$ | Adjusted $R^2$ | Std. Error of the Estimate | Change Statistics | | | | |
| | | | | | $R^2$ Change | F Change | df1 | df2 | Sig. F Change |
| 1_Latencies | .517 | .267 | -.110 | 2.87758 | .267 | .709 | 18 | 35 | .779 |
| 2_Amplitudes1 | .748 | .560 | -.227 | 3.02580 | .293 | .791 | 16 | 19 | .679 |
| 3_Amplitudes2 | .832 | .692 | -.631 | 3.48867 | .132 | .477 | 9 | 10 | .860 |
| Significant predictors | | | B | Beta | | | | | |
| N2-amplitude1_O1 | | | -.521* | -.810* | | | | | |
| N2-amplitude1_O2 | | | -.478* | -.929* | | | | | |

* p<0.05 ** p<0.01

Analyzing the possible significant predictors for Strelau's temperament dimensions (Table 14), it could be seen that again, same as previously, neither regression analyses resulted with significant prediction model. However, some evoked brain potentials' parameters are significant predictors for temperament dimensions. P2-latencies on parietal electrodes and N1-P3-amplitudes in the first trial at parietal electrodes are significant predictors for strength of excitation. The significant predictors of strength of inhibition are N2-amplitudes from the first trail on parietal electrodes.

Finally, N2-P2-latencies mostly on parietal electrodes are significant predictors of mobility. Again, similar to prior results, some significant predictors have no ground on prior correlation analyses results, what could be explained by significant inter-correlations between personality traits. These predictions reflect individual contribution of analyzed predictors, what is very interesting. In addition, it should be emphasized, significant predictors within visual evoked potentials for one personality dimensions have got different direction of predictability (positive and negative) what could be explained with different psychological and functional role of each EP-component.

In addition, within Table 14, hierarchical regression analysis results and significant predictors for depression are shown also. It could be seen, that regression model was not significant in general, but N1-latency on parietal electrodes showed to be the significant predictor of depression, what could be hypothesized regarding the previously run correlation analyses.

Table 15 presents the results of five hierarchical regression analyses which have tested prediction power of N1, P2, N2, P3 and Sw latencies (the first step), N1, P2, N2 and P3 amplitudes in the first trial (the second step) and N1, P2, N2 and P3 amplitudes in the second trial (the third step) for addiction, criminality, impulsivity, adventurousness and empathy. Overall, only

*Table 14. Four Regression analyses of N1, P2, N2, P3 and Sw latencies (the first step), N1, P2, N2 and P3 amplitudes in the first trial (the second step) and N1, P2, N2 and P3 amplitudes in the second trial (the third step) as predictors of strength of excitation, strength of inhibition, mobility and depression*

| Model Summary: Strength of Excitation | | | | | | | | | |
|---|---|---|---|---|---|---|---|---|---|
| Model | R | $R^2$ | Adjusted $R^2$ | Std. Error of the Estimate | Change Statistics | | | | |
| | | | | | $R^2$ Change | F Change | df1 | df2 | Sig. F Change |
| 1_Latencies | .523 | .273 | -.100 | 9.17603 | .273 | .732 | 18 | 35 | .757 |
| 2_Amplitudes1 | .826 | .682 | .114 | 8.23468 | .409 | 1.529 | 16 | 19 | .187 |
| 3_Amplitudes2 | .854 | .730 | -.433 | 10.47325 | .047 | .194 | 9 | 10 | .989 |
| Significant predictors | | | B | Beta | | | | | |
| P2-latency_P3 | | | -1.170* | -3.300* | | | | | |
| P2-latency_P4 | | | -1.152* | -3.282* | | | | | |
| N1-amplitude1_P3 | | | .653** | .560* | | | | | |
| P3-amplitude1_P3 | | | -1.018* | -.806* | | | | | |
| **Model Summary: Strength of Inhibition** | | | | | | | | | |
| Model | R | $R^2$ | Adjusted $R^2$ | Std. Error of the Estimate | Change Statistics | | | | |
| | | | | | $R^2$ Change | F Change | df1 | df2 | Sig. F Change |
| 1_Latencies | .602 | .362 | .034 | 6.80568 | .362 | 1.103 | 18 | 35 | .389 |
| 2_Amplitudes1 | .850 | .723 | .228 | 6.08360 | .361 | 1.550 | 16 | 19 | .180 |
| 3_Amplitudes2 | .953 | .908 | .510 | 4.84527 | .184 | 2.217 | 9 | 10 | .115 |
| Significant predictors | | | B | Beta | | | | | |
| N2-amplitude1_P3 | | | .791* | .700* | | | | | |
| N2-amplitude1_P4 | | | .947* | .714* | | | | | |
| **Model Summary: Mobility** | | | | | | | | | |
| Model | R | $R^2$ | Adjusted $R^2$ | Std. Error of the Estimate | Change Statistics | | | | |
| | | | | | $R^2$ Change | F Change | df1 | df2 | Sig. F Change |
| 1_Latencies | .600 | .360 | .030 | 9.26611 | .360 | 1.091 | 18 | 35 | .399 |
| 2_Amplitudes1 | .795 | .633 | -.024 | 9.52255 | .273 | .884 | 16 | 19 | .595 |
| 3_Amplitudes2 | .905 | .820 | .043 | 9.20213 | .187 | 1.150 | 9 | 10 | .413 |
| Significant predictors | | | B | Beta | | | | | |
| N2-latency_O1 | | | -2.331* | -8.918* | | | | | |
| P2-latency_P3 | | | -1.214* | -3.184* | | | | | |
| P2-latency_P4 | | | -1.292* | -3.421* | | | | | |
| N2-latency_P4 | | | -.094* | -.515* | | | | | |

*continued on following page*

*Table 14. Continued*

| Model Summary: Depression | | | | | | | | | |
|---|---|---|---|---|---|---|---|---|---|
| Model | R | $R^2$ | Adjusted $R^2$ | Std. Error of the Estimate | Change Statistics | | | | |
| | | | | | $R^2$ Change | F Change | df1 | df2 | Sig. F Change |
| 1_Latencies | .661 | .436 | .146 | 6.94933 | .436 | 1.505 | 18 | 35 | .147 |
| 2_Amplitudes1 | .848 | .719 | .217 | 6.65556 | .283 | 1.197 | 16 | 19 | .350 |
| 3_Amplitudes2 | .922 | .850 | .205 | 6.70549 | .131 | .969 | 9 | 10 | .514 |
| Significant predictors | | | B | Beta | | | | | |
| N1-latency_P3 | | | .903* | 3.607* | | | | | |
| N1-latency_P4 | | | .970* | 3.913* | | | | | |

* p<0.05 ** p<0.01

*Table 15. Five Regression analyses of N1, P2, N2, P3 and Sw latencies (the first step), N1, P2, N2 and P3 amplitudes in the first trial (the second step) and N1, P2, N2 and P3 amplitudes in the second trial (the third step) as predictors of addiction, criminality, impulsivity, adventurousness and empathy*

| Model Summary: Addiction | | | | | | | | | |
|---|---|---|---|---|---|---|---|---|---|
| Model | R | $R^2$ | Adjusted $R^2$ | Std. Error of the Estimate | Change Statistics | | | | |
| | | | | | $R^2$ Change | F Change | df1 | df2 | Sig. F Change |
| 1_Latencies | .598 | .358 | .028 | 3.85293 | .358 | 1.084 | 18 | 35 | .405 |
| 2_Amplitudes1 | .825 | .680 | .108 | 3.69010 | .322 | 1.197 | 16 | 19 | .350 |
| 3_Amplitudes2 | .935 | .874 | .333 | 3.19039 | .194 | 1.713 | 9 | 10 | .207 |
| Significant predictors | | | B | Beta | | | | | |
| N1-latency_P3 | | | -.535* | -4.114* | | | | | |
| N1-latency_P4 | | | -.561* | -4.354* | | | | | |
| N2-latency_P4 | | | -.046* | -.608* | | | | | |
| P3-amplitude2_O2 | | | -1.886* | -1.292* | | | | | |
| Model Summary: Criminality | | | | | | | | | |
| Model | R | $R^2$ | Adjusted $R^2$ | Std. Error of the Estimate | Change Statistics | | | | |
| | | | | | $R^2$ Change | F Change | df1 | df2 | Sig. F Change |
| 1_Latencies | .617 | .380 | .062 | 4.56080 | .380 | 1.193 | 18 | 35 | .318 |
| 2_Amplitudes1 | .857 | .734 | .257 | 4.05794 | .353 | 1.576 | 16 | 19 | .171 |
| 3_Amplitudes2 | .950 | .903 | .486 | 3.37608 | .169 | 1.939 | 9 | 10 | .158 |
| Significant predictors | | | B | Beta | | | | | |
| N1-latency_P4 | | | -.060* | -.657* | | | | | |
| P3-amplitude2_O2 | | | -2.232* | -1.268* | | | | | |

continued on following page

*Table 15. Continued*

| Model Summary: Impulsivity | | | | | | | | | |
|---|---|---|---|---|---|---|---|---|---|
| Model | R | $R^2$ | Adjusted $R^2$ | Std. Error of the Estimate | Change Statistics | | | | |
| | | | | | $R^2$ Change | F Change | df1 | df2 | Sig. F Change |
| 1_Latencies | .397 | .157 | -.276 | 3.89783 | .157 | .363 | 18 | 35 | .988 |
| 2_Amplitudes1 | .806 | .650 | .024 | 3.40851 | .493 | 1.673 | 16 | 19 | .142 |
| 3_Amplitudes2 | .865 | .748 | -.338 | 3.99089 | .097 | .429 | 9 | 10 | .891 |
| Significant predictors | | | B | Beta | | | | | |
| P3-amplitude1_O1 | | | -1.210* | -1.021* | | | | | |
| P3-amplitude1_O2 | | | -1.059* | -.985* | | | | | |
| P2-amplitude1_P4 | | | -.405* | -1.072* | | | | | |
| **Model Summary: Adventurousness** | | | | | | | | | |
| Model | R | $R^2$ | Adjusted $R^2$ | Std. Error of the Estimate | Change Statistics | | | | |
| | | | | | $R^2$ Change | F Change | df1 | df2 | Sig. F Change |
| 1_Latencies | .670 | .449 | .165 | 3.29141 | .449 | 1.583 | 18 | 35 | .120 |
| 2_Amplitudes1 | .847 | .718 | .214 | 3.19485 | .269 | 1.134 | 16 | 19 | .392 |
| 3_Amplitudes2 | .904 | .817 | .032 | 3.54386 | .099 | .605 | 9 | 10 | .769 |
| Significant predictors | | | B | Beta | | | | | |
| P3-amplitude1_O1 | | | -1.256* | -1.015* | | | | | |
| **Model Summary: Empathy** | | | | | | | | | |
| Model | R | $R^2$ | Adjusted $R^2$ | Std. Error of the Estimate | Change Statistics | | | | |
| | | | | | $R^2$ Change | F Change | df1 | df2 | Sig. F Change |
| 1_Latencies | .557 | .310 | -.044 | 3.15813 | .310 | .875 | 18 | 35 | .609 |
| 2_Amplitudes1 | .822 | .675 | .094 | 2.94096 | .365 | 1.335 | 16 | 19 | .271 |
| 3_Amplitudes2 | **.960** | **.922** | **.587** | 1.98572 | **.247** | **3.520** | **9** | **10** | **.031** |
| Significant predictors | | | B | Beta | | | | | |
| N1-amplitude2_P4 | | | .263* | .666* | | | | | |

* p<0.05 ** p<0.01

one regression model was statistically significant, i.e. visual evoked potentials are significant predictors of empathy. Specifically, N1-amplitude in the second trial on one parietal electrode is significant predictor of empathy in this sample of students.

Furthermore, even though overall models were not significant, some individual latencies and amplitudes of evoked potentials are significant predictors of other personality traits. Therefore, addiction could be significantly predicted by N1-N2-latencies at parietal electrodes and by P3-amplitude in the second trial on one occipital electrode. In addition, criminality could be predicted by N1-latency on one parietal electrode and P3-amplitude in the second trial on one occipital electrode – the same EP-parameters that are significant predictors for addiction. This is not surprising since these two traits are measured by different items that reflect extraversion, neuroticism, psychoticism and social desirability (conformism).

Furthermore, it is interesting to see determined significant predictors of impulsivity and adventurousness. P2-amplitude on occipital electrodes and P3-amplitude on one parietal electrode are significant predictors of impulsivity and P3-amplitude on one occipital electrode is significant predictor of adventurousness. Determined predictors are rather different in comparison to previously determined correlations what could be explained by significant inter-correlations between personality traits.

However, general conclusion of presented hierarchical regression analyses results could be that the relationship between human personality and visual evoked potentials is definitely very complex. Due to significant inter-correlations between personality traits, the high visual evoked potentials' variability, specific sample, monotonous visual oddball task and not so contemporary ERP-measurement instrument (manual EP-marking), it is not possible to have single-way and clear conclusion, what is a solid ground for creating new research direction in the field of electrophysiology of human personality.

## REFERENCES

Baal, G. C. M. van, Geus, E. J. C. & de, Boomsma, D. I. (1997). Longitudinal Study of Genetic Influences on ERP-P3 during Childhood. In G. C. M. van Baal (Ed.), *A Genetic Perspective on the Developing Brain* (pp. 37-61). Vrije Universiteit, Print Partners Ipskamp.

Bruder, G. E., Tenke, C., Stewart, J. E., Towey, J. P., Leite, P., Voglmaier, M., & Quitkin, F. M. (1995). Brain event-related potentials to complex tones in depressed patients: Relations to perceptual asymmetry and clinical features. *Psychophysiology*, *32*(4), 373–381. doi:10.1111/j.1469-8986.1995.tb01220.x PMID:7652114

Bruin, K. J., Kenemans, J. L., Verbaten, M. N., & Van der Heijden, A. C. H. (2000). Habituation: An event-related potential and dipole source analysis study. *International Journal of Psychophysiology*, *36*(3), 199–209. doi:10.1016/S0167-8760(99)00114-2 PMID:10754194

Coles, M. G. H., Gratton, G., Kramer, A. F., & Miller, G. A. (1986). Principles of signal acquisition and analysis. In M. G. H. Coles, E. Donchin, & S. W. Porges (Eds.), *Psychophysiology: Systems, Processes and Applications* (pp. 183–221). New York: The Guilford Press.

Dabić-Jeftić, M., & Mikula, I. (1994a). Evocirani potencijali kore mozga – Osnovne postavke i klinička primjena [Evoked brain potentials – Fundamental postulates and clinical application]. Školska knjiga.

Dalebout, S. D., & Robey, R. R. (1997). Comparison of the intersubject and intrasubject variability of exogenous and endogenous auditory evoked potentials. *Journal of the American Academy of Audiology*, *8*(5), 342–354. PMID:9328896

De Pascalis, V. (1993). Hemispheric Asymmetry, Personality and Temperament. *Personality and Individual Differences*, *14*(6), 825–834. doi:10.1016/0191-8869(93)90095-K

De Pascalis, V. (1994). Personality and temperament in the event-related potentials during stimulus recognition tasks. *Personality and Individual Differences*, *16*(6), 877–889. doi:10.1016/0191-8869(94)90232-1

Diner, B. C., Holcomb, P. J., & Dykman, R. A. (1985). P300 in major depressive disorder. *Psychiatry Research*, *15*(3), 175–184. doi:10.1016/0165-1781(85)90074-5 PMID:3862153

Donchin, E. (1979). Event-related brain potentials: A tool in the study of human information processing. In H. Begleiter (Ed.), *Evoked brain potentials and behavior* (pp. 13–88). New York: Plenum Press. doi:10.1007/978-1-4684-3462-0_2

Eysenck, H. J., & Eysenck, S. B. G. (1994). *Priručnik za Eysenckove skale ličnosti: EPS-odrasli [The Manual for Eysenck's personality scales: EPS-adults]*. Jastrebarsko, Croatia: Naklada Slap.

Faber, B. (1980). Artefakti u elektroencefalografiji [Artifacts in Electroencephalography]. Psychiatric Hospital Jankomir, Zagreb.

Gangadhar, B. N., Ancy, J., Janakiramaiah, N., & Umapathy, C. (1993). P300 amplitude in non-bipolar, melancholic depression. *Journal of Affective Disorders*, *28*(1), 57–60. doi:10.1016/0165-0327(93)90077-W PMID:8326081

Hansenne, M., Pitchot, W., Pinto, E., Reggers, J., Papart, P., & Ansseau, M. (2000). P300 Event-related Brain Potential and Personality in Depression. *European Psychiatry*, *15*(6), 1–8. doi:10.1016/S0924-9338(00)00505-8 PMID:11004732

Hoormann, J., Falkenstein, M., Schwarzenau, P., & Hohnsbein, J. (1998). Methods for the Quantification and Statistical Testing of ERP Differences across Conditions. *Behavior Research Methods, Instruments, & Computers*, *30*(1), 103–109. doi:10.3758/BF03209420

Ippolitov, F. V. (1972). Interanalyser differences in the sensitivity – strenght parameter of vision, hearing and cutaneous modalities. In V. D. Nebylitsyn & J. A. Gray (Eds.), *Biological bases of individual behaviour* (pp. 43–61). New York: Academic Press. doi:10.1016/B978-0-12-515350-8.50009-0

Krizmanić, M. & Kolesarić, V. (1994). *Priručnik za primjenu Skale depresiivnosti D-92* [The Manual for the application of Depression Scale- D]. Naklada Slap.

Lin, E., & Polich, J. (1999). P300 habituation patterns: Individual differences from ultradian rhythms. *Perceptual and Motor Skills*, *88*(3c), 1111–1125. doi:10.2466/pms.1999.88.3c.1111 PMID:10485091

Lučev, I., Tadinac, M., & Tatalović Vorkapić, S. (2006). Krosvalidacija hrvatske verzije Pavlovijanskog upitnika temperamenta (PTS) [Cross-validation of Croatian version of Pavlov's Temperament Survey (PTS)]. *Suvremena Psihologija*, *9*(1), 35–45.

Lučev, I., Tadinac Babić, M., & Tatalović, S. (2002). Konstrukcija hrvatske verzije Pavlovijanskog upitnika temperamenta (PTS) [Construction of Croatian version of Pavlov's Temperament Survey (PTS)]. *Suvremena Psihologija*, *5*, 207–226.

Medelec/TECA Sapphire[II] 4E device – the portable part. (n.d.). Retrieved from www.admarneuro.com/eeg_emg.html

Muir, W. J., St Clair, D. M., & Blackwood, D. H. R. (1991). Long-latenca auditory event-related potentials in schizophrenia and in bipolar and unipolar affective disorder. *Psychological Medicine*, *21*, 867–879. doi:10.1017/S003329170002986X PMID:1780401

Nishida, S., Nakamura, M., & Shibasaki, H. (1999). Physiological Variability of Peak Latency in Evoked Potentials: Use of a Property of Asynchronous Averaging. *Medical Engineering & Physics*, *21*(10), 681–687. doi:10.1016/S1350-4533(99)00100-9 PMID:10717548

Novalić, D. (1991). *Standardizacija vidnih evociranih potencijala pobuđenih reverzibilnom šahovskom pločom* [Standardization of visual evoked potentials evoked by reversibile chessboard. In Croatian] (Graduate thesis). Department of Psychology, Faculty of Humanities and Social Sciences, University of Zagreb, Zagreb, Croatia.

Nuwer, M. R., Comi, G., Emerson, R., Fuglsang-Frederiksen, A., Guérit, J.-M., Hinrichs, H., & ..., Rappelsburger, P. (1998). IFCN Standards for Digital Recording of Clinical EEG. *Electroencephalography and Clinical Neurophysiology*, *106*, 259–261. doi:10.1016/S0013-4694(97)00106-5 PMID:9743285

Picton, T. W., Bentin, S., Berg, P., Donchin, E., Hillyard, S. A., Johnson, R. Jr, & Taylor, M. J. et al. (2000). Guidelines for Using Human Event-Related Potentials to Study Cognition: Recording Standards and Publication Criteria – Committee Report. *Psychophysiology*, *37*(2), 127–157. doi:10.1111/1469-8986.3720127 PMID:10731765

Polich, J. (1989). Habituation of P300 from Auditory Stimuli. *Psychobiology (Austin, Tex.)*, *17*(1), 19–28.

Polich, J. (1998). P300 Clinical Utility and Control of Variability. *Journal of Clinical Neurophysiology*, *15*(1), 14–33. doi:10.1097/00004691-199801000-00004 PMID:9502510

Polich, J. (1999). P300 in clinical applications. In E. Niedermeyer & F. Lopes de Silva (Eds.), Electroencephalography: Basic Principles, Clinical Applications and Related Fields (4th ed.; pp. 1073-1091). Baltimore, MD: Urban & Schwarzenberg.

Polich, J. (2002). Neuropsychology of P3a and P3b: A Theorethical Overwiev. In K. Arikan & N. Moore (Eds.), Advances in Electrophysiology in Clinical Practice and Research. Academic Press.

Polich, J., & Kok, A. (1995). Cognitive and Biological Determinants of P300: An Integrative Review. *Biological Psychology*, *41*(2), 103–146. doi:10.1016/0301-0511(95)05130-9 PMID:8534788

Pritchard, W. S. (1981). Psychophysiology of P300. *Psychological Bulletin, 89*(3), 506–540. doi:10.1037/0033-2909.89.3.506 PMID:7255627

Revelle, W., Humphreys, M. S., Simon, L., & Gilliland, K. (1980). The interactive effect of personality, time of day, and caffeine: A test of the arousal model. *Journal of Experimental Psychology. General, 109*(1), 1–31. doi:10.1037/0096-3445.109.1.1 PMID:6445402

Šantić, A. (1995). Biomedicinska elektronika [Biomedical electronics]. Školska knjiga.

*Sapphire*[II] *User manual 003W009A*. (1996). Medelec, Vickers Medical & Teca Vickers Medical. Medical Device Directive, Medelec Ltd.

Saxena, N., Bhatia, M., Joshi, Y. K., Garg, P. K., & Tandon, R. K. (2001). Utility of P300 auditory event-related potential in detecting cognitive dysfunction in patients with cirrhosis of the liver. *Neurology India, 49*, 350–354. PMID:11799406

Shaughnessy, J. J., & Zechmeister, E. B. (1997). Ethical Issues in the conduct of psychological research. In *Research methods in psychology* (4th ed.; pp. 38–75). McGraw-Hill Companies, Inc., Usa.

Soysal, A., Atakli, D., Atay, T., Altintas, H., Baybas, S., & Arpaci, B. (1999). Auditory event-related potentials (P300) in partial and generalized epileptic patients. *Seizure, 8*(2), 107–110. doi:10.1053/seiz.1998.0234 PMID:10222303

Soysal, A., Atay, T., Aysal, F., Ozturk, M., Altunkaynak, Y., Baybas, S., & Arpaci, B. (2001). Pattern reversal visual evoked potentials and EEG in migraine patients with-and without visual aura. *Journal of Neurological Sciences, 18*(1). Retrieved from http://www.med.ege.edu.tr/norolbil/2001/NBD14401.html

Strelau, J. (1972). A diagnosis of temperament by nonexperimental techniques. *Polish Psychological Bulletin, 3*, 97–105.

Strelau, J. (1983a). *Temperament, Personality, Activity*. London: Academic Press.

Strelau, J., Angleitner, A., & Newberry, B. H. (1999). Pavlovian Temperament Survey (PTS): An international handbook. Göttingen: Hogrefe & Huber Publishers.

Strelau, J., Angleitner, A., Bantelmann, J., & Ruch, W. (1990). The Strelau Temperament Inventory – Revised (STI-R): Theoretical considerations and scale development. *European Journal of Personality*, *4*(3), 209–235. doi:10.1002/per.2410040304

Tadinac, M. (1988). The partiality phenomenon in investigation of strenght of the nervous system. *Psychologische Beiträge*, *30*, 166–172.

Tadinac Babić, M., Kulenović, A. & Ledinski, D. (1989). On the structure of Strelau Temperament Inventory (STI). *Revija za psihologiju*, *19*(1-2), 25-32.

Tatalović Vorkapić, S. (2009). Biological correlates of P300 and its relationship with extraversion. *Collegium Antropologicum*, *33*(4), 1215–1222. PMID:20102071

Tatalović Vorkapić, S. (2010). Odnos između temperamenta, temeljnih dimenzija ličnosti i evociranih mozgovnih potencijala (The relationship between temperament, basic personality dimensions and evoked brain potentials. *In Croatian*). *Doctoral dissertation*. Faculty of Humanities and Social Sciences, University of Zagreb, Croatia.

Tatalović Vorkapić, S. (2011). Electrocortical differences in sanguine, choleric, phlegmatic and melancholic. *Romanian Journal of Psychology. Psychotherapy and Neuroscience*, *1*(2), 67–96.

Tatalović Vorkapić, S., & Tadinac, M. (2011a). Does the abstract thinking have a significant role in the relationship between extraversion and evoked brain potentials? *Review of Psychology*, *18*(2), 63–70.

Tatalović Vorkapić, S. (2014a). The relationship between concordance of some personality dimensions and visual evoked potentials. *Studia Psychologica*, *56*(4), 323–336.

Tatalović Vorkapić, S. (2015). The relationship between social desirability and visual evoked potentials: Implications for personality measurement. *Cognition, Brain, Behavior /Cogniţie, creier, comportament. 19*, *2*, 99–113.

Tatalović Vorkapić, S., & Tadinac, M., & Rudež, J. (2010). P300 and extraversion in the visual oddball paradigm. *Studia Psychologica*, *52*(1), 3–14.

Tatalović Vorkapić, S., & Tadinac, M. (2016). The relationship of neuroticism, psychoticism and depression with visual evoked potentials. *Acta Neuropsychologica*, *14*(3), 241–254. doi:10.5604/17307503.1222838

Tatalović Vorkapić, S., Tadinac, M., & Lučev, I. (2013). Electrocortical correlates of temperament. *Polish Psychological Bulletin*, *44*(1), 92–101. doi:10.2478/ppb-2013-0010

van Beijsterveldt, C. E. M., Molenaar, P. C. M., Geus, E. J. C., & de Boomsma, D. I. (1996a). Heritability of human brain functioning as assessed by electroencephalography. In C. E. M. van Beijsterveldt (Ed.), *The Genetics of Electrophysiological Indices of Brain Activity* (pp. 29–49). Dissertatierecks, Faculteit Psychologie, Universiteit van Amsterdam.

Vorkapić, S. T., & Tadinac, M. (2011b). Electrophysiological Correlates of Empathy. *The Romanian Journal of Psychology. Psychotherapy and Neuroscience*, *1*(1), 19–37.

Zuckerman, M. (1969). Theoretical formulations. In J. P. Zubek (Ed.), *Sensory deprivation: Fifteen years of research* (pp. 407–432). New York: Appleton-Century-Crofts.

# Chapter 5
# Conclusions and Future Research Guidelines


## ABSTRACT

*The main aim of this book is to present contemporary research findings in the field of brain activity and human personality. Certain psychological and electrophysiological attributes of human personality and their relationship were presented. The contribution of this research and the whole book is described here. Also, the focus has been given to the novelty of research findings. In addition, like many other studies, this study has given some answers but at the same time has revealed many more questions. Therefore, various guidelines for future research, and some innovative measurement/methodology proposals have been presented in this last section.*


## OPPORTUNITIES AND CHALLENGES IN ELECTROPHYSIOLOGICAL RESEARCH ON PERSONALITY

*One of the hallmarks of the field of personality psychology is the breadth and sophistication of its methods. Thumbing through a typical issue of a personality journal, one encounters a rich array of research designs, assessment procedures, and statistical techniques… Just as personality psychologists appreciate the complexity of human nature and individual variability, so too*

DOI: 10.4018/978-1-5225-2283-6.ch005

*do we appreciate the diverse ways in which that complexity can be assessed, quantified, and examined. (Robins, Fraley & Krueger, 2007, ix)*

A large number of authors who systematically study the interrelationship between cognition, personality and their biological basis, has strived to find the causes of the existing disagreements, both among theoretical assumptions as well as in the chain of inconsistent findings, which have a specifically strong presence in the field of analyzing the relation between personality and brain evoked potentials. Matthews and Gilliland (2001) concluded that there are two fundamental factors: the absence of the best research strategy to improve the biological personality theories and insufficient prominence of individual differences in cognition as a significant factor in the context of the personality traits theory.

Considering the first cause, the main obstacle is the extreme complexity of experiment data, and the difficulty of achieving consistent results, leading to biological theories that are ignoring a growing number of evidence that personality traits are in very different ways associated with multiple and independent systems of the brain and not only them. As for the second cause, there are discussions in the direction that some phenomena are best explained by means of integrated bio-cognitive explanations, while others can be explained in terms of the cognitive constructs without a direct relation with nervous system processes, resulting in the formation of an excessively large number of biological personality theories and situations in which cognitive explanations are preferred to the neurological. On the other hand, Eysenck (1997) emphasized in his study of the uniqueness of psychology and the possibility of creating a paradigm for both the person and intelligence that excessive and artificial separation of correlational and experimental approaches, which have resulted in a lack of necessary research paradigms in the study of individual differences, which was discussed in the introduction of work, and which was later enriched by Stelmack's examples (1997).

## CONCEPTUAL PROBLEMS IN PERSONALITY TRAITS THEORIES

Regarding Eysenck's (1967) personality theory, it is clear that it is supported by a range of evidence from the behavioral genetics circle since their consistent psychophysiological paradigms reject the possibility that personality traits are social constructs without biological components, which was the starting point in this paper. However, Mathews and Gilliland (1999) provided a critical review of the fact that particular psychophysiological findings on the threshold of sensitivity and conditioning truly support Eysenck's view on the relation between extraversion and lower levels of cortical-reticular excitation. They have pointed out that an exaggerated generalization of interaction effects of extraversion and stimulus intensity occurs in different research paradigms, although the determined nervous systems that underlie these responses have not been specified. The existing biological theories have yet to decide how to conceptualize the complexity that is evident in the empirical data.

Corr and colleagues (Pickering et al, 1997) highlighted that an interaction between the systems is extremely important, i.e. access the "related sub-systems." Although system interaction has always been a part of the theory - e.g. in Eysenck's personality theory (1967) interaction E *x* N dimension is present, a large number of researchers have ignored it. The interaction itself absolutely makes sense, but the complexity of its effects often reflects other factors. For example, personality traits can be distributed across multiple brain systems, such as the "cortical-reticular" and "dopaminergic" aspects of extraversion (Matthews & Gilliland, 1999). Also, there are a number of findings about the relation between extraversion and a similar BAER wave V reflecting CNS arousal (Bullock and Gilliland, 1993), or extraversion is possible even when it is independently associated with more peripheral neural mechanisms (Stelmack, Campbell & Bell, 1993).

Work in the field of linguistic differences between extraverts and introverts (Dewaele & Furnham, 1999, 2000) suggest that personality is associated with the "language centers" in the brain. Similarly, it appears that anxiety/neuroticism is associated with systems that are not motivational (Derryberry & Reed, 1997, according to Matthews and Gilliland, 2001), while personality is generally associated with circulating hormones, as well as with discrete brain areas (Zuckerman, 1991). Theorists of personality traits assume a hierarchical system that contributes to personality. We can imagine that every personality trait is supported by a number of brain systems, such as multiple systems supporting a stimulating motivation (Depu & Collins, 1999). Within such a hierarchy, it is possible to identify dimensions E and N of the specific systems that facilitate the prediction of behavior. However, perhaps this assumption is wrong.

Zuckerman (1991) strongly opposed any kind of simplified isomorphism between personality traits and brain systems: one system can contribute to several different personality traits, each of which reflects several systems. If this is copied to a finer level, this could greatly limit the contribution to molecular genetic studies. The relation between genes and brain systems can be just as non-isomorphic (Canli, 2006). If so, only a small association between specific genes and personality traits can be expected, which greatly reduces the value of molecular genetic studies (Plomin & Caspi, 1998).

In addition, studies that have attempted to make conclusions about arousal based on behavioral indicators in experimental manipulations are not popular because of the tendency to support arbitrary *post hoc* explanations and circular reasoning (Hockey, 1984, according to Matthews & Gilliland, 2001), which after all, also poses a threat in this research. They also provided similar criticism regarding Gray's Reinforcement Sensitivity Theory (RST) (Gray, 1991), noting that this theory underestimates the multiplicity of the possible biological personality origin. Although the RST is on its way to provide quality answers about how it is possible to distinguish between the motivational effects and other sources of individual differences in personality, the problem of determining the precise relationship between brain motivational subsystems and personality traits nevertheless remains. Within the context of the aforementioned, they found that the most neglected, on the one hand, is the effect of motivational factors in biological theories of personality, which have a role in moderating the impact of personality on psychophysiological and behavioral responses, especially in studies that use evoked brain potentials (Bartusssek et al., 1996).

Problems related to Strelau's temperament theory based on Pavlov's Theory of the Central Nervous System Properties (Strelau, Angleitner & Newberry, 1999) are added, which in their title reflects the significant biological determinants of human personality, but with a very low level of empirical validation in that sense. On the other hand, Corr (2000) pointed out the dominant, but also ignored, impact of cognitive factors such as expectations in the simple paradigm of conditioning, which then again in a way affects the subcortical brain system.

Regarding the above mentioned, Corr (2000) and Matthews and Gilliland (1999) considered the cognitive constructs to be more suitable than biological in explaining most of the behavior samples, and that the explanations provided by Eysenck's and Gray's theories are relevant only for a limited part of the overall human behavior. They thereby emphasized that they do not want to discourage attempts of directly relating to individual differences in behavior of brain functions, such as the P300-wave, since the personality theory can be more complete if adopts diversity and soundness of approach in explaining individual differences. However, they pointed out that the cognitive constructs associated with personality traits proved reliable predictors of laboratory and actual performance of neurological constructs, whose representatives are psychophysiological measures.

On the other hand, they suggested that cognitive constructs provide a more consistent image of how the influence of personality traits is moderated by environmental and inter-human factors, unlike biological constructs. Therefore, the authors proposed the integration of cognitive and biological theories, which cover two aspects. The first concerns the development of a model that links the operation of the nerve system and processing information to the proposal of connectionist theorists, (the Connectionist model represents level-processing constructs as activation samples within the neural network unit).

Siegle (1999), and Siegle and Ingram (1997, all according to Matthews & Gilliland, 2001) developed a model of feedback between nerve units representing semantic constructs and units representing emotions that stimulate aspects of depressive cognition, which is in accordance with the emotional processing in the amygdala, the hippocampus and frontal lobe. The second relates to the recognition of the limitations of biological models for understanding self-regulatory control to adapt to situational demands, and the need to apply different levels of explanation for the different problems in psychology (Matthews & Gilliland, 2001).

Finally, Canli (2006) highlighted in his book that, although there are various research designs, theories, and methods of measuring human personality, in fact, the genetic studies of personality traits and the application of the method of functional magnetic resonance imaging are the most promising in the research of human personality.

## TOWARDS A PARADIGM DEVELOPMENT: GUIDELINES FOR FURTHER RESEARCH

Be as it may, the overall behavior depends on the brain, and the overall behavior is biological. The most important issue is related to whether the theory thrives as a better science when the psychological constructs that explain personality are described in neurological or cognitive terms. The advantage of cognitive constructs is that they are more clearly operationalized and measurable in contrast to the neurological constructs and permit accurate predictions of experimental consequences. Starting from the broader framework of those who are placed in relation to the important role of personality biology of the individual, further development of science requires methods and theories that will allow researchers to distinguish and separate the biological components of cognitive research in the field of personality, as well as that genetic testing model requires differentiation of environmental effects (Mann, 1994).

In relation to this, Eysenck (1997) pointed out that the need for psychology uniqueness undoubtedly lies in the capacity of psychology as a science. Therefore, he emphasized that psychologists study people, not atoms. It is the person who enters the research laboratory: a person with his/her ideas, emotions, prejudices, a certain amount of knowledge, and information; a person with a specific position in a two-dimensional space of the fundamental personality dimensions; a person with a certain IQ and specific abilities. All of the above is in interaction, and enters this interaction in different ways, be it from the performance in the laboratory to experimental conditions; it affects the memory, learning, perception, conditioning, emotional reactions, psychophysiology - in fact, everything that a participant does at the given time. It is not possible to draw any conclusions based on this evidence of such a large interaction scale (Eysenck & Eysenck, 1985), which implies an imperative on the inclusion of relevant personality factors in any type of experimental design. In other words, relating correlational and experimental drafts, which would be set within a specific holistic theoretical personality framework, should provide an opportunity to improve the existing theory and the creation of paradigms.

## Conclusions About These Research Results in the Light of Future Studies

In fact, this question is clearly visible in this study, since the correlation of all personality analysis and visual evoked potentials did not fully reflect the significant predictors in the visual evoked potentials for each personality trait separately. In addition, in the previous article (Tatalović Vorkapić, Tadinac & Rudež, 2010), the effect of habituation is described in detail, which is analyzed only by EP amplitudes in the two series on the four recorded electrodes, considering that EP latencies represent a constant for labeling evoked potentials in the second series of recordings. An important finding has been established that points to the existence of habituation in the subsequent P3-wave component. This finding is commonly recognized as significant only in subsequent components, given that a significant amount of their variability can be attributed to the participant's attention, awareness, and focus on the task. This fact reflects the late components sensitivity of the participant's psychological state. The level of attention in which the participant accesses a task will have a significant impact on the length of the late component's amplitude (Davis, 1964; Picton & Hillyard, 1974). In addition, this difference in the habituation effect of exogenous EP-components, in relation to the endogenous once, is in accordance with the included functioning of the higher order that is associated with such structures as the frontal cortex and hippocampus.

Based on this finding it is clear that a visual oddball paradigm, which was applied in this study, represents a monotonous and simple task for the participants, which is obviously a significant interaction with the studied personality traits, both theoretically and empirically. Furthermore, although the descriptive analysis of personality traits data and visual evoked potentials in the questioned sample of psychology students only confirmed previous findings, as it has already been explained, the correlation analysis of personality traits and latency amplitude of evoked brain potentials together resulted in a smaller number of significant correlations, mostly between adventurousness and social desirability with EP-latencies, and psychoticism and mobility with EP-amplitudes. More specifically, this study has significant relation between brain evoked potentials (N1, P1, N2, P3, and SW) and personality operationalized within Eysenck's dimensional personality typology and Pavlov's central nervous system characteristics theory, in the following ways: there was a significant relation between increased amplitudes of the N1-P2-N2-P3 components recorded in the first and second series of parietal electrodes and a higher power excitation and mobility and lower inhibition power, which was expected considering the established effect of habituation. No significant relations between the EP latency and mobility were found. Although the elevated levels of cortical arousal were related with introverts, during the effect of habituation there was no significant relation between extraversion and EP-amplitudes.

However, a significant relation of shorter latencies of P3 slow-wave activity and extraversion was found, which is interpreted in terms of faster information processing among extravert participants. In the end, there was a significant relation of lower amplitude and prolonged latency with higher neuroticism and depression, and prolonged latency with social desirability, while psychoticism showed a significant relation with shorter latencies and high amplitudes of evoked potentials. These findings suggest a different relation direction between these two personality models with electro-cortical correlates, but the PTS-dimensions have showed a more consistent and significant overall relation with evoked potentials. In addition, adventurousness has showed the most consistent negative correlation with EP-latencies, empathy a negative significant correlation with the N2-amplitude on one parietal electrode, and impulsivity with N2-amplitudes on both occipital electrodes and in the first series of positive correlation and in the second series a negative correlation.

Furthermore, regarding the relationship between evoked potentials and behavioral variables, the following was identified. A prolonged P3-latency on both occipital electrodes in participants who are not using any vision corrections (lenses or glasses); significantly shorter Sw-latencies on both occipital electrodes with participants who drink coffee; significantly shortened slow-latency on both parietal electrodes and the P3-latency on the P4-electrode in participants who smoke. Apart from age, out of eight behavioral variables only drinking alcoholic beverages and sports activity showed no significant relation with EP-amplitudes, which indicates a significant conditionality of the EP-amplitude measured with behavioral variables.

At the end, it can be concluded that this work contributes not only to the determination of some basic associations between evoked potentials and different operationalized and theoretically compelling personality traits, but it also represents a significant methodological contribution in the identification of a set of variables that moderate this relation, which is in EP-research often neglected for various reasons. The obtained findings are explained in detail in the theoretical personality framework in relation to the existing effect of habituation, and confirmed previous studies (Tatalović Vorkapić, 2009, 2011, 2014a, 2015; Tatalović Vorkapić & Tadinac, 2011a,b, 2016; Tatalović Vorkapić, Tadinac & Rudež, 2010; Tatalović, Tadinac & Lučev, 2013). However, a significant contribution of this book lies in the implementation of the analysis of predicting personality traits based on the measured visual evoked potentials. As stated in the research, the conducted correlation analyses did not fully comply with the individual hierarchical analysis, precisely for the reason that Eysenck (1997) stated as being the most important.

First and foremost, these are inconsistent and although significant, relatively low correlations between personality traits and visual evoked potentials. Second, the hierarchical analysis has showed that the general effect of predictions based on visual evoked potentials was determined at the level of 5% of significance, only for empathy, emphasizing only one EP-component as significant predictor (N1-amplitude in the second trial on one parietal electrode). Third, individual analysis of each personality trait has resulted in fewer and different types of EP predictors, than it was possible to conclude based on a common correlation analysis. For example, in addiction and criminality that are operationalized and measured within Eysenck's theory of personality, and as such are composed of a combination of particles from a subscale of extraversion, psychoticism, neuroticism, and social desirability (conformism), there are several significant EP-predictors determined as significant. In detail, a separate regression hierarchical analysis has indicated that there are four different parameters of evoked potentials that are significant predictors of addiction, and two of criminality, although the overall prediction effect of these two personality traits based on the visual evoked potential is not significant. On the other side, it was only one significant positive correlation between addiction and slow-wave latency activities on one parietal electrode.

Considering this, one really old question needs to be asked, but now for a completely new and different reason: How to study the relation between human personality and evoked brain potentials? Should the holistic approach be emphasized, which is present in the correlation analysis, or the elementary approach, which is present in the hierarchical regression analyses? Depending on which approach is adopted, it will greatly affect the results obtained concerning the electrophysiology of human personality. What certainly can be concluded is that a highly expressed sensitivity of visual evoked potentials has been determined, which has resulted in a broad physiological and other variability in this study, and can be avoided by using oddball tasks that require a technically advanced device for recording the evoked brain potentials.

By summarizing the factors that should to be taken into consideration in such a specific study, it can be observed that they relate to: the variation and controlling difficulty/modality of the task; more recording series; variation of time between series; a numerically larger and more heterogeneous sample of participants with respect to gender, age, and study interests/occupations; a technically modern device to record evoked potentials using a number of relevant electrodes; the application of laboratory measured dimensions of personality and not just questionnaire dimensions; and similar. This, perhaps, would not provide the answers to questions of this research, but it would certainly result in better insight into this complicated yet very interesting relation between personality and evoked potentials.

## Identity Models and Evoked Brain Potentials as Future Research Guideline?

In addition to these very clear guidelines, by applying a theoretical approach to this type of research, and representing a holistic approach to understanding the electrophysiology of human personality, it is possible to examine the relation between the identity model and evoked brain potentials. One part of this study has contributed to this segment about research methodology in electrophysiology of human personality and it refers to the results of the factor analysis. Namely, fifteen factors were ultimately extracted within which certain individual characteristics of personality on the one side and evoked potentials on the other had a high saturation, which indicates that in rotated space they commonly explain the variances of individual factors.

First, these results have confirmed the explanation of significant inter-correlations of individual personality traits that may be underlying the non-compliant findings group correlation analyses and individual hierarchical regression analyses.

Second, there is a need for researching the one-factor unified model of personality (Musek, 2007) and its relation to the electrophysiological parameters in studies of personality psychology.

Third, an interesting finding is that individual personality traits had a higher saturation factors which are predominantly characterized by evoked potentials, and not by other personality traits, such as adventurousness, psychoticism, and empathy - does that mean that these personality traits are biologically strongly determined or something else? In any case, each of the analyses in this study has resulted with new results, contributed to previous studies of biological determination of human personality, and opened up new questions.

However, going back to the idea of a studying the association between the identity model with electrophysiological parameters, it is important to argument this idea at the beginning - why identity models rather than the current theoretical models of personality? Besides, the development of identity models has been the result of constraints arising not only from a large number of personality theories that have quite different starting points, but also from the internal structure of theoretical models, such as the model of extraversion (Tatalović Vorkapić, 2008b). In addition, a number of methodological problems have been pointed out within the framework of the existing theoretical models of personality in psychology (Bratko, 2002; Hogan & Roberts, 2004; McAdams & Pals, 2006; Musek, 1999; Tatalović Vorkapić, 2014b).

Generally, they relate to the amount of information that contain answers to questions about the personality of a person and the level of our understanding of the personality of that same person in a given time and situation, for example, using a standardized personality questionnaire as the only measure that is thereby applied. Although the scientific methodology meets the fundamental purpose of science (Milas, 2005; Cohen, Manion & Morrison, 2007), it is also limiting. It is clear that models of personality traits are nowadays ranked very high on the scientific scale. Nevertheless, is this justified? The principal difference between models of personality and models of identity is that according to the personality traits' perspective, personality development is more influenced by genetic rather than environmental factors, which determine temporal stability of personality. In other words, personality traits in the Five-factor model are expressions of human biology, and in the beginning stages of the development of this model it was considered that they are not affected by the environment.

In addition to this problem of the dominant biological determination of personality traits, this model contains a problem of connecting personality structure with personality processes, as well as the problem that it emphasizes that all individuals possess these five factors, which is not derived from available research evidence. Although the authors in a later revision of the model took into account the importance of the environment in the development of personality, they pointed out that future research should investigate in detail and explain developmental psychology of characteristic adaptations (McCrae & Costa, 2008). Thus, models of identity attach significantly more importance to the impact of the environment and to the interaction between the individual and the environment. They provide detailed instructions of how stability but also changes in certain personality traits are achieved, not only under the influence of genetic factors, but also the very maturation and activity between the individual and the environment.

McAdams and Pals (2006) pointed out that explanations of human personality should include its three basic aspects: a) understanding the features specific to humans as a species - that is, how a person resembles all other members of its species; b) understanding individual characteristics as common characteristics – i.e. the way in which a person resembles others; and c) understanding the unique pattern of one personality - that is, in what way and how a person is not like any other.

The most contemporary identity model today is the neo-socio-analytical model of personality, which represents a structural and integrated personality model that includes personal characteristics, motives, abilities, biographies and social roles (Roberts, 2006). In his model he describes the four basic elements of analysis or basic domains that form the foundation of human personality and the most important categories of individual differences: personality traits (again, usually from the domain of the Five-factor personality theory), motives and values (goals, interests, life tasks, and desires), skills (verbal, numerical, and spatial intelligence), and biographies (life histories, significant memories, and memories). All these elements strongly influence each other, as well as the identity (self-evaluation that represents a conscious subjective experience) and reputation (evaluation by others, and reflects the unconscious processes), which are the two psychological and methodological entities. Formed identity and reputation directly affect the four key elements of personality, culture, and social roles that reflect status and belonging, which explicitly implements the social environment (Hogan & Roberts, 2000). This model, on the one hand, keeps in mind the factor of culture, which is closely associated with identity, reputation and social roles, and, on the other, the important role of genes in the stability of personality traits. As it is observable, in addition to genetic research, it is possible to implement electrophysiological research, and explore with holistic approach the relation of this identity model and evoked brain potentials.

## Concordance for Personality Traits and Evoked Brain Potentials as Future Research Guideline?

Finally, it is important to briefly present the results of the analysis carried out and presented in the work about the relation between the concordance of some personality dimensions and visual evoked brain potentials (Tatalović Vorkapić, 2014a). Chernyshev and colleagues (2011) pointed out that it is necessary to focus research efforts to study concordance levels of personality dimensions regarding their relationship with various psychophysiological measures. They stated a number of reasons. The first relates to the fact that based on the expected high construct validity, most personality traits show significant and high inter-correlations, which proved to be important in this research as well. In particular, when self-evaluation questionnaires are applied in research, the determination of significant inter-correlations between the examined personality traits is expected, both within the same and between different personality theory models (Rusalov, 2000). These Russian authors believed that these are the most common determining significant correlations between a certain personality traits indicator of standard behavioral samples, affective and cognitive specifications, rather than their own individual personality traits. They also stated that it is theoretically possible that there are people in whom the concordance between some or all of the personality traits is significantly lower than the average. Consequently, they believed that this difference in concordance between personality traits has an effect on psychophysiological measures, especially on brain evoked potentials. While testing this hypothesis (Tatalović Vorkapić, 2014a), it was found that there are significant differences between the groups of students who have demonstrated a low concordance between personality traits and a high concordance between personality traits. In other words, students with low concordance also had a significantly lower EP amplitude and EP latency in all measured visual evoked potentials.

In addition, there was significant correlation between the years of study and concordance between personality traits, where the students during the research showed higher levels of concordance, which is discussed in the framework of the maturation process. The method that the authors proposed to determine the concordance groups of subjects relates to the implementation of two steps in the analysis. The first step relates to a subjects divided into three groups: the first group includes those participants who have scores lower than the difference between the arithmetic mean and standard deviation ($X < M - SD$); the second group includes those participants with results from the difference and the sum of the arithmetic mean and standard deviation ($SD - M < X < M + SD$); and in the third group are those participants with results higher than the sum of the mean and standard deviation ($X > M + SD$). In the second step, the high concordance group consists of those subjects in which all tested personality traits are in the same category of the above three, the low concordance group includes those subjects whose personality traits are in different categories.

This paper approached the more lenient criterion, where in the low concordance group those participants are included whose two or more characteristics were in different categories, not just one. This more lenient criterion was used in this study (Tatalović Vorkapić, 2014a) because there were very few female participants who had all the personality traits in the same category. This raises the question, what criterion of distribution into concordance groups should be used, and to what extent would this way of studying electrophysiology of human personality contribute to its understanding?

## Personality Traits, Evoked Brain Potentials, and Neurofeedback as Future Research Guideline?

Within the frame of investigating biological determination of personality, it is important to mention the research that connects the evoked brain potentials, neurofeedback and personality traits. Optimal cognitive functioning is an essential prerequisite of effective learning. However, during the learning process, in addition to basic cognitive processes and abilities, from the perspective of intrapersonal factors, the personality of the learner significantly influences on his/her learning outcomes. Prior psychological research demonstrated significant differences in teaching methods and learning outcomes between people who have high and low levels of extraversion. This moderating effect of personality is especially visible in certain learning models, such as the operant conditioning. Taking into account the biological basis of cognition and personality, the question is whether it is possible that different personality traits are the cause of some contradictory findings in operant conditioning of brainwaves (neurofeedback)? In other words, is it possible to explain the current large number of contradictory findings on the in-effectiveness of neurofeedback based on the moderation effect of personality traits, especially extraversion? Therefore, one of the future research directions could be aimed at validation of the neurofeedback training on cognitive performance regarding the personality effect on a normal and clinical sample. In the experiment, not only Eysenck's personality theory could be the only theoretical background of personality. It could be expected to determine that personality traits, especially extraversion could have a significant moderation effect on the congition-neurofeedback training relationship (Gruzelier & Egner, 2005).

## CONCLUSION

Finally, what to conclude? There is no doubt that this research has significantly contributed to the understanding of electrophysiology of human personality, as indeed there are very few similar studies. By including a large number of personality traits and behavioral variables, and their study in relation to visual evoked potentials on a homogeneous sample of female students, this has enabled insight into the complexity of the investigated relationships. On the other hand, the methodology which was applied, method of measuring evoked potentials both from aspect of the simple visual oddball task and the technically limited device aspect for recording evoked potentials, the homogeneous and non-random sample, and the personality theories that have been used, not only points to significant restrictions of the research, but significantly opens up new research questions for future studies.

In addition to the above mentioned new research questions, there is an open question of the existing theoretical personality models, and to the very approaches to researching personality by using electrophysiology in methodology. Therefore, the contribution of this book lies in the fact that it refers readers to existing knowledge in this field and encourages them to continue to explore, paving the way for new insights in the understanding of the measurement of Psychological and Electrophysiological Attributes of Human Personality.

## REFERENCES

Bartussek, D., Becker, G., Diedrich, O., Naumann, E., & Maier, S. (1996). Extraversion, neuroticism, and event-related brain potentials in response to emotional stimuli. *Personality and Individual Differences*, *20*(3), 301–312. doi:10.1016/0191-8869(95)00175-1

Bratko, D. (2002). Teorijski i metodološki problemi pri istraživanju kontinuiteta i promjena ličnosti [Theoretical and methodological problems in research of continuity and changes in personality. In Croatian]. Društvena istraživanja, 4-5(60-61), 603-622.

Bullock, W. A., & Gilliland, K. (1993). Eysencks arousal theory of introversion/ekstraversion: A converging measures investigation. *Journal of Personality and Social Psychology*, *64*(1), 113–123. doi:10.1037/0022-3514.64.1.113 PMID:8421248

Canli, T. (2006). *Biology of Personality and Individual Differences*. London: The Guilford Press.

Chernyshev, B. V., Chernysheva, E. G., Ramendik, D. M., & Zinchenko, V. P. (2011). Manifestations of temperament and perception in auditory evoked potentials. In B. Kokinov, A. Karmiloff-Smith, & N. J. Nersessian (Eds.), *European Perspectives on Cognitive Science*. New Bulgarian University Press. Retrieved from http://nbu.bg/cogs/eurocogsci2011/proceedings/contents.html

Cohen, L., Manion, L., & Morrison, K. (2007). Metode istraživanja u obrazovanju [Research Methods in education]. Naklada Slap.

Corr, P. J. (2000). Testing problems in J. A. Grays personality theory: A commentary on Matthews and Gilliland (1999). *Personality and Individual Differences*, *30*(2), 333–352. doi:10.1016/S0191-8869(00)00028-3

Davis, H. (1964). Enhancement of evoked cortical potentials in humans related to a task requiring a decision. *Science*, *145*(3628), 182–183. doi:10.1126/science.145.3628.182 PMID:14171564

Depu, R. A., & Collins, P. F. (1999). Neurobiology of the structure of personality: Dopamine, facilitation of incentive motivation, and extraversion. *Behavioral and Brain Sciences*, *22*, 491–533. PMID:11301519

Dewaele, J.-M., & Furnham, A. (1999). Extraversion: The unloved variable in applied linguistic research. *Language Learning*, *43*(3), 509–544. doi:10.1111/0023-8333.00098

Dewaele, J.-M., & Furnham, A. (2000). Personality and speech production: A pilot study of second language learners. *Personality and Individual Differences*, *28*(2), 355–365. doi:10.1016/S0191-8869(99)00106-3

Eysenck, H. J. (1967). *Biological basis of personality*. Springfield, IL: Charles C Thomas Publisher.

Eysenck, H. J. (1997). Personality and Experimental Psychology: The Unification of Psychology and the Possibility of a Paradigm. *Journal of Personality and Social Psychology*, *73*(6), 1224–1237. doi:10.1037/0022-3514.73.6.1224

Eysenck, H. J., & Eysenck, M. W. (1985). Chapter eight: The psychophysiology of personality. In *Personality and individual differences: A natural science approach* (pp. 217–236). New York: Plenum Press. doi:10.1007/978-1-4613-2413-3_8

Gray, J. A. (1991). Neural systems, emotion and personality. In J. Madden IV, (Ed.), *Neurobiology of learning, emotion and affect* (pp. 273–306). New York: Raven Press.

Gruzelier, J., & Egner, T. (2005). Critical validation studies of neurofeedback. *Child and Adolescent Psychiatric Clinics of North America*, *14*(1), 83–104. doi:10.1016/j.chc.2004.07.002 PMID:15564053

Hogan, R., & Roberts, B. W. (2004). A socioanalytic model of maturity. *Journal of Career Assessment*, *12*(2), 207–217. doi:10.1177/1069072703255882

Hogan, R. T., & Roberts, B. W. (2000). A socioanalytic perspective on person/environment interaction. In W. B. Walsh, K. H. Craik, & R. H. Price (Eds.), *New directions in person-environment psychology* (pp. 1–24). Mahwah, NJ: Erlbaum.

Mann, C. C. (1994). Behavioral genetics in transition. *Science*, *264*(5166), 1686–1689. doi:10.1126/science.8209246 PMID:8209246

Matthews, G., & Gilliland, K. (1999). The personality theories of H. J. Eysenck and J. A. Gray: A comparative review. *Personality and Individual Differences*, *26*(4), 583–626. doi:10.1016/S0191-8869(98)00158-5

Matthews, G., & Gilliland, K. (2001). Personality, biology and cognitive science: A reply to Corr (2001). *Personality and Individual Differences*, *30*(2), 353–362. doi:10.1016/S0191-8869(00)00029-5

McAdams, D. P., & Pals, J. L. (2006). A New Big Five: Fundamental Principles for an Integrative Science of Personality. *The American Psychologist*, *61*(3), 204–217. doi:10.1037/0003-066X.61.3.204 PMID:16594837

McCrae, R. R., & Costa, P. T. Jr. (2008). The five-factor theory of personality. In O. P. John, R. W. Robins, & L. A. Pervin (Eds.), *Handbook of personality: Theory and research* (pp. 151–181). New York: Guilford Press.

Milas, G. (2005). *Istraživačke metode u psihologiji i drugim društvenim znanostima [Research Methods in Psychology and other Social Sciences]*. Naklada Slap, Jastrebarsko.

Musek, J. (1999). Psihološki modeli in teorije osebnosti [Psychological models in personality theories]. Ljubljana: Filozofska fakulteta.

Musek, J. (2007). A general factor of personality: Evidence for the Big One in the five-factor model. *Journal of Research in Personality*, *41*(6), 1213–1233. doi:10.1016/j.jrp.2007.02.003

Pickering, A. D., Corr, P. J., Powell, J. H., Kumari, V., Thornton, J. C., & Gray, J. A. (1997). Individual differences in reactions to reinforcing stimuli are neither black nor white: To what extent are they Gray? In H. Nyborg (Ed.), *The scientific study of human nature: Tribute to Hans J. Eysenck at eighty* (pp. 36–67). Oxford, UK: Pergamon Press.

Picton, T. W., Hillyard, S. A., Krausz, H. T., & Galambos, R. (1974). Human auditory evoked potentials. I Evaluation of components. *Electroencephalography and Clinical Neurophysiology*, *36*, 179–190. doi:10.1016/0013-4694(74)90155-2 PMID:4129630

Plomin, R., & Caspi, A. (1998). DNA and personality. *European Journal of Personality*, *12*(5), 387–407. doi:10.1002/(SICI)1099-0984(1998090)12:5<387::AID-PER330>3.0.CO;2-U

Roberts, B. W. (2006). Personality development and organizational behavior. In B. M. Staw (Ed.), *Research on organizational behavior* (pp. 1–41). New York: Elsevier Science/JAI Press.

Robins, R. W., Fraley, R. C., & Krueger, R. F. (2007). *Handbook of Research Methods in Personality Psychology*. London: The Guilford Press.

Rusalov, V. M. (2000). Natural preconditions and individual-psychophysiological peculiarities of personality. In *Psychology of personality in works of Russian psychologists*. St. Petersburg: Piter.

Siegle, G. J. (1999). A neural network model of attention biases in depression. In J. A. Reggia, E. Ruppin, & D. L. Glanzman (Eds.), Disorders of brain, behavior, and cognition: The neurocomputational perspective (pp. 415-441). New York: Elsevier.

Siegle, G. J., & Ingram, R. E. (1997). Modeling individual differences in negative information processing biases. In G. Matthews (Ed.), *Cognitive science perspectives on personality and Siegle et al, Sustained Amygdala Activity in Depression 36 emotion*. New York, NY: Elsevier. doi:10.1016/S0166-4115(97)80124-0

Stelmack, R. M., Campbell, K. B., & Bell, I. (1993). Extraversion and brainstem auditory evoked potentials during sleep and wakefulness. *Personality and Individual Differences*, *14*(3), 447–453. doi:10.1016/0191-8869(93)90314-S

Strelau, J., Angleitner, A., & Newberry, B. H. (1999). Pavlovian Temperament Survey (PTS): An international handbook. Göttingen: Hogrefe & Huber Publishers.

Tatalović Vorkapić, S. (2008b). Brebner-Cooperov model ekstraverzije [Brebner-Cooper's model of extraversiono]. *Suvremena Psihologija*, *11*(2), 261–272.

Tatalović Vorkapić, S. (2009). Biological correlates of P300 and its relationship with extraversion. *Collegium Antropologicum*, *33*(4), 1215–1222. PMID:20102071

Tatalović Vorkapić, S., & Tadinac, M. (2011a). Does the abstract thinking have a significant role in the relationship between extraversion and evoked brain potentials? *Review of Psychology*, *18*(2), 63–70.

Tatalović Vorkapić, S. (2014a). The relationship between concordance of some personality dimensions and visual evoked potentials. *Studia Psychologica*, *56*(4), 323–336.

Tatalović Vorkapić, S. (2014b). Je li privilegirani status modela osobina ličnosti u psihologiji ličnosti opravdan? – Prikaz modela identiteta [Is privileged status of personality traits' models in personality psychology justified? – Description of identity models]. *Suvremena Psihologija*, *17*(2), 181–198.

Tatalović Vorkapić, S. (2015). The relationship between social desirability and visual evoked potentials: Implications for personality measurement. *Cognition, Brain, Behavior /Cogniţie, creier, comportament. 19*, *2*, 99–113.

Tatalović Vorkapić, S., & Tadinac, M., & Rudež, J. (2010). P300 and extraversion in the visual oddball paradigm. *Studia Psychologica*, *52*(1), 3–14.

Tatalović Vorkapić, S., & Tadinac, M. (2011b). Electrophysiological Correlates of Empathy. *The Romanian Journal of Psychology. Psychotherapy and Neuroscience*, *1*(1), 19–37.

Tatalović Vorkapić, S., & Tadinac, M. (2016). The relationship of neuroticism, psychoticism and depression with visual evoked potentials. *Acta Neuropsychologica*, *14*(3), 241–254. doi:10.5604/17307503.1222838

Tatalović Vorkapić, S., Tadinac, M., & Lučev, I. (2013). Electrocortical correlates of temperament. *Polish Psychological Bulletin*, *44*(1), 92–101. doi:10.2478/ppb-2013-0010

Vorkapić, S. T. (2011). Electrocortical differences in sanguine, choleric, phlegmatic and melancholic. *Romanian Journal of Psychology, Psychotherapy and Neuroscience*, *1*(2), 67–96.

Zuckerman, M. (1991). Psychobiology of personality. Cambridge University Press.

# Related Readings

To continue IGI Global's long-standing tradition of advancing innovation through emerging research, please find below a compiled list of recommended IGI Global book chapters and journal articles in the areas of psychology, human cognition, and human behavior. These related readings will provide additional information and guidance to further enrich your knowledge and assist you with your own research.

Abdolshah, M., Farazmand, N., Mollaaghamirzaei, A., Eshragh, F., & Nezhad, K. G. (2017). Analyzing and Studying the Selection Tests based on their Capabilities in Evaluation of Various Jobs Proficiencies and Abilities. In A. Bhattacharya (Ed.), *Strategic Human Capital Development and Management in Emerging Economies* (pp. 90–109). Hershey, PA: IGI Global. doi:10.4018/978-1-5225-1974-4.ch005

Abuljadail, M. H., Ha, L., Wang, F., & Yang, L. (2015). What Motivates Online Shoppers to "Like" Brands' Facebook Fan Pages? In A. Mesquita & C. Tsai (Eds.), *Human Behavior, Psychology, and Social Interaction in the Digital Era* (pp. 279–293). Hershey, PA: IGI Global. doi:10.4018/978-1-4666-8450-8.ch014

Akbar, S., & Khurana, H. (2017). Chronic Mental Illness in Old Age Homes: An International Perspective. In B. Prasad (Ed.), *Chronic Mental Illness and the Changing Scope of Intervention Strategies, Diagnosis, and Treatment* (pp. 21–39). Hershey, PA: IGI Global. doi:10.4018/978-1-5225-0519-8.ch002

Alcántara-Pilar, J. M., del Barrio-García, S., Crespo-Almendros, E., & Porcu, L. (2015). A Review of Psycho- vs. Socio-Linguistics Theories: An Application to Marketing Research. In J. Alcántara-Pilar, S. del Barrio-García, E. Crespo-Almendros, & L. Porcu (Eds.), *Analyzing the Cultural Diversity of Consumers in the Global Marketplace* (pp. 227–255). Hershey, PA: IGI Global. doi:10.4018/978-1-4666-8262-7.ch011

Alcántara-Pilar, J. M., del Barrio-García, S., Crespo-Almendros, E., & Porcu, L. (2015). The Moderating Role of Language on Perceived Risk and Information-Processing Online. In J. Alcántara-Pilar, S. del Barrio-García, E. Crespo-Almendros, & L. Porcu (Eds.), *Analyzing the Cultural Diversity of Consumers in the Global Marketplace* (pp. 320–345). Hershey, PA: IGI Global. doi:10.4018/978-1-4666-8262-7.ch015

Antonietti, A., Caravita, S. C., Colombo, B., & Simonelli, L. (2015). Blogs' Potentialities in Learning: What Are the Key Variables to Promote Cognitive Empowerment. In A. Mesquita & C. Tsai (Eds.), *Human Behavior, Psychology, and Social Interaction in the Digital Era* (pp. 21–44). Hershey, PA: IGI Global. doi:10.4018/978-1-4666-8450-8.ch002

Antonova, A. (2015). How Social Factors Influence Implicit Knowledge Construction on the Internet. In Z. Jin (Ed.), *Exploring Implicit Cognition: Learning, Memory, and Social Cognitive Processes* (pp. 205–215). Hershey, PA: IGI Global. doi:10.4018/978-1-4666-6599-6.ch010

Araujo, B. H., & Nasseh, I. E. (2017). Understanding the Interdisciplinary Meaning of Beauty to Neuroscience: Designing Beauty to Neuroscience. In R. Zuanon (Ed.), *Projective Processes and Neuroscience in Art and Design* (pp. 103–118). Hershey, PA: IGI Global. doi:10.4018/978-1-5225-0510-5.ch007

Athota, V. S. (2017). Foundations and Future of Well-Being: How Personality Influences Happiness and Well-Being. In S. Háša & R. Brunet-Thornton (Eds.), *Impact of Organizational Trauma on Workplace Behavior and Performance* (pp. 279–294). Hershey, PA: IGI Global. doi:10.4018/978-1-5225-2021-4.ch012

Bandy, J. (2017). Employee Wellness Programs: An International Examination. In F. Topor (Ed.), *Handbook of Research on Individualism and Identity in the Globalized Digital Age* (pp. 359–379). Hershey, PA: IGI Global. doi:10.4018/978-1-5225-0522-8.ch016

Barone, P. A. (2017). Defining and Understanding the Development of Juvenile Delinquency from an Environmental, Sociological, and Theoretical Perspective. In S. Egharevba (Ed.), *Police Brutality, Racial Profiling, and Discrimination in the Criminal Justice System* (pp. 215–238). Hershey, PA: IGI Global. doi:10.4018/978-1-5225-1088-8.ch010

Barratt, J., & Bishop, J. (2015). The Impacts of Alcohol on E-Dating Activity: Increases in Flame Trolling Corresponds with Higher Alcohol Consumption. In J. Bishop (Ed.), *Psychological and Social Implications Surrounding Internet and Gaming Addiction* (pp. 186–197). Hershey, PA: IGI Global. doi:10.4018/978-1-4666-8595-6.ch011

Beard, R. L., & O'Connor, M. K. (2015). Listening to Alzheimer's: The Role of Social Location in Illness Narratives. In C. Dick-Muehlke, R. Li, & M. Orleans (Eds.), *Psychosocial Studies of the Individual's Changing Perspectives in Alzheimer's Disease* (pp. 1–32). Hershey, PA: IGI Global. doi:10.4018/978-1-4666-8478-2.ch001

Bedi, D. (2017). Efficacy of Art Therapy in Treating Patients with Paranoid Schizophrenia. In B. Prasad (Ed.), *Chronic Mental Illness and the Changing Scope of Intervention Strategies, Diagnosis, and Treatment* (pp. 308–320). Hershey, PA: IGI Global. doi:10.4018/978-1-5225-0519-8.ch017

Bermeitinger, C. (2015). Priming. In Z. Jin (Ed.), *Exploring Implicit Cognition: Learning, Memory, and Social Cognitive Processes* (pp. 16–60). Hershey, PA: IGI Global. doi:10.4018/978-1-4666-6599-6.ch002

Bishop, J. (2015). Determining the Risk of Digital Addiction to Adolescent Targets of Internet Trolling: Implications for the UK Legal System. In J. Bishop (Ed.), *Psychological and Social Implications Surrounding Internet and Gaming Addiction* (pp. 31–42). Hershey, PA: IGI Global. doi:10.4018/978-1-4666-8595-6.ch003

Bishop, J. (2015). Using "On-the-Fly Corpus Linguistics" to Systematically Derive Word Definitions Using Inductive Abstraction and Reductionist Correlation Analysis: Considering Seductive and Gratifying Properties of Computer Jargon. In J. Bishop (Ed.), *Psychological and Social Implications Surrounding Internet and Gaming Addiction* (pp. 153–170). Hershey, PA: IGI Global. doi:10.4018/978-1-4666-8595-6.ch009

Boesch, B. (2017). Enabling Creativity: Using Garden Exploration as a Vehicle for Creative Expression and Analysis. In N. Silton (Ed.), *Exploring the Benefits of Creativity in Education, Media, and the Arts* (pp. 117–135). Hershey, PA: IGI Global. doi:10.4018/978-1-5225-0504-4.ch006

Bozoglan, B., & Demirer, V. (2015). The Association between Internet Addiction and Psychosocial Variables. In J. Bishop (Ed.), *Psychological and Social Implications Surrounding Internet and Gaming Addiction* (pp. 171–185). Hershey, PA: IGI Global. doi:10.4018/978-1-4666-8595-6.ch010

Byrd-Poller, L., Farmer, J. L., & Ford, V. (2017). The Role of Leaders in Facilitating Healing After Organizational Trauma. In S. Háša & R. Brunet-Thornton (Eds.), *Impact of Organizational Trauma on Workplace Behavior and Performance* (pp. 318–340). Hershey, PA: IGI Global. doi:10.4018/978-1-5225-2021-4.ch014

Cacho-Elizondo, S., Shahidi, N., & Tossan, V. (2015). Giving Up Smoking Using SMS Messages on your Mobile Phone. In A. Mesquita & C. Tsai (Eds.), *Human Behavior, Psychology, and Social Interaction in the Digital Era* (pp. 72–94). Hershey, PA: IGI Global. doi:10.4018/978-1-4666-8450-8.ch004

Card, S., & Wang, H. (2015). Taking Care to Play: Meaningful Communication in Dementia Care in Chinese Culture. In C. Dick-Muehlke, R. Li, & M. Orleans (Eds.), *Psychosocial Studies of the Individual's Changing Perspectives in Alzheimer's Disease* (pp. 76–103). Hershey, PA: IGI Global. doi:10.4018/978-1-4666-8478-2.ch004

Carrasco, G., & Kinnamon, E. (2017). An Examination of Selfish and Selfless Motives: A Review of the Social Psychological and Behavioral Economics Literature. In R. Ianole (Ed.), *Applied Behavioral Economics Research and Trends* (pp. 93–109). Hershey, PA: IGI Global. doi:10.4018/978-1-5225-1826-6.ch006

Cejka, P., & Mohelska, H. (2017). National Culture Influence on Organisational Trauma: A Conceptual Framework Review. In S. Háša & R. Brunet-Thornton (Eds.), *Impact of Organizational Trauma on Workplace Behavior and Performance* (pp. 162–186). Hershey, PA: IGI Global. doi:10.4018/978-1-5225-2021-4.ch007

Chen, R., Lin, T., & Xie, T. (2015). Towards Intelligent Window Layout Management: The Role of Mental Map. In A. Mesquita & C. Tsai (Eds.), *Human Behavior, Psychology, and Social Interaction in the Digital Era* (pp. 146–161). Hershey, PA: IGI Global. doi:10.4018/978-1-4666-8450-8.ch007

Chuang, S., Lin, S., Chang, T., & Kaewmeesri, R. (2017). Behavioral Intention of Using Social Networking Site: A Comparative Study of Taiwanese and Thai Facebook Users. *International Journal of Technology and Human Interaction, 13*(1), 61–81. doi:10.4018/IJTHI.2017010104

Cialdella, V. T., Lobato, E. J., & Jordan, J. S. (2017). Wild Architecture: Explaining Cognition via Self-Sustaining Systems. In J. Vallverdú, M. Mazzara, M. Talanov, S. Distefano, & R. Lowe (Eds.), *Advanced Research on Biologically Inspired Cognitive Architectures* (pp. 41–62). Hershey, PA: IGI Global. doi:10.4018/978-1-5225-1947-8.ch003

Cleve, R. A., Işık, İ., & Pecanha, V. D. (2017). Sexual Identities in the Workplace: Avoiding Organizational Trauma When Disclosure Occurs – Current Perspectives. In S. Háša & R. Brunet-Thornton (Eds.), *Impact of Organizational Trauma on Workplace Behavior and Performance* (pp. 188–220). Hershey, PA: IGI Global. doi:10.4018/978-1-5225-2021-4.ch008

Contier, A. T., & Torres, L. (2017). Neuroaesthetics: Insights into the Aesthetic Experience of Visual Art. In R. Zuanon (Ed.), *Projective Processes and Neuroscience in Art and Design* (pp. 87–102). Hershey, PA: IGI Global. doi:10.4018/978-1-5225-0510-5.ch006

Crawford, C. M., & Smith, M. S. (2015). Rethinking Bloom's Taxonomy: Implicit Cognitive Vulnerability as an Impetus towards Higher Order Thinking Skills. In Z. Jin (Ed.), *Exploring Implicit Cognition: Learning, Memory, and Social Cognitive Processes* (pp. 86–103). Hershey, PA: IGI Global. doi:10.4018/978-1-4666-6599-6.ch004

de Soir, E., & Kleber, R. (2017). Understanding the Core of Psychological Trauma: Trauma in Contemporary French Theory. In S. Háša & R. Brunet-Thornton (Eds.), *Impact of Organizational Trauma on Workplace Behavior and Performance* (pp. 57–75). Hershey, PA: IGI Global. doi:10.4018/978-1-5225-2021-4.ch003

Delgado, J. J. (2017). How Is the Personality of Facebook Customers?: Cloninger's Psychobiological Model of Temperament as a Predictor of SNSs. In M. Dos Santos (Ed.), *Applying Neuroscience to Business Practice* (pp. 191–229). Hershey, PA: IGI Global. doi:10.4018/978-1-5225-1028-4.ch009

Dentale, F., Vecchione, M., & Barbaranelli, C. (2015). Applying the IAT to Assess Big Five Personality Traits: A Brief Review of Measurement and Validity Issues. In Z. Jin (Ed.), *Exploring Implicit Cognition: Learning, Memory, and Social Cognitive Processes* (pp. 1–15). Hershey, PA: IGI Global. doi:10.4018/978-1-4666-6599-6.ch001

Díez, J. C., & Saiz-Alvarez, J. M. (2016). Leadership in Social Entrepreneurship: Is It Ability or Skill? In J. Saiz-Álvarez (Ed.), *Handbook of Research on Social Entrepreneurship and Solidarity Economics* (pp. 134–153). Hershey, PA: IGI Global. doi:10.4018/978-1-5225-0097-1.ch008

Dikici, A. (2017). Revisiting the Relationships between Turkish Prospective Teachers' Thinking Styles and Behaviors Fostering Creativity. In N. Silton (Ed.), *Exploring the Benefits of Creativity in Education, Media, and the Arts* (pp. 136–157). Hershey, PA: IGI Global. doi:10.4018/978-1-5225-0504-4.ch007

Eapen, V., & Walter, A. (2016). Mind the Gap: Developmental Vulnerability and Mental Health. In R. Gopalan (Ed.), *Handbook of Research on Diagnosing, Treating, and Managing Intellectual Disabilities* (pp. 11–32). Hershey, PA: IGI Global. doi:10.4018/978-1-5225-0089-6.ch002

Fallon, F. (2017). Integrated Information Theory (IIT) and Artificial Consciousness. In J. Vallverdú, M. Mazzara, M. Talanov, S. Distefano, & R. Lowe (Eds.), *Advanced Research on Biologically Inspired Cognitive Architectures* (pp. 1–23). Hershey, PA: IGI Global. doi:10.4018/978-1-5225-1947-8.ch001

Fang, L., & Ha, L. (2015). Do College Students Benefit from Their Social Media Experience?: Social Media Involvement and Its Impact on College Students' Self-Efficacy Perception. In A. Mesquita & C. Tsai (Eds.), *Human Behavior, Psychology, and Social Interaction in the Digital Era* (pp. 259–278). Hershey, PA: IGI Global. doi:10.4018/978-1-4666-8450-8.ch013

Farmer, L. (2014). Technology Impact on New Adult Behavior about Health Information. In V. Wang (Ed.), *Handbook of Research on Adult and Community Health Education: Tools, Trends, and Methodologies* (pp. 68–81). Hershey, PA: IGI Global. doi:10.4018/978-1-4666-6260-5.ch005

Fasko, D. (2017). Creativity in the Schools: Educational Changes Lately? In N. Silton (Ed.), *Exploring the Benefits of Creativity in Education, Media, and the Arts* (pp. 92–116). Hershey, PA: IGI Global. doi:10.4018/978-1-5225-0504-4.ch005

Fazio, S., & Mitchell, D. B. (2015). Self-Preservation in Individuals with Alzheimer's Disease: Empirical Evidence and the Role of the Social Environment. In C. Dick-Muehlke, R. Li, & M. Orleans (Eds.), *Psychosocial Studies of the Individual's Changing Perspectives in Alzheimer's Disease* (pp. 183–207). Hershey, PA: IGI Global. doi:10.4018/978-1-4666-8478-2.ch008

Feitosa-Santana, C. (2017). Understanding How the Mind Works: The Neuroscience of Perception, Behavior, and Creativity. In R. Zuanon (Ed.), *Projective Processes and Neuroscience in Art and Design* (pp. 239–252). Hershey, PA: IGI Global. doi:10.4018/978-1-5225-0510-5.ch014

Ferris, A. (2017). Creativity in the Emerging Adult. In N. Silton (Ed.), *Exploring the Benefits of Creativity in Education, Media, and the Arts* (pp. 26–49). Hershey, PA: IGI Global. doi:10.4018/978-1-5225-0504-4.ch002

Fogliano, F., & Oliveira, H. C. (2017). Neuroesthetics: Perspectives and Reflections. In R. Zuanon (Ed.), *Projective Processes and Neuroscience in Art and Design* (pp. 52–70). Hershey, PA: IGI Global. doi:10.4018/978-1-5225-0510-5.ch004

Folk, J. R., & Eskenazi, M. A. (2017). Eye Movement Behavior and Individual Differences in Word Identification During Reading. In C. Was, F. Sansosti, & B. Morris (Eds.), *Eye-Tracking Technology Applications in Educational Research* (pp. 66–87). Hershey, PA: IGI Global. doi:10.4018/978-1-5225-1005-5.ch004

Franco, M., Ortiz, T. V., Amorim, H. A., & Faber, J. (2017). Can We Induce a Cognitive Representation of a Prosthetic Arm by Means of Crossmodal Stimuli? In R. Zuanon (Ed.), *Projective Processes and Neuroscience in Art and Design* (pp. 182–204). Hershey, PA: IGI Global. doi:10.4018/978-1-5225-0510-5.ch011

Gallego, J. (2017). Organizational Trauma and Change Management. In S. Háša & R. Brunet-Thornton (Eds.), *Impact of Organizational Trauma on Workplace Behavior and Performance* (pp. 140–161). Hershey, PA: IGI Global. doi:10.4018/978-1-5225-2021-4.ch006

Galvin, J. E., & Kelleher, M. E. (2015). Dementia and Other Neurocognitive Disorders: An Overview. In C. Dick-Muehlke, R. Li, & M. Orleans (Eds.), *Psychosocial Studies of the Individual's Changing Perspectives in Alzheimer's Disease* (pp. 104–130). Hershey, PA: IGI Global. doi:10.4018/978-1-4666-8478-2.ch005

Gardner, M. K., & Strayer, D. L. (2017). What Cognitive Psychology Can Tell Us About Educational Computer Games. In R. Zheng & M. Gardner (Eds.), *Handbook of Research on Serious Games for Educational Applications* (pp. 1–18). Hershey, PA: IGI Global. doi:10.4018/978-1-5225-0513-6.ch001

Garg, B., Khanna, P., & Khanna, A. (2017). Chronic Mental Illness and the Changing Scope of Intervention Strategies, Diagnosis, and Treatment in Child and Adolescent Population. In B. Prasad (Ed.), *Chronic Mental Illness and the Changing Scope of Intervention Strategies, Diagnosis, and Treatment* (pp. 258–269). Hershey, PA: IGI Global. doi:10.4018/978-1-5225-0519-8.ch014

Giannouli, V. (2017). Creativity and Giftedness: A Study of Attitudes. In N. Silton (Ed.), *Exploring the Benefits of Creativity in Education, Media, and the Arts* (pp. 179–197). Hershey, PA: IGI Global. doi:10.4018/978-1-5225-0504-4.ch009

Gopalan, R. T. (2016). Intellectual Disability: From History to Recent Trends. In R. Gopalan (Ed.), *Handbook of Research on Diagnosing, Treating, and Managing Intellectual Disabilities* (pp. 1–10). Hershey, PA: IGI Global. doi:10.4018/978-1-5225-0089-6.ch001

Hacker, D. J. (2017). The Role of Metacognition in Learning via Serious Games. In R. Zheng & M. Gardner (Eds.), *Handbook of Research on Serious Games for Educational Applications* (pp. 19–40). Hershey, PA: IGI Global. doi:10.4018/978-1-5225-0513-6.ch002

Halder, S., & Mahato, A. (2017). Cognitive Remediation Therapy in Chronic Schizophrenia. In B. Prasad (Ed.), *Chronic Mental Illness and the Changing Scope of Intervention Strategies, Diagnosis, and Treatment* (pp. 292–307). Hershey, PA: IGI Global. doi:10.4018/978-1-5225-0519-8.ch016

Heins, S., Heins, G., & Dick-Muehlke, C. (2015). Steve's Story: Living with Mild Cognitive Impairment. In C. Dick-Muehlke, R. Li, & M. Orleans (Eds.), *Psychosocial Studies of the Individual's Changing Perspectives in Alzheimer's Disease* (pp. 33–60). Hershey, PA: IGI Global. doi:10.4018/978-1-4666-8478-2.ch002

Isik, I. (2017). Organizations and Exposure to Trauma at a Collective Level: The Taxonomy of Potentially Traumatic Events. In S. Háša & R. Brunet-Thornton (Eds.), *Impact of Organizational Trauma on Workplace Behavior and Performance* (pp. 18–56). Hershey, PA: IGI Global. doi:10.4018/978-1-5225-2021-4.ch002

Jančec, L., Vorkapić, S. T., & Vodopivec, J. L. (2015). Hidden Curriculum Determinants in (Pre)School Institutions: Implicit Cognition in Action. In Z. Jin (Ed.), *Exploring Implicit Cognition: Learning, Memory, and Social Cognitive Processes* (pp. 216–242). Hershey, PA: IGI Global. doi:10.4018/978-1-4666-6599-6.ch011

Jerabek, I., & Muoio, D. (2017). The Stress Profile: The Influence of Personal Characteristics on Response to Occupational Trauma. In S. Háša & R. Brunet-Thornton (Eds.), *Impact of Organizational Trauma on Workplace Behavior and Performance* (pp. 77–119). Hershey, PA: IGI Global. doi:10.4018/978-1-5225-2021-4.ch004

Jha, S., Khanna, A., & Khanna, P. (2017). Advanced Intervention Strategies for Suicide in Patients with Chronic Mental Illness. In B. Prasad (Ed.), *Chronic Mental Illness and the Changing Scope of Intervention Strategies, Diagnosis, and Treatment* (pp. 271–291). Hershey, PA: IGI Global. doi:10.4018/978-1-5225-0519-8.ch015

Johard, L., Lippi, V., Safina, L., & Mazzara, M. (2017). Mind and Matter: Why It All Makes Sense. In J. Vallverdú, M. Mazzara, M. Talanov, S. Distefano, & R. Lowe (Eds.), *Advanced Research on Biologically Inspired Cognitive Architectures* (pp. 63–82). Hershey, PA: IGI Global. doi:10.4018/978-1-5225-1947-8.ch004

Kasemsap, K. (2017). Investigating the Roles of Neuroscience and Knowledge Management in Higher Education. In S. Mukerji & P. Tripathi (Eds.), *Handbook of Research on Administration, Policy, and Leadership in Higher Education* (pp. 112–140). Hershey, PA: IGI Global. doi:10.4018/978-1-5225-0672-0.ch006

Kasemsap, K. (2017). Mastering Cognitive Neuroscience and Social Neuroscience Perspectives in the Information Age. In M. Dos Santos (Ed.), *Applying Neuroscience to Business Practice* (pp. 82–113). Hershey, PA: IGI Global. doi:10.4018/978-1-5225-1028-4.ch005

Kaushik, P., & Singh, T. B. (2017). Predictors of Expressed Emotion, Caregiver's Burden, and Quality of Life in Chronic Mental Illness. In B. Prasad (Ed.), *Chronic Mental Illness and the Changing Scope of Intervention Strategies, Diagnosis, and Treatment* (pp. 143–163). Hershey, PA: IGI Global. doi:10.4018/978-1-5225-0519-8.ch008

Keyser, A. K., & Corning, M. (2017). Creative Aging: Stimulating Creativity in Middle and Late Adulthood. In N. Silton (Ed.), *Exploring the Benefits of Creativity in Education, Media, and the Arts* (pp. 50–66). Hershey, PA: IGI Global. doi:10.4018/978-1-5225-0504-4.ch003

Kılıç, B. (2017). An Organizational Trauma Intervention: A Case From Turkey. In S. Háša & R. Brunet-Thornton (Eds.), *Impact of Organizational Trauma on Workplace Behavior and Performance* (pp. 264–277). Hershey, PA: IGI Global. doi:10.4018/978-1-5225-2021-4.ch011

Kirsch, C., Lubart, T., de Vries, H., & Houssemand, C. (2017). Scientific Creativity in Psychology: A Cognitive-Conative Approach. In C. Zhou (Ed.), *Handbook of Research on Creative Problem-Solving Skill Development in Higher Education* (pp. 51–73). Hershey, PA: IGI Global. doi:10.4018/978-1-5225-0643-0.ch003

Kleinmintz, O. M. (2017). Train Yourself to Let Go: The Benefits of Deliberate Practice on Creativity and Its Neural Basis. In N. Silton (Ed.), *Exploring the Benefits of Creativity in Education, Media, and the Arts* (pp. 67–90). Hershey, PA: IGI Global. doi:10.4018/978-1-5225-0504-4.ch004

Kučera, D. (2017). The Potential of Spirituality for the Treatment of Organizational Trauma. In S. Háša & R. Brunet-Thornton (Eds.), *Impact of Organizational Trauma on Workplace Behavior and Performance* (pp. 295–317). Hershey, PA: IGI Global. doi:10.4018/978-1-5225-2021-4.ch013

Kukreti, P., Khanna, P., & Khanna, A. (2017). Chronic Mental Illnesses and Homelessness. In B. Prasad (Ed.), *Chronic Mental Illness and the Changing Scope of Intervention Strategies, Diagnosis, and Treatment* (pp. 1–20). Hershey, PA: IGI Global. doi:10.4018/978-1-5225-0519-8.ch001

Kuss, D. J. (2015). "I Can't Do It by Myself": An IPA of Clients Seeking Psychotherapy for Their MMORPG Addiction. In J. Bishop (Ed.), *Psychological and Social Implications Surrounding Internet and Gaming Addiction* (pp. 78–110). Hershey, PA: IGI Global. doi:10.4018/978-1-4666-8595-6.ch006

Landim, P. D. (2017). Design and Emotion: Contributions to the Emotional Design. In R. Zuanon (Ed.), *Projective Processes and Neuroscience in Art and Design* (pp. 119–136). Hershey, PA: IGI Global. doi:10.4018/978-1-5225-0510-5.ch008

Lebraty, J., & Godé, C. (2015). Assessing the Performance of Decision Support Systems in Military Environment: The 3C Method. In A. Mesquita & C. Tsai (Eds.), *Human Behavior, Psychology, and Social Interaction in the Digital Era* (pp. 45–70). Hershey, PA: IGI Global. doi:10.4018/978-1-4666-8450-8.ch003

Lehenbauer-Baum, M., & Fohringer, M. (2015). Internet Gaming Disorder: A Deeper Look into Addiction vs. High Engagement. In J. Bishop (Ed.), *Psychological and Social Implications Surrounding Internet and Gaming Addiction* (pp. 1–15). Hershey, PA: IGI Global. doi:10.4018/978-1-4666-8595-6.ch001

Lei, M., Liu, W., Gao, Y., & Zhu, T. (2015). Mobile User Behaviors in China. In Z. Yan (Ed.), *Encyclopedia of Mobile Phone Behavior* (pp. 1110–1128). Hershey, PA: IGI Global. doi:10.4018/978-1-4666-8239-9.ch091

Leote, R. (2017). Perceptual Processes and Multisensoriality: Understanding Multimodal Art from Neuroscientific Concepts. In R. Zuanon (Ed.), *Projective Processes and Neuroscience in Art and Design* (pp. 1–14). Hershey, PA: IGI Global. doi:10.4018/978-1-5225-0510-5.ch001

Lin, L., & Lipsmeyer, B. (2015). The Environmental and Technological Factors of Multitasking. In A. Mesquita & C. Tsai (Eds.), *Human Behavior, Psychology, and Social Interaction in the Digital Era* (pp. 1–20). Hershey, PA: IGI Global. doi:10.4018/978-1-4666-8450-8.ch001

Lin, T., Wu, Z., & Chen, Y. (2015). Using High-Frequency Interaction Events to Automatically Classify Cognitive Load. In A. Mesquita & C. Tsai (Eds.), *Human Behavior, Psychology, and Social Interaction in the Digital Era* (pp. 210–228). Hershey, PA: IGI Global. doi:10.4018/978-1-4666-8450-8.ch010

Liu, X., & Zhu, T. (2017). Comparing Online Personality of Americans and Chinese. In I. Management Association (Ed.), Gaming and Technology Addiction: Breakthroughs in Research and Practice (pp. 339-351). Hershey, PA: IGI Global. doi:10.4018/978-1-5225-0778-9.ch016

Lopes, M. M. (2017). Inside/Out: Looking Back into the Future. In R. Zuanon (Ed.), *Projective Processes and Neuroscience in Art and Design* (pp. 15–39). Hershey, PA: IGI Global. doi:10.4018/978-1-5225-0510-5.ch002

Lu, Y. Y., & Austrom, M. G. (2015). Disease Awareness, Cognitive Decline, and Communication in Persons with Mild Cognitive Impairment and Caregivers. In C. Dick-Muehlke, R. Li, & M. Orleans (Eds.), *Psychosocial Studies of the Individual's Changing Perspectives in Alzheimer's Disease* (pp. 254–270). Hershey, PA: IGI Global. doi:10.4018/978-1-4666-8478-2.ch011

Lytras, M. D., Raghavan, V., & Damiani, E. (2017). Big Data and Data Analytics Research: From Metaphors to Value Space for Collective Wisdom in Human Decision Making and Smart Machines. *International Journal on Semantic Web and Information Systems, 13*(1), 1–10. doi:10.4018/IJSWIS.2017010101

MacKinlay, E., & Trevitt, C. (2015). Spiritual Factors in the Experience of Alzheimer's Disease and Other Dementias. In C. Dick-Muehlke, R. Li, & M. Orleans (Eds.), *Psychosocial Studies of the Individual's Changing Perspectives in Alzheimer's Disease* (pp. 230–253). Hershey, PA: IGI Global. doi:10.4018/978-1-4666-8478-2.ch010

Mahato, A., & Halder, S. (2017). Disability in Schizophrenia: The Psychosocial and Neurocognitive Perspective. In B. Prasad (Ed.), *Chronic Mental Illness and the Changing Scope of Intervention Strategies, Diagnosis, and Treatment* (pp. 188–202). Hershey, PA: IGI Global. doi:10.4018/978-1-5225-0519-8.ch010

Manthiou, A., Chiang, L. L., & Tang, L. R. (2015). Developing a Successful Facebook Fan Page Based on Costumers' Needs. In A. Mesquita & C. Tsai (Eds.), *Human Behavior, Psychology, and Social Interaction in the Digital Era* (pp. 189–209). Hershey, PA: IGI Global. doi:10.4018/978-1-4666-8450-8.ch009

McCutcheon, J. L. (2017). Emerging Ethical Issues in Police and Public Safety Psychology: Reflections on Mandatory vs. Aspirational Ethics. In C. Mitchell & E. Dorian (Eds.), *Police Psychology and Its Growing Impact on Modern Law Enforcement* (pp. 314–334). Hershey, PA: IGI Global. doi:10.4018/978-1-5225-0813-7.ch016

Menezes, M. (2017). Cells, Organisms, and the Living Brain as New Media for Art: A Pursuit in Art Research. In R. Zuanon (Ed.), *Projective Processes and Neuroscience in Art and Design* (pp. 40–50). Hershey, PA: IGI Global. doi:10.4018/978-1-5225-0510-5.ch003

Mitchell, C. L. (2017). Preemployment Psychological Screening of Police Officer Applicants: Basic Considerations and Recent Advances. In C. Mitchell & E. Dorian (Eds.), *Police Psychology and Its Growing Impact on Modern Law Enforcement* (pp. 28–50). Hershey, PA: IGI Global. doi:10.4018/978-1-5225-0813-7.ch002

Mittlböck, K. (2015). Dangers of Playing with the Virtual Other in Mind: A Psychoanalytical View on Digital Role-Playing Games and the Edge between Facilitating Personality Development and Endangering the Player's Psyche. In J. Bishop (Ed.), *Psychological and Social Implications Surrounding Internet and Gaming Addiction* (pp. 44–61). Hershey, PA: IGI Global. doi:10.4018/978-1-4666-8595-6.ch004

Moraru, A. (2017). Student's Psychological Factors and Metacognitive Skills in Higher Education. In E. Railean, A. Elçi, & A. Elçi (Eds.), *Metacognition and Successful Learning Strategies in Higher Education* (pp. 176–199). Hershey, PA: IGI Global. doi:10.4018/978-1-5225-2218-8.ch009

Morhardt, D., & Spira, M. (2015). Cognitive Decline and the Changing Self in Relationship. In C. Dick-Muehlke, R. Li, & M. Orleans (Eds.), *Psychosocial Studies of the Individual's Changing Perspectives in Alzheimer's Disease* (pp. 61–75). Hershey, PA: IGI Global. doi:10.4018/978-1-4666-8478-2.ch003

Nakamura, D. (2015). Individual Differences in Implicit Learning: Current Problems and Issues for Research. In Z. Jin (Ed.), *Exploring Implicit Cognition: Learning, Memory, and Social Cognitive Processes* (pp. 61–85). Hershey, PA: IGI Global. doi:10.4018/978-1-4666-6599-6.ch003

Navarro, A. B., Díaz-Orueta, U., Martín-Niño, L., & Sánchez-Sánchez, M. E. (2015). Art, Drawing Task Processes, and Identity Awareness: A Case Study on the Retro-Genesis Phenomenon as an Indicator of the Progress of Dementia. In C. Dick-Muehlke, R. Li, & M. Orleans (Eds.), *Psychosocial Studies of the Individual's Changing Perspectives in Alzheimer's Disease* (pp. 208–228). Hershey, PA: IGI Global. doi:10.4018/978-1-4666-8478-2.ch009

Nina, B., & Nadejda, B. (2017). Metacognitive Strategies in Higher Education: Development of Spiritual Intelligence Strategies Within Training of the Academic Staff. In E. Railean, A. Elçi, & A. Elçi (Eds.), *Metacognition and Successful Learning Strategies in Higher Education* (pp. 109–136). Hershey, PA: IGI Global. doi:10.4018/978-1-5225-2218-8.ch006

Norris, S. E., & Porter, T. H. (2017). The Influence of Spirituality in the Workplace and Perceived Organizational Support on Organizational Citizenship Behaviors for Strategic Success. In V. Wang (Ed.), *Encyclopedia of Strategic Leadership and Management* (pp. 1140–1162). Hershey, PA: IGI Global. doi:10.4018/978-1-5225-1049-9.ch080

O'Reilly, A. G., Roche, B., & Cartwright, A. (2015). Function over Form: A Behavioral Approach to Implicit Attitudes. In Z. Jin (Ed.), *Exploring Implicit Cognition: Learning, Memory, and Social Cognitive Processes* (pp. 162–182). Hershey, PA: IGI Global. doi:10.4018/978-1-4666-6599-6.ch008

Pandey, J. M., Mishra, P., Garg, S., & Mshra, B. P. (2017). Chronic Mental Illness and Dumping Patients: A Concern towards Management. In B. Prasad (Ed.), *Chronic Mental Illness and the Changing Scope of Intervention Strategies, Diagnosis, and Treatment* (pp. 40–57). Hershey, PA: IGI Global. doi:10.4018/978-1-5225-0519-8.ch003

Pantos, A. J. (2015). Implicit Social Cognition and Language Attitudes Research. In Z. Jin (Ed.), *Exploring Implicit Cognition: Learning, Memory, and Social Cognitive Processes* (pp. 104–117). Hershey, PA: IGI Global. doi:10.4018/978-1-4666-6599-6.ch005

Park, L. Q., & Busson, B. (2015). The Impact of Decline on Everyday Life in Alzheimer's Disease. In C. Dick-Muehlke, R. Li, & M. Orleans (Eds.), *Psychosocial Studies of the Individual's Changing Perspectives in Alzheimer's Disease* (pp. 327–338). Hershey, PA: IGI Global. doi:10.4018/978-1-4666-8478-2.ch014

Pellas, N. (2015). Unraveling a Progressive Inquiry Script in Persistent Virtual Worlds: Theoretical Foundations and Decision Processes for Constructing a Socio-Cultural Learning Framework. In Z. Jin (Ed.), *Exploring Implicit Cognition: Learning, Memory, and Social Cognitive Processes* (pp. 243–280). Hershey, PA: IGI Global. doi:10.4018/978-1-4666-6599-6.ch012

Pena, P. A., Van den Broucke, S., Sylin, M., Leysen, J., & de Soir, E. (2017). Definitions, Typologies, and Processes Involved in Organizational Trauma: A Literature Review. In S. Háša & R. Brunet-Thornton (Eds.), *Impact of Organizational Trauma on Workplace Behavior and Performance* (pp. 1–17). Hershey, PA: IGI Global. doi:10.4018/978-1-5225-2021-4.ch001

Photiadis, T., & Souleles, N. (2015). A Theoretical Model, Including User-Experience, Aesthetics, and Psychology, in the 3D Design Process. In J. Bishop (Ed.), *Psychological and Social Implications Surrounding Internet and Gaming Addiction* (pp. 139–152). Hershey, PA: IGI Global. doi:10.4018/978-1-4666-8595-6.ch008

Pontes, H. M., & Griffiths, M. D. (2015). New Concepts, Old Known Issues: The DSM-5 and Internet Gaming Disorder and its Assessment. In J. Bishop (Ed.), *Psychological and Social Implications Surrounding Internet and Gaming Addiction* (pp. 16–30). Hershey, PA: IGI Global. doi:10.4018/978-1-4666-8595-6.ch002

Power, G. A. (2015). Changing Perception in Alzheimer's: An Experiential View. In C. Dick-Muehlke, R. Li, & M. Orleans (Eds.), *Psychosocial Studies of the Individual's Changing Perspectives in Alzheimer's Disease* (pp. 271–300). Hershey, PA: IGI Global. doi:10.4018/978-1-4666-8478-2.ch012

Reinert, L. (2017). Qualia and Extended Field of Contemporary Design. In R. Zuanon (Ed.), *Projective Processes and Neuroscience in Art and Design* (pp. 138–154). Hershey, PA: IGI Global. doi:10.4018/978-1-5225-0510-5.ch009

Rios, J. A., Nonato, E. D., Sales, M. V., & Carneiro, T. K. (2014). U-Learning Pedagogical Management: Cognitive Processes and Hypermediatic Resources Involved in Web-Based Collaborative Workspace. In F. Neto (Ed.), *Technology Platform Innovations and Forthcoming Trends in Ubiquitous Learning* (pp. 270–288). Hershey, PA: IGI Global. doi:10.4018/978-1-4666-4542-4.ch015

Ross, D. B., Exposito, J. A., & Kennedy, T. (2017). Stress and Its Relationship to Leadership and a Healthy Workplace Culture. In V. Bryan & J. Bird (Eds.), *Healthcare Community Synergism between Patients, Practitioners, and Researchers* (pp. 213–246). Hershey, PA: IGI Global. doi:10.4018/978-1-5225-0640-9.ch010

Saberi, M. (2016). Personality-Based Cognitive Design of Characters in Virtual Environments. In J. Turner, M. Nixon, U. Bernardet, & S. DiPaola (Eds.), *Integrating Cognitive Architectures into Virtual Character Design* (pp. 124–150). Hershey, PA: IGI Global. doi:10.4018/978-1-5225-0454-2.ch005

Sharma, R., & Lohan, A. (2016). Psychosocial Interventions for Individuals with Intellectual Disability. In R. Gopalan (Ed.), *Handbook of Research on Diagnosing, Treating, and Managing Intellectual Disabilities* (pp. 262–282). Hershey, PA: IGI Global. doi:10.4018/978-1-5225-0089-6.ch014

Sharon, D. (2015). The Sleep-Wake System and Alzheimer's Disease. In C. Dick-Muehlke, R. Li, & M. Orleans (Eds.), *Psychosocial Studies of the Individual's Changing Perspectives in Alzheimer's Disease* (pp. 339–365). Hershey, PA: IGI Global. doi:10.4018/978-1-4666-8478-2.ch015

Simuth, J. (2017). Psychological Impacts of Downsizing Trauma. In S. Háša & R. Brunet-Thornton (Eds.), *Impact of Organizational Trauma on Workplace Behavior and Performance* (pp. 120–139). Hershey, PA: IGI Global. doi:10.4018/978-1-5225-2021-4.ch005

Sinha, P., Garg, A., Khanna, P., & Khanna, A. (2017). Management of Chronic Mental Illnesses and Substance Use Disorders. In B. Prasad (Ed.), *Chronic Mental Illness and the Changing Scope of Intervention Strategies, Diagnosis, and Treatment* (pp. 101–122). Hershey, PA: IGI Global. doi:10.4018/978-1-5225-0519-8.ch006

Siqueira de Freitas, A. (2017). A Study on the Interface between Arts and Sciences: Neuroesthetics and Cognitive Neuroscience of Art. In R. Zuanon (Ed.), *Projective Processes and Neuroscience in Art and Design* (pp. 71–86). Hershey, PA: IGI Global. doi:10.4018/978-1-5225-0510-5.ch005

Solo, A. M., & Bishop, J. (2015). Avoiding Adverse Consequences from Digital Addiction and Retaliatory Feedback: The Role of the Participation Continuum. In J. Bishop (Ed.), *Psychological and Social Implications Surrounding Internet and Gaming Addiction* (pp. 62–77). Hershey, PA: IGI Global. doi:10.4018/978-1-4666-8595-6.ch005

Soni, S. C. P., & Ahamed, P. C. (2017). Understanding and Management of Caregivers' Stress and Burden of Person with Obsessive Compulsive Disorder. In B. Prasad (Ed.), *Chronic Mental Illness and the Changing Scope of Intervention Strategies, Diagnosis, and Treatment* (pp. 124–142). Hershey, PA: IGI Global. doi:10.4018/978-1-5225-0519-8.ch007

Srivastav, D., & Singh, T. B. (2017). Comorbidity Issues and Treatment in Chronic Mental Illness. In B. Prasad (Ed.), *Chronic Mental Illness and the Changing Scope of Intervention Strategies, Diagnosis, and Treatment* (pp. 77–100). Hershey, PA: IGI Global. doi:10.4018/978-1-5225-0519-8.ch005

Strang, K. D. (2017). Predicting Student Satisfaction and Outcomes in Online Courses Using Learning Activity Indicators. *International Journal of Web-Based Learning and Teaching Technologies, 12*(1), 32–50. doi:10.4018/IJWLTT.2017010103

Svanström, R. (2015). Fragmented Existence: Living Alone with Dementia and a Manifest Care Need. In C. Dick-Muehlke, R. Li, & M. Orleans (Eds.), *Psychosocial Studies of the Individual's Changing Perspectives in Alzheimer's Disease* (pp. 302–326). Hershey, PA: IGI Global. doi:10.4018/978-1-4666-8478-2.ch013

Swiatek, L. (2017). Accessing the Finest Minds: Insights into Creativity from Esteemed Media Professionals. In N. Silton (Ed.), *Exploring the Benefits of Creativity in Education, Media, and the Arts* (pp. 240–263). Hershey, PA: IGI Global. doi:10.4018/978-1-5225-0504-4.ch012

Szymanski, M., & Schindler, E. (2017). Embracing Organizational Trauma: Positive Effects of Death Experiences on Organizational Culture – Three Short Case Studies. In S. Háša & R. Brunet-Thornton (Eds.), *Impact of Organizational Trauma on Workplace Behavior and Performance* (pp. 247–263). Hershey, PA: IGI Global. doi:10.4018/978-1-5225-2021-4.ch010

Tavaragi, M. S. (2017). Chronic Mental Illness in Prisons: Global Scenario. In B. Prasad (Ed.), *Chronic Mental Illness and the Changing Scope of Intervention Strategies, Diagnosis, and Treatment* (pp. 203–224). Hershey, PA: IGI Global. doi:10.4018/978-1-5225-0519-8.ch011

Terras, M. M., & Ramsay, J. (2014). E-Learning, Mobility, and Time: A Psychological Framework. In E. Barbera & P. Reimann (Eds.), *Assessment and Evaluation of Time Factors in Online Teaching and Learning* (pp. 63–90). Hershey, PA: IGI Global. doi:10.4018/978-1-4666-4651-3.ch003

Tietze, R. L. (2017). Creativity and the Arts. In N. Silton (Ed.), *Exploring the Benefits of Creativity in Education, Media, and the Arts* (pp. 337–375). Hershey, PA: IGI Global. doi:10.4018/978-1-5225-0504-4.ch016

Toms, G., Lawrence, C., & Clare, L. (2015). Awareness, Self, and the Experience of Dementia: Foundations of a Psychologically Minded Approach. In C. Dick-Muehlke, R. Li, & M. Orleans (Eds.), *Psychosocial Studies of the Individual's Changing Perspectives in Alzheimer's Disease* (pp. 132–158). Hershey, PA: IGI Global. doi:10.4018/978-1-4666-8478-2.ch006

Tran, B. (2014). The Foundation of Cultural Intelligence: Human Capital. In B. Christiansen, S. Yıldız, & E. Yıldız (Eds.), *Handbook of Research on Effective Marketing in Contemporary Globalism* (pp. 348–376). Hershey, PA: IGI Global. doi:10.4018/978-1-4666-6220-9.ch020

Tran, B. (2017). Impact of Organizational Trauma on Workplace Behavior and Performance: Workplace Bullying Due to (In)Competency. In S. Háša, & R. Brunet-Thornton (Eds.), Impact of Organizational Trauma on Workplace Behavior and Performance (pp. 221-245). Hershey, PA: IGI Global. doi:10.4018/978-1-5225-2021-4.ch009

Tran, B. (2017). Psychological (and Emotional) Architecture: The Values and Benefits of Nature-Based Architecture – Biophilia. In G. Koç, M. Claes, & B. Christiansen (Eds.), *Cultural Influences on Architecture* (pp. 200–230). Hershey, PA: IGI Global. doi:10.4018/978-1-5225-1744-3.ch008

Tran, B. (2017). The Architect of Organizational Psychology: The Geert Hofstede's Dimensions of Cultural (Corporate and Organizational) Identity. In G. Koç, M. Claes, & B. Christiansen (Eds.), *Cultural Influences on Architecture* (pp. 231–258). Hershey, PA: IGI Global. doi:10.4018/978-1-5225-1744-3.ch009

Triberti, S., & Chirico, A. (2017). Healthy Avatars, Healthy People: Care Engagement Through the Shared Experience of Virtual Worlds. In G. Graffigna (Ed.), *Transformative Healthcare Practice through Patient Engagement* (pp. 247–275). Hershey, PA: IGI Global. doi:10.4018/978-1-5225-0663-8.ch010

Tripathi, M. A., & Sridevi, G. (2017). Psychotherapeutic Interventions in Emotional and Behavioural Problems with Adolescents. In B. Prasad (Ed.), *Chronic Mental Illness and the Changing Scope of Intervention Strategies, Diagnosis, and Treatment* (pp. 321–333). Hershey, PA: IGI Global. doi:10.4018/978-1-5225-0519-8.ch018

Trompetter, P. S. (2017). A History of Police Psychology. In C. Mitchell & E. Dorian (Eds.), *Police Psychology and Its Growing Impact on Modern Law Enforcement* (pp. 1–26). Hershey, PA: IGI Global. doi:10.4018/978-1-5225-0813-7.ch001

Valencia, E. (2017). Neuromarketing Step by Step: Based on Scientific Publications. In M. Dos Santos (Ed.), *Applying Neuroscience to Business Practice* (pp. 18–48). Hershey, PA: IGI Global. doi:10.4018/978-1-5225-1028-4.ch002

Valeyeva, N. S., Kupriyanov, R., & Valeyeva, E. R. (2017). Metacognition and Metacognitive Skills: Intellectual Skills Development Technology. In E. Railean, A. Elçi, & A. Elçi (Eds.), *Metacognition and Successful Learning Strategies in Higher Education* (pp. 63–84). Hershey, PA: IGI Global. doi:10.4018/978-1-5225-2218-8.ch004

Vallverdú, J., & Talanov, M. (2017). Naturalizing Consciousness Emergence for AI Implementation Purposes: A Guide to Multilayered Management Systems. In J. Vallverdú, M. Mazzara, M. Talanov, S. Distefano, & R. Lowe (Eds.), *Advanced Research on Biologically Inspired Cognitive Architectures* (pp. 24–40). Hershey, PA: IGI Global. doi:10.4018/978-1-5225-1947-8.ch002 von Kutzleben, M., & Panke-Kochinke, B. (2015). Stable Self-Concepts and Flexible Coping Strategies of People with Dementia Attending Dementia Self-Help Groups in Germany: Results from the Qualitative Longitudinal SEIN Study. In C. Dick-Muehlke, R. Li, & M. Orleans (Eds.), *Psychosocial Studies of the Individual's Changing Perspectives in Alzheimer's Disease* (pp. 159–182). Hershey, PA: IGI Global. doi:10.4018/978-1-4666-8478-2.ch007

Vorkapić, S. T. (2017). Personality and Education: Contemporary Issues in Psychological Science about Personality in Teacher Education. In C. Martin & D. Polly (Eds.), *Handbook of Research on Teacher Education and Professional Development* (pp. 163–186). Hershey, PA: IGI Global. doi:10.4018/978-1-5225-1067-3.ch009

Vorkapić, S. T., Vujičić, L., & Čepić, R. (2014). Preschool Teacher Identity. In P. Breen (Ed.), *Cases on Teacher Identity, Diversity, and Cognition in Higher Education* (pp. 22–60). Hershey, PA: IGI Global. doi:10.4018/978-1-4666-5990-2.ch002

Wagner, C., & Schlough, D. E. (2017). Creativity: A Childhood Essential. In N. Silton (Ed.), *Exploring the Benefits of Creativity in Education, Media, and the Arts* (pp. 1–25). Hershey, PA: IGI Global. doi:10.4018/978-1-5225-0504-4.ch001

Wang, L., Li, C., & Wu, J. (2017). The Status of Research into Intention Recognition. In J. Wu (Ed.), *Improving the Quality of Life for Dementia Patients through Progressive Detection, Treatment, and Care* (pp. 201–221). Hershey, PA: IGI Global. doi:10.4018/978-1-5225-0925-7.ch010

Wehle, M., Weidemann, A., & Boblan, I. W. (2017). Research on Human Cognition for Biologically Inspired Developments: Human-Robot Interaction by Biomimetic AI. In J. Vallverdú, M. Mazzara, M. Talanov, S. Distefano, & R. Lowe (Eds.), *Advanced Research on Biologically Inspired Cognitive Architectures* (pp. 83–116). Hershey, PA: IGI Global. doi:10.4018/978-1-5225-1947-8.ch005

Wilson, J. G. (2017). Social Psychology: The Seduction of Consumers. In C. Martins & M. Damásio (Eds.), *Seduction in Popular Culture, Psychology, and Philosophy* (pp. 206–231). Hershey, PA: IGI Global. doi:10.4018/978-1-5225-0525-9.ch010

Wu, F., Tang, X., Ren, Y., Yang, W., Takahashi, S., & Wu, J. (2017). Effects of Visual Contrast on Inverse Effectiveness in Audiovisual Integration. In J. Wu (Ed.), *Improving the Quality of Life for Dementia Patients through Progressive Detection, Treatment, and Care* (pp. 187–200). Hershey, PA: IGI Global. doi:10.4018/978-1-5225-0925-7.ch009

Wu, Z., Lin, T., Tang, N., & Wu, S. (2015). Effects of Display Characteristics on Presence and Emotional Responses of Game Players. In A. Mesquita & C. Tsai (Eds.), *Human Behavior, Psychology, and Social Interaction in the Digital Era* (pp. 130–145). Hershey, PA: IGI Global. doi:10.4018/978-1-4666-8450-8.ch006

Xie, T., Zhu, Y., Lin, T., & Chen, R. (2015). Modeling Human Behavior to Reduce Navigation Time of Menu Items: Menu Item Prediction Based on Markov Chain. In A. Mesquita & C. Tsai (Eds.), *Human Behavior, Psychology, and Social Interaction in the Digital Era* (pp. 162–187). Hershey, PA: IGI Global. doi:10.4018/978-1-4666-8450-8.ch008

Yang, C., Ha, L., Yun, G. W., & Chen, L. (2015). From Relationship to Information: A Study of Twitter and Facebook Usage in Terms of Social Network Size among College Students. In A. Mesquita & C. Tsai (Eds.), *Human Behavior, Psychology, and Social Interaction in the Digital Era* (pp. 241–258). Hershey, PA: IGI Global. doi:10.4018/978-1-4666-8450-8.ch012

Yartey, F. N., & Ha, L. (2015). Smartphones and Self-Broadcasting among College Students in an Age of Social Media. In A. Mesquita & C. Tsai (Eds.), *Human Behavior, Psychology, and Social Interaction in the Digital Era* (pp. 95–128). Hershey, PA: IGI Global. doi:10.4018/978-1-4666-8450-8.ch005

# About the Author

**Sanja Tatalović Vorkapić** was born on July 18th 1972, in Rijeka, Croatia. After finishing her primary and secondary education in Rijeka, she enrolled in Psychology course at the Department for Psychology at Faculty of Humanities and Social Sciences, Rijeka, Croatia. After she has graduated in 1997, she couldn't find a job, so she volunteered at the Clinical Hospital Center and Primary school "Zamet" in Rijeka. After that, she worked in kindergarten, primary school, secondary school, social welfare system, healthcare system within substance abuse work and Psychiatric Hospital Lopača. In the meantime, she got her master degree in the field of biological psychology at the Department of Psychology at Faculty of Humanities and Social Sciences in Zagreb, at 2005. That same year, she started to work as the part-time lecturer for the Faculty of Teacher Education and enrolled the Doctoral studies in Psychology in Zagreb. In 2007, she got a part-time job at the Faculty of Teacher Education and half-time job at the Department for Quality Assurance at the University of Rijeka. She got her doctoral degree in the field of personality psychology and biological psychology in 2010 at the Department of Psychology at Faculty of Humanities and Social Sciences in Zagreb. During her master and doctoral studies, she was mentored by Ph.D. Meri Tadinac, full professor. After getting her doctoral degree, she got a full-time job at the Faculty of Teacher Education as an Assistant Professor. Today she is an Associate Professor at the Faculty of Teacher Education, who is teaching future pre-school and primary school teachers the following subjects: General psychology, Developmental psychology, Psychology of an early learning and teaching, The Basics of psychology of learning and teaching, Developmental Psychopathology, Positive psychology, Emotional Intelligence and Methodology of quantitative research. Some courses are joint, so other students, such as future psychologists, pedagogics and specific subject teachers are enrolled. Her research interest are following personality psychology (biological and environmental correlates of personality, personality in education); biological psychology (the relationship between evoked brain potentials and personality); positive psychology (children's well-being, resilience and positive psychology in education) and research methodology (development and validation of measures for personality measurement and measures for educational context). She has achieved the Award for the best scientist in the field of Humanities and social sciences in the 2013/2014 ac. year from the University of Rijeka Foundation. She has been an Erasmus coordinator at her faculty, the member of quality assurance board at the university and faculty level, the member of Ethical board, the Vice-dean for quality assurance at her faculty and the member of the University board of crediting students. She is the Head of Department for Educational Sciences at her faculty now. She has participated and organized numerous scientific, professional projects, and conferences and symposia. She has mentored 35 students. She has written three manuals for students and 85 scientific papers. She is the member of two international editorial boards and regular reviewer for Elsevier journals. She is happily married and has two beautiful children.

# Index

www.ingramcontent.com/pod-product-compliance
Ingram Content Group UK Ltd.
Pitfield, Milton Keynes, MK11 3LW, UK
UKHW051028041026
15470UKWH00015B/1651

9 781522 522836